D0325415

LIFE AS WE KNOW IT

LIFE AS WE KNOW IT

A COLLECTION OF PERSONAL
ESSAYS FROM SALON.COM

Edited by

Jennifer Foote Sweeney

With a foreword by Jane Smiley

WASHINGTON SQUARE PRESS
New York London Toronto Sydney Singapore

Washington Square Press
1230 Avenue of the Americas
New York, NY 10020

ISBN: 0-7434-7686-7

First Washington Square Press trade paperback edition October 2003

10 9 8 7 6 5 4 3 2 1

WASHINGTON SQUARE PRESS and colophon are
registered trademarks of Simon & Schuster, Inc.

Manufactured in the United States of America

For information regarding special discounts for bulk purchases,
please contact Simon & Schuster Special Sales at 1-800-456-6798
or business@simonandschuster.com

To my brother Michael,
for coming back.

CONTENTS

THE CALCULUS OF LOVE

Pluses and Minuses

Multiplication

POST-NUCLEAR FAMILY LIFE

The 'Rents

The Reared

WORLD WITHOUT END

Loss

Remembrance

FOREWORD
By Jane Smiley

LAST YEAR, WHEN I left to go on my book tour, I had everything arranged. My son would be staying with his dad, my former husband, who also would be working with my partner (male) at my house, tiling and drywalling. My partner planned to divide his time between my house, where he would also take care of the dogs, and his place, where he planned to do some plumbing so that his former wife (the mother of his two children) and her new partner (female) could get better water pressure in their house, and he could get the washer and dryer installed at his house. He had been using the washer and dryer in the guest house, where his former wife's former partner (male) lives. On the days when my partner was planning to join me, my former husband was to take care of the dogs, and my partner's former wife was to feed the horses.

I'm not one of those who laments the decline of the traditional family. I'm one of those who suspects that familial arrangements in previous centuries were more diverse than we have been led to believe. I'm one of those who suspects that the traditional family we hear of all the time and are supposed to miss was more about preserving property and keeping women in line than it was about rearing children, obeying the word of God, or, indeed, anything else. A short course of nineteenth century novels like *Vanity Fair* and *Madame Bovary* and *Portrait of a Lady,* not to mention *Anna Karenina,* is enough to demonstrate that the motives earlier generations brought to marrying and reproducing were no less foolish and maybe more venal than similar motives in generations now alive. I'm one of those who thinks that the great experiment is being conducted by the baby boomers, an experiment in living and marrying according to desire, love, and companionship rather than survival, practicality, and conformity, and that this experiment, whatever its outcome, is one that had to be conducted somewhere, sometime.

Of course my own family life is the result of that experiment. All of us looked for love and companionship, found it, lost it, found it again. Those were the facts of our existence. But whatever those facts, the children, five in all, seemed to need ready access to both parents. And, here in California, the kinks of the real estate boom led to some nonstandard housing options. And horses, dogs, and home remodeling kept turning up as shared themes and common interests, maybe because we are all too old to develop new interests. Anyway, old grievances gave way to a habit of cooperation, and here we are, a twenty-first century extended family where the favorite aunt is an ex-wife or the guy fixing the waterheater is an ex-husband. Of course, we baby boomers don't know the outcome of our experiment; in spite of the premature handwringing of the traditional-family cheerleading squad, we won't know that until our children have made their own choices. In the same way that we baby boomers showed what we thought of our parents' frustrations with suburban monogamy fifties' and sixties' style, we know that our children will try something else that will demonstrate their own conclusions about how best to marry and reproduce. More power to them.

Even so, living in my own unorthodox family did not preserve me from amazement at the unorthodox families described and celebrated in the following essays. Gathered together, these essays are jewels of the unexpected, and in introducing them, I don't want to steal any of their surprise. Suffice it to say that family life in America (and especially in California) at the turn of the millennium is alive and well, but it is not like anything you ever read about before in your life. Each of the authors of the following pieces is trying something new, in some cases, something very new in the history of the world. Erin Aubrey Kaplan tried crossing racial boundaries and getting to know someone she didn't expect to like or respect. Eve Parnell tried reconnecting with an old boyfriend through the internet. Carol Mithers looked for cheaper fertility drugs on the black market, and found herself entering the lives of people she had never imagined. And believe me, we are not even scratching the surface here of what these writers tried, and what they came up with.

Each essay in this book is a preliminary finding, a report from our grand and sometimes terrifying experiment. Together, these essays report that, even if the ways we get into families today may be unusual and even astonishing, the family is not dead, or even moribund. People still long to link up, and to believe those connections are solid and permanent; the desire for children is still so unappeasable that any arrangement, any technique that achieves the pregnancy, is acceptable; there is still no one more sanguine than someone who is about to have a baby; raising children continues to be harder in a million different ways than anyone ever thinks it is going to be, and sometimes it is as satisfying as it is difficult; and also, family life (in spite of the American myth, purveyed on TV and in women's magazines and advertising) is still where we learn about tragedy as well as about situation comedy.

If all of the sociological analyses and how-to manuals, all the surveys and advice books, all the polemics and sermons about American family life at the beginning of the twenty-first century were to vanish (an appealing idea, actually), and only this book were left, a hypothetical reading public a thousand years from now would know enough about us—would know who we are and how we think, how we love and what we want.

INTRODUCTION

By Jennifer Foote Sweeney

FROM THE BEGINNING, when the Life site of Salon was called Mothers Who Think, our intention has been to provide refuge to readers battered by the judgment, irrelevance, and surrealism of mainstream "family" journalism. The plan was—and still is—to offer writing that acknowledges the way we really are, and rejects the idea that we want or need to be better or best or just like everyone else. It is a commitment that requires courage—from the writer above all. Writing in the first person is hard, even for the self-satisfied egotist who crows and blushes through a fantasy version of their past. To tell a true story, a messy, naked account of flunking out, or crawling back, or finding love, or losing faith, is an act of bravery; as editor of Life, I have been humbled by the daily offering of such heroic work.

The stories in this anthology share classic traits: They are honest, surprising, heartbreaking, infuriating, and often very funny. The writers are not at all alike, except that they are like us: They march, limp and muddle through familiar, and sometimes completely unexpected, territory—cursing, laughing, sometimes muttering poetry. They write about family values, not the ones tied to a certain religion or a specific constellation of relationships, but the ones—love, respect, community—that exist outside the sanctity of the now-mythical nuclear family. The romance in arranged marriage, the melancholy of a conjugal visit, the exhilaration of sperm donation, the eroticism of age and intelligence—the stuff of life as it is now is the stuff of Life as it is represented in this book.

A couple of years ago, I wrote a story that questioned whether a certain study about the impact of child care could be taken seriously, given the data it relied upon and its mode of collection. I got a lot of letters after it was published, but one in particular stood out. It said: "Why do I get the sinking suspicion that you hand your children over to a kid kennel every morning in order to drive the latest BMW and want not to feel guilty about it?"

It made me laugh, and not just because it got me all wrong. It made me laugh because I felt impervious to such ham-fisted bullying. I know who's got my back. Hundreds of voices have been heard in this site during the time I have been its editor; hundreds more have spoken to me through essays and letters that never got to print. This is a community that speaks the truth about how we live, and has faith in the choices of its members. These are voices that can be heard above the din of intolerance—a lusty chorus to put some soul into the occasional "I know you are, but what am I?"

I wish it were possible to print it all. This collection, like so many anthologies, is haunted by terrific work that could not fit. The essays that we picked, corralled under headings that reference life's milestones and mysteries, are some of the best. With luck, there always will be more.

THE CALCULUS OF LOVE

THE COLOR OF LOVE

Erin Aubry Kaplan

TWO YEARS AGO, if anyone had asked, I would have said that I would probably never marry. I had nothing against the institution, but by my middle thirties I had come to believe that the marriage I'd always imagined might never happen. I didn't find this tragic; I found it liberating. Not getting married meant absolution from a number of entanglements I could do without—a deadwood relationship, compromised living space, the half-hearted internal debate about whether to have babies. While I embraced the idea of marriage, I embraced solitude in equal measure. I found a certain elation in the prospect of a future in which I could allow my emotions and shoe-buying impulses to run free. At age thirty-seven, my desire for freedom seemed to have neatly trumped my yearning for anything, or anyone, else. And that was fine with me.

In this rare state of contentment, I met Alan Kaplan, who was forty-three and in a state of extreme discontent. We met at his house on a Sunday afternoon, though he didn't want to meet me at all, let alone on a weekend. He was a white public high school teacher who had become the epicenter of a racially charged controversy at his campus. Because I am a journalist with a particular interest in matters of racial justice, I had been enlisted by an irate group of black parents at the school, and subsequently by my paper, to do a story about it.

According to the parents pushing the story, Kaplan was guilty of racial impertinence. (These parents hoped that, as a black woman, I would be sympathetic to their viewpoint.) They said he was intellectually arrogant in a white-privilege sort of way, eager to overwhelm his black students' frail sense of self-esteem by, among other things, extending the discussion of slavery to issues of latter-day segregation in his classroom. Kaplan insisted that the system failed black and white students alike, and asked his students to confront the racial achievement gap in his classroom and to question why teachers have different sets of expectations for black and white students.

The parents felt that identifying latter-day segregation was not his business or his purview. According to them, Kaplan's insistence that he was only trying to do the right thing was merely a cover for the fact that he was improperly fixated on race—he had issued himself a street-gang name, K-Dawg, and even dated black women. "You know the type," the leader of the parent group said meaningfully, and a bit wearily.

I did. This also was not the first I'd heard of Kaplan or his exploits: my younger sister, Heather, had been his student in the 1980s and had complained regularly about his intransigence. Many of her complaints, I vaguely recalled, had to do with race. Heather's an attorney now, and when I asked her whether she thought Kaplan had been racist, she argued vehemently with herself for about ten minutes before giving something of an answer.

"He was harder on black students than on other students," she said. "He definitely had issues about race, and he wasn't always diplomatic about expressing them. And he'd get mad with me because he felt I was squandering my potential, not living up to myself. I don't think that was racist per se."

I thought of all this as I rang Kaplan's doorbell one Sunday in April. Yet I was more than willing to get his side of the story. I was also intrigued: What sort of white man would keep pushing the racial envelope in this day and age? He was either exceedingly honest or exceedingly boorish, or both. In spite of everything, I had liked his voice on the phone when we talked to arrange this visit—rough-edged, with the nearly unconscious authority of a veteran teacher, but younger than I had expected.

He didn't bother to hide his uncertainty. "I must tell you, I'm very reticent about seeing you," he said, already sounding regretful. I gave him my usual pledge of open-mindedness and then said we had to meet right away, as I was on deadline. Sunday, at his place? I heard a startled silence and prayed I hadn't pushed too far—without him, there wasn't much of a story. "All right," he said. "Do you take cream in your coffee?"

It turned out to be the powdered stuff, which I don't really like but took because he gave it to me. I sat on the floor of his tiny living room because he had no coffee table, and I preferred the floor as a writing surface. Kaplan was dressed in jeans and an old T-shirt. He had the resigned look of a man headed for the gallows. He was nothing like the odd, obsessive recluse I'd imagined, the sort who would erect a wall of racial self-righteousness around himself and loudly proclaim himself to be K-Dawg. Instead, he had tousled brown hair, a graying goatee, and sad eyes that nonetheless burned bright and curious: he wanted to see exactly how his death would unfold.

I stayed at Kaplan's house for nearly five hours. Talking to him was terribly easy. He had a native charm that was rooted not in assurance but in attentiveness and honesty, even as he detailed the ugliest moments in his ongoing battles with nervous parents and administrators who objected to his teaching style and his determination to impart the hard lessons of race in American history. (As for the moniker K-Dawg, he said one student had given it to him as a kind of joke, because despite being very familiar with racial issues, Kaplan was as unhip—and un-hip-hop—as they come.)

He sat on the floor opposite me and offered more powdered cream, and I said yes. Nearly three hours into our interview, he asked if I was hungry. Did I want dinner? It was my turn to hesitate and his turn to look abashed, afraid that he had overstepped his boundaries. "Dinner?" I asked, pretending to mull it over. "That'd be good."

He gave me a place setting, salad, and lasagna that he'd heated up in a microwave. He didn't eat because he didn't have any more, I learned later. I also learned that 364 days out of the year, Kaplan, a quintessential bachelor, never had anything to eat in the house. His refrigerator typically contained nothing more than a couple of jugs of ice water and a pack of batteries; he used the stove so infrequently that he'd had it turned off several months before my visit.

We sat at his dining table, and the climate between us shifted as the sun shifted and day lengthened into early night. He leaned forward on the table with his hands clasped tightly together, as if in prayer or anticipation. I noted that he smelled faintly woodsy, that he wore a diving watch and no other jewelry, that the fluorescent light above the table revealed his eyes to be perhaps more green than brown.

He cocked his head, furrowed his brow in mock gravity, and asked me about myself: How did I get started as a writer? How was my sister doing? Did I work out? "Nice arms," he said, as decidedly as he had said anything all day. He didn't look abashed now. I thanked him, feeling inexplicably delighted, because I didn't work out at all and knew somehow that he knew that.

As a reporter, I was somewhat used to this kind of intimate

rapport. He was trying to save his skin, and I must say I have always been prone to falling in love with my subjects—for an hour, or a day or two at most—taking the prolonged conversations and forced intimacy to heart before writing a story that either favors them or does not, and then filing it all away in my professional memory.

I welcomed such encounters because they stood in—briefly—for genuine love and connection. I could believe what I wanted about my subjects in my mind's eye, without ever crossing a line or committing my prejudice to paper. My professional encounters serviced my romantic ideals, illuminating them briefly, sometimes even brilliantly, before I moved on.

In such a context, I could allow that Alan Kaplan was sweet, affecting, a perfect gentleman, a wonderful listener, good-looking even. If he was a villain, I could still give him the due afforded by my writer's license and the vast but inconsequential space between interview and story.

At 10 P.M., he walked me out to my car and stood at the curb, waving until I was out of sight. I felt less like I'd had an interview and more like I'd been on a date.

I'm still trying to sort out what happened next, though admittedly, I'm not trying very hard. The skeletal sequence of events goes something like this: Kaplan and I talked some more; I interviewed more people, wrote a story in the span of about five days, and published it. The story sympathized with the racial inequities in public education, but disagreed with the black parents' indictment of Kaplan. I never heard from them again.

Kaplan and I never stopped hearing from each other. He showed up at my door, unannounced, with flowers, a thank-you for the story, he said. I got more flowers. We began meeting regularly on weeknights at a coffeehouse to unofficially confirm that we had to keep meeting. We talked on the phone one night from midnight to six without saying anything of consequence, hanging up bleary-eyed but completely bewitched by the fact that we had staggered through the strangest and most intimate hours of the night together.

His eyes began looking less sorrowful and more hopeful. He talked about his frustrations with racial dishonesty, and he told me scores of other things about himself as well—his romantic failings and underdeveloped ambitions, his passion for jazz, guitars, and baseball.

This time, I didn't write anything down. I didn't want to. We were so obviously in love that neither one of us bothered to say so. We did wonder aloud about the propriety of a reporter falling for a source, but we couldn't do anything about it except keep a low profile for a while. On our first official date beyond the coffeehouse, we thought we'd go to a movie, but instead we wound up driving around Los Angeles to avoid being seen together. We sat in his big old Lincoln on a road high up in the Sepulveda Pass, among the hills that divide L.A. from itself, and talked for hours more.

There was never any question that I would marry Alan. I did, in October, roughly a year and a half after we first met. My sister is still flabbergasted that I married the teacher who loomed the largest in her adolescence—she sometimes slips and calls him "Kaplan." There is and always will be the race issue—the raised eyebrows on both sides of the color line, the people who question our ethnic loyalty and politics. This is no surprise, especially considering the ethnic rancor that brought us together in the first place.

We understand the questions others may have about our relationship, and we often raise them ourselves. The concerns we each had about race before we met remain firmly in place, perhaps even more firmly than before. We do not want to be poster children for interracial marriage or the latest diversity campaign. Love for us is a triumph not of integration but of imagination, the wild-card coupling of a pair of resolutely lonely hearts who chose to navigate the same rough, but potentially magical, course.

SAUCY SOCCER MOMS

Matthew DeBord

THE *SPORTS ILLUSTRATED* swimsuit issue—annual apex of service journalism for boys—is supposed to bring every red-blooded straight male, or his trousers, to his knees. And yet, the specially wrapped pack o' porn, accessories included, did nothing for me this year.

There was no pop-eyed lust, no furtive boner, no drooling over dusky bazooms and stiletto gams. I could not be moved by Teutonic nubility, taut bellies, or thong-flossed buttocks. In fact, the entire 3-D section conjured up only the grim image of near-sighted shut-ins with red-and-blue cardboard glasses perched on their trembling noses, soiled BVDs clumped around their vari-cosed ankles.

I tossed my copy on a groaning pile of erotically benign rags: *Harper's*, the *New Yorker, Golf Digest*. I was saving myself for the superior stroke book, my own true erotic bible, the glossy guide to honeys most likely to succeed with me, myself, and a box of Kleenex: the Lands' End "America's Ultimate Swimwear" catalog, demurely billed as "26 pages of the kindest cut anywhere."

To hell with coltish babefests and contrived 3-D hooey. They wither in the face of this robust confidence, these sturdy thighs, those downy arms. What is a collagen-plumped pout and a belly ring in the face of a tender grin and the endless promise of maturity? I am over the supermodel; we're not even friends. These days, most nights, I belong to the soccer mom.

That's right, she of the coveted vote and the Plymouth Voyager. Am I the only one to have discovered her sultry poignancy, the sexy affirmation that everything—and I do mean everything—is possible after childbirth at the age of thirty-five? Nope. We are legion (though still somewhat stealthy and apologetic).

I know, I know. The Lands' End models are fairly young women, but that's only because catalog models usually are. What they project is unabashedly adult. These are still proto-soccer moms, here to dispel the ridicule and denigration heaped on their sisters by smarmy comedians and jealous Type A urbanettes. This subtle swan might require a kinder cut, but that's about all the supermodel has on this Venus in a tankini.

I am not the first guy to complain (others in a suspiciously defensive tone, I with great sincerity) that the overwhelming majority of women promoted by *Sports Illustrated*, *Vogue*, *Harper's Bazaar*, *Cosmopolitan*, *Allure*—the whole panoply of publications dedicated to starvation chic—tend to be about as sexy as plaster mannequins. Beautiful, yes—if you subscribe to the criteria of Hugh Hefner and Hamish Bowles—but also unapproachable, unreal, and kind of cadaverous.

The typical supermodel is, to my eye, oddly lifeless, sterile. Does she have genitals? Or is her authentic sexuality subsumed by the awesome austerity of her calculated media presence?

Could I really contrive a convincing fantasy in which I would throw down Heidi Klum and blitz her fleshy battlements? Nah. For that I need a real woman. For that I need a soccer mom.

A soccer mom implies an inner life; she bristles with knowledge and heat and can-do sexuality. Her alluring humanity and softness—coupled with the expectation that she has a lot more on her plate every day than rolling out of bed and posing for dollars—brings to mind novelist Nicholson Baker's observation, made in his highbrow trash novel *Vox*, that an orgasm in the mind of an intelligent woman is far more exciting than one that occurs in an outwardly gorgeous void. Soccer moms are smart, not just brainy in that librarian-about-to-take-her-hair-down way, but charged with a brand of common sense that conveys sufficiency of a superior, and way-sexy, grade.

In some quarters (pretty much everywhere but deepest, darkest suburbia), soccer moms have a bad rep, not to mention an aesthetically displeasing habitat (the mall), boring priorities (marriage and children), and bad footwear (white leather Keds). But how blind we are to interpret their sweet suburban industriousness as repressed and sexless. What could be more seductive to the active sexual imagination than pluck and verve and white cotton underpants?

I wasn't nuts for the postmodern meanderings of Dave Eggers's phenom-book *A Heartbreaking Work of Staggering Genius*, but at least one aspect of the work resonated for me: Eggers's desire to get over on one of his fellow parents. "I was looking to score," he writes of attending Back to School Night with his younger brother. "I expected attractive single mothers and flirting." I would probably have hatched the same plot, given the chance. Eggers, unfortunately, sees his plan wrecked on the shoals of his fellow single parents' unattractiveness. I, on the other hand, have kept my fantasies intact.

I see myself cruising soccer practice. The moms arrive in Dodge Caravans, hulking Suburbans, Volvo station wagons with Raffi thumping hard from the speakers, kids yelping in the back seat. I'm well prepared. I have SnackWells and nonalcoholic beer, baggies full of those dwarf carrots, and tiny boxes of raisins tucked in my pockets. I ogle the moms from a louche distance, voyeuristically pondering the rustle of L. L. Bean "Freeport Studio" separates against calves and biceps made sinewy by the aerobic exertions that only chasing seven-year-olds all day long can promote.

I shamble over to my quarry, who is perusing a copy of *Real Simple* on a beach towel redolent of Tide. I lay down my mojo, thick as the Welch's grape jelly I will lick from her heaving bosom in the back seat of her tinted-window SUV. I break the ice by asking if she voted for Christie Todd Whitman in the last New Jersey gubernatorial election. I suggest that maybe we've met someplace before, possibly at the big Nordstrom shoe sale.

Finally, I ask for the digits. She fishes around in the pocket of her willowy sundress and comes up with a crayon and a report card. "Call me," she whispers. I crack open another O'Doul's and offer her a pull. She tosses her nape-length chestnut tresses. She hiccups nervously—and we're off.

As seductions go, I think it's pretty compelling. And thanks to an ever-enlightening popular culture, it doesn't even involve much in the way of imagination. Ever since Sela Ward hefted the banner, during her *Sisters* days, for foxy maternity, more than a few of us have had a thing for babes with babies under their belts. Now Ward and her dark chevron forty-something eyebrows and come-hither half-smile (her overbite alone should be declared a national treasure) are starring in ABC's hit postdivorce, single-parent series *Once and Again,* and every week, I'm vibrating with lust.

When Sela hollers at her girls, I pop a woody. I had the same reaction to the Hope character on *thirtysomething:* infant on her hip, her house tumbling down around her, she still managed to embody the kind of woman you'd want to fuck so often that she'd get pregnant a few more times.

This is one of the core differences between soccer moms and supermodels: soccer-mom fertility inflames masculine virility. Supermodels would rather smoke cigarettes and get a pedicure; soccer moms want to fuck all night (once they get the kids to sleep, of course).

For guys who share my devotion to the Lifetime cable demographic, to the siren call of the estrogen set, the best soccer mom to score with is probably the single-mother soccer mom. (Just ask Nick Hornby.) I recall fondly (and with predictable firmness) that old IKEA TV ad that featured a recent divorcée on a shopping spree for new furniture, talking about how she might even want to have a guy over to her new bachelorette pad someday. "Oh, yeah," I thought. "Put the kids in front of Elmo, and I'll help you break in that new mattress."

There is a saucy sensibility, calibrated with a tad of neediness and unwanted celibacy, in these women. Plus, if I am to be completely honest, they represent the whole enchilada—sexy, appreciative women with kids and a no-nonsense approach to marriage.

Then again, I am susceptible to a melancholy reverence (and shivering horniness) when confronted by the married soccer mom. She, too, is saucy and, if statistics are correct, not averse to the stray romp with a young man. I adore her and am forced to envy her husband, one lucky dude by my measurement. Down deep, and despite my bacheloric protestations, there's a big part of me that wants to be him. After all, he gets to spend Saturdays studying the toggle of her proud soccer-mom ass as she navigates the fluorescent aisles of the supermarket, stocking up on Fruit Roll-Ups and Trix and gallons and gallons of reduced-fat milk.

And I, as the story always goes, am not alone. Ostensibly raffish single men—real lady-killers—have been mooning over moms forever. Does the acronym MILF (Mother I'd Like to Fuck) ring a bell? It might sound juvenile, but in truth it's an expression of desire for elegant maturity. And we are not talking here about the cross-generational couplings of a Benjamin Braddock and a Mrs. Robinson. The idea here is to be not a Young Turk out of his element with an older woman, but a youthful gentleman brought into his element through the ministrations of a woman bashful enough to wear a sarong, gentle enough to mop the drool from a baby's chin.

Literature is rife with images that derive from hallowed observations of soccer-mom lust. The hands-down sexiest paperback novel cover in my bookcases belongs to *The Sportswriter* by Richard Ford. It depicts sad-sack narrator Frank Bascombe's estranged suburban golf-pro wife in full, leggy, short-skirted follow-through. I stared at this cover for a solid ten minutes in the bookstore one day, considering all the smutty possibilities. No kohl-eyed urban slattern, this one. Not a *Sex and the City* floozy, vamped out in Pat Field skankwear and bounding from sack to sack in a futile quest for love and multiple orgasms. No, this woman had made her peace. This woman had once been spoken for, but not necessarily satisfied. She had experienced contractions. She was sexy and secure. She was June Cleaver, post–Summer of Love. She was Donna Reed with a diaphragm.

And then there is the quintessential cinematic soccer mom, Joan Allen, who managed, in Oliver Stone's *Nixon*, to make Tricky Dick's Pat a sort of simmering Republican sex symbol. She did even better in *The Ice Storm*, where, pitted against Sigourney Weaver's New Canaan swinger, it was Joan who got shtupped in the station wagon while Weaver struggled with Kevin Kline's guilty natterings. This is the thing about the saucy soccer mom and her transgressions: when she takes the plunge, she takes it deep.

Not that I know from experience. Alas, I have never shared a fling with a soccer mom. I've never slipped that mug of herbal tea from her hand and slid my tongue between her parted, unpainted lips. I've never consummated the Lands' End swimsuit issue smut that percolates in my reptile brain.

But I am confident that the day will come. Part of the soccer-mom charm, after all, is the suggestion of attainability. And if these women constitute a viable political constituency, there can't be a shortage of them out there. I imagine that sometime I will find myself in an American suburb on a crickety evening in late summer, and all the soccer moms will be sipping vodka tonics on the patio, and the moonlight will be illuminating their delicate crow's-feet and the enticing strands of gray that flicker in their no-muss, no-fuss dos. It is then that I'll strike.

I just worry that by that time, there will be a waiting list. It can't be long before, smitten by the Nordstrom "Reinvent the soccer mom" ads or the hottie mommy around the block, many, many fellows like me will be prostrating themselves before our bemused and eternally tolerant idols.

For the sake of fantasy, we must assume there will be enough to go around, a battalion of unconditional lovers who will smooth our rumpled khakis, run their fingers over our incipient bald spots, and nurture our brains out.

DERANGED MARRIAGE

Sridhar Pappu

IN THE DAYS before last Christmas, a girl I had never met or spoken to called me to see if I wanted to marry her. It wasn't the girl, really, but her family. And they didn't call me, exactly. They called my mother.

Thus began a series of events that concluded on a Saturday night in January with me sitting in the dark, sobbing into a pillowcase, drinking a bottle of He'brew beer that I'd saved from a friend's Hanukkah party, and listening to Merle Haggard. I had taken on the antiquated custom of arranged marriage, in its modern incarnation, and it had beaten me into a state of previously unfathomable self-pity that happened to include very bad beer.

This was new terrain for me. I am Indian by birth, but I grew up as a white kid in southwest Ohio. I drank beer in open fields in high school and still consider my greatest adolescent achievement the night I walked into the homecoming dance with the prettiest girl in my senior class. I worship Johnny Bench. And until last December, the prospect of an arranged marriage was an abstract idea to me, the appropriate narrative vein for someone else's story; my grandparents', my parents', even my sister's, but never my own.

Of course, I had distaste for all of it: a feeling, which informed every John Hughes movie I ever saw, that any kind of outside involvement in finding that "someone" was, well, wrong. I can say truthfully now that I felt the right girl would just come to me on, say, the Wilson Avenue Bridge in Chicago, or within the basement-level environs of the old Knitting Factory in New York. Tabula rasa. I'm here.

I believed my future would be spent in apartments on the Upper East Side or in Greenwich Village, where, my hands shoved into the pockets of a tweed sports coat, I would find myself asking a waiflike brunet why she was leaving me or coming back to me, or if she had ever loved me at all. I saw my brows furrowed and my eyes drawn close. "Jenny," I'd say, "what's this all about?"

The fact of the matter is that I have passed through nearly half of my twenties without experiencing anything close to that exchange, and I realize that, on some level, the idea of an arranged marriage has always been with me. It has served as both an emboldening force against loneliness and the precise cause of that loneliness, since it has hovered in the background as Plan B while I have searched for nothing less than the perfect girl.

Which brings us to the events of the past few months.

It all began with my hesitant approval of my mother's decision to start "the process." I did this without knowing precisely where or to whom that process might lead. Arranged marriage has changed a great deal since it was shipped to this country in the late 1960s, having been forced to embrace the exterior trappings of a world that it is designed to circumvent. There are (or can be) phone calls, dates, and months of courtship, supposedly meant to give the participants access to traits, qualities, and annoying habits not obvious at first glance. More important, these new aspects of the ritual seek to first simulate, then stimulate the intermittent passion, the plain pining, experienced in unmatched love.

My own faux dating started with a match to a girl from Louisiana that never got past the picture-viewing stage, then moved to a match with a soon-to-be-graduating medical school student from Florida. Nearly giddy in the days before Christmas, my mother and father called to say that, yes, "this one" was pretty, and soon, in a hotel room in Boston, they showed me her picture—with résumé.

The photograph showed her standing in profile, her face turned just slightly. She was wearing a sari with her hands placed over one another in an attempt to display a kind of grace. Her vita said her career goals include a "fellowship in gastroenterology" and listed her interests as "Languages, Literature" as well as travel and running. It went on to say that she enjoyed "people, social and fun loving." My father said she'd be coming to Chicago on the residency-interview trail in January, and that was when I could meet her.

"For now," said my father as I sat on the edge of the bed, pretending to only half-listen while watching *The Sopranos*, "we're going to just concentrate on doctors."

I met her two weeks later on a cold, sunless day. She had on a long, dark coat and a blue shawl, and a smile—bright and assured and unironic—that made her seem irreducibly pretty. We were, I felt, what a young couple should look like: well dressed and un-wrinkled, what Eudora Welty once described as a "matched team—like professional, Spanish dancers wearing masks."

We spent seven hours together—beginning with a tense el ride and a tenser, chitchatty lunch at the Berghoff meant to create casualness where there was none. Of course, the easiest way for characters in any story to address the large, overarching dilem-mas and issues (Why am I with you? What is going on between the two of us? How can I make things better?) is to talk about them, which, initiated by her, is what we did.

"Are your parents traditional?" she asked as we walked around the Art Institute.

"I guess they have traditional ideas," I said. "My dad likes to play the liberal, but my mom's the real heavy. They're pretty great, though. I dunno. I mean, what do you mean by 'traditional'?"

"I guess," she said, "I mean, what do they expect out of this?"

"I'm not sure," I said, and I wasn't.

"What do you expect out of this?"

"I don't know," I said, taken by her matter-of-factness. "How about you?"

She went on to tell me that her parents first brought up the idea a year ago, saying that as long as she was going to visit these cities, she "might as well" begin to meet "these" boys.

Listening to this, I felt my limbs entirely weaken and my head grow light. I thought about the Cincinnati Bengals' inability to keep their lead against the San Francisco 49ers in the 1989 Super Bowl, about the need for the Cincinnati Reds to pick up another quality starting pitcher. I saw my picture pasted on a bulletin board along with those of other earnest, nearsighted young Indian men. How did my looks rate next to theirs? My clothes? My hair? How did she feel when I told her that I felt unnerved around large groups of Indian people, that most of my close friends were Jewish?

I wanted to go home, but of course I didn't. Instead, I finished the museum tour with her and walked north up Michigan Avenue, talking to her about city politics in Chicago and Miami. She told me that she loved Cuban coffee, and I said that my father had raised my sister and me to drink Maxwell House black. She said there was nothing so pretty as a Florida sunset, but that she wanted to live in a place with hip, young professionals. I didn't ask but was pretty certain that she really, really liked *Friends*.

"So, Sridhar," she said before we entered a Starbucks, "what else?"

"About me," I replied, "or about this?"

"About this," she said. "What are your concerns?"

That night in my notebook, I would write that I was "gripped by an acute sensation to hold her and only let go 30 or 40 years later." I know, yeech. But I suppose that a good deal of me had thought this was a moment of real definition, where she could see something that set me apart from the rest of the Sanjays and Ajays, the would-be radiologists and software engineers. The future had in fact unfolded. Now it just needed ironing out.

Inside, over a tall mocha and a tall house coffee, we spoke about our problems with the process and what we expected from a potential spouse. She said she didn't want to get married for two more years, and that she wanted to move to Houston. Proximity, she said, was a definite issue. I expressed the sentiment that part of me didn't feel Indian enough, that I wanted someone not entirely freaked out by my intention to eventually write a novel.

Smitten is the word for what I felt. In the course of the day I had premonitions of attending her medical school graduation in May, of buying a fixer-upper in Houston's Rice Village with a large sunporch and a home office in the attic. Premature feelings perhaps, but not entirely out of line with the heightened sense that comes with these things, where every word choice, every pause, every action takes on 400 to 500 additional pounds in emotional weight.

I told her that I'd like to see her before she left town, and she said that she felt the same. When I called her two days later, however, she said seeing me again wasn't possible, that she had gone ahead and made plans with other people. "I guess," she said, "it's just not going to happen."

A pretty good piece of dialogue for someone who is not a writer, good enough to plunge me into a rueful weekend of darkness and "Mama Tried."

Since then, however, in talks with my parents and my sister, I have come to see this experience for what it was: the first match, the initial act in a process that seeks to remove the randomness from life, that deals with affection directly and is meant to eliminate the ambiguities and missed signals that plague us once we enter the love life of adults.

I'm not sure if it will ever "happen" for me, not in this way. But for now I'm willing to try.

FORESKIN AND SEVERAL YEARS FROM NOW

Kim Lane

"YOU'RE gonna wha, what?"

My husband had just announced his newest do-it-yourself project.

"I'm going to regrow my foreskin. Here's a book about it."

As the book slid across the table, my mind swirled with *Young Frankenstein*–type images of Gene Wilder holding a home skin-grafting kit and Marty Feldman standing near a refrigerator full of gelatinous brown blobs growing in petri dishes.

"How, w-w-what?" I continued to fumble.

"It'll take a while; it's a very gradual process," he said.

"See"—his hands began an illustrated dance in the air—"you pull the skin from the shaft up over the top of the penis, tape it, then apply constant tension, causing it to stretch and grow. It's called 'tugging.' Eventually, after a few years, the extra skin is long enough to cover the glans and act as a makeshift foreskin.

"I'm going back to do some research on the internet," he said, and casually tra-la-la'd past my petrified cadaver of a body, practically skipping on his way to the room he uses as a home office.

What just happened here? I thought. Did I hear the word *years*? I followed in hot pursuit.

"Where did you hear about this?" I questioned.

"In men's group," he mumbled, barely looking up from the computer. "They say once you're restored, you can have up to a 30 percent increase in sensation. Plus, I really want to look like our sons."

I knew it! That damned men's group, the one I frequently credit with saving my husband's life and our marriage, as well as making him emotionally whole again, is also the one that has introduced him to the sometimes radical ideas of the new men's movement: that smaller, fewer-axes-to-grind, reverse-gendered twin of the 1960s feminist confab.

Invariably, the morning after group night there is a large leaflet strategically positioned on the suspiciously bare kitchen table. Curious, I wander over with my cup of coffee, sit down, and begin reading about the unbelievable orgasmic nirvana I could provide my male sex partner if only I'd strap on an elbow-length latex glove slathered with about a jar of lubrication, enter what's usually an exit, then fish around for the male G-spot located just an inch or so below said partner's Adam's apple. If I'm lucky, there'll be a grotesquely detailed accompanying diagram with "You Are Here" marked on the anus.

My husband's group must reserve the last five minutes of each session for wife-shocking leaflet distribution. "Sorry, Tom, we'd really like to hear more about your feelings of unimportance, but it's LEAFLET TIME!" High-fives and whoops abound.

What baffles me is how I'd missed the foreskin-restoration leaflet.

Worry rapidly filled my thoughts. Had anyone done this successfully before? Surely there is a risk of permanent disfigurement when you decide to grow new pieces of your body. Did my husband draw the shortest straw at men's group?

I was a bundle of festering questions, but I decided it was best not to grill my husband just yet. I was afraid that if I made too strong a case against this process, or especially if I questioned its validity too quickly or vehemently, I might stoke his desire to proceed. Maybe he's just exploiting the shock value of it all, I lied to myself. Maybe it's a Drama King thing, and in a short while he'll lose interest.

It was a day or two later that they started appearing all over the house: miniature treasures left behind by the absentminded Foreskin Fairy. Coin-shaped pieces of tape, some featuring crudely hacked holes in the center and others festooned with clumps of gnarled pubic hair, would stick to the bottoms of my feet. A thin white strip of elastic, formed into a loop and then sewn together with erratic, black, big-as-a-staple stitches, like some *Flintstones* hair holder, showed up. And then there was my favorite: a warped little disk of forged and hardened clay possessing what appeared to be a teeny-tiny handle right in the center. It was like the Lilliputian Refuse Service had accidentally left behind a trashcan lid.

Then my five-year-old son's suspenders started disappearing.

"Honey, have you seen Greyson's blue suspenders?" I called from my son's closet, where I'd been on the floor rifling ineffectively through train tracks, stray Legos, and other fragments of boyhood in search of my elasticized quarry.

"I'll be out in a minute," my husband trilled from behind the bathroom door.

An hour later I heard him emerge and scuttle back to his office, closing the door behind him. I thought nothing of it until I noticed the frayed chunks of leftover suspenders scattered in the bathroom trash.

"Did you cut up these suspenders?" I asked hesitantly.

"Yeah, I needed them. I'll get Greyson some more."

I could just barely see a section of suspender peeking out of his T-shirt.

"What's that?" I asked.

So began my introduction to the first in my foreskin farmer's series of cobbled-together suspender-remnant contraptions known as: the Devices.

Crude, yes, but fascinating in an *Inspector Gadget* sort of way. The first one featured a large loop to slide the left arm through, leaving the remainder of the suspender strap to trail down the left side of the body. A clip at the end of the strap attached to tape stuck around the penis. At first glance, the whole ensemble sort of resembled a stop-gap holster and quickly earned the name the OK Corral-er.

His poor penis looked miserable, strained and reddened, like it was struggling in some Torquemada-inspired mechanism from the Oscar Mayer Inquisition.

"Oh, God! Does it hurt?" I asked, trying not to scream.

"Not too much. It's a little sore."

A few weeks later came the Formal—so named because at a

distance it appeared as though my husband was wearing a long black necktie. One rather tight elastic loop fitted around his neck, with the remainder of the strap trailing down his chest and belly to the taped penis. I have a fondness for this model because it's the only one I laughed at out loud—to his face, anyway. It just looked so damned dangerous. What if the loop suddenly cut off his air somehow, like when he was driving?

"If you have an accident with that thing on," I remarked, "don't expect me to come claim your body."

After the first full day of wearing the Formal, my husband seemed to be hobbling around more than usual. He said his penis was once again sore from the constant "attention." Seconds later, our four-year-old bounded into the room, jumped on my husband's lap, yanked the elastic strap, and said, "Hey! What's THIS?" I'd never seen a person completely fold in half so quickly.

Finally, after a brief trial-and-rejection period of the Fred Mertz—consisting of a strap leading from the clip on the penis down the right leg to a tight loop just below the right knee, resembling an upside-down sock garter popular with some older men—the Hipster made its debut as the most discreetly designed and popular model. It featured a strap made into a hip belt with a perpendicular segment in front that clipped to the taped penis. At least this device was hidden completely from John and Jane Q. Public. But then again, John Q. himself might be a tugger.

While waiting for my husband to grow disenchanted with his project, I did a little independent tugger research of my own. According to statistics provided by NORM (the National Organization of Restoring Men), there are approximately 18,000 known tuggers, as well as countless more unreported members (ahem), mostly in the United States.

Printed along with the statistics were stories promising the heightened glans sensation to which my husband had referred, as well as details regarding a much-desired effect known as the "gliding sensation," a perk that occurs during sex. Apparently, once the restored penis is inserted, the extra skin on its shaft causes the exterior to remain relatively static while the interior of the shaft does its business. This gliding effect, done with little or no friction, is purportedly much more pleasurable for both sex partners. Could be interesting, I thought.

Like my husband, some tuggers are using the elastic strap method to stretch the skin around their penises, while others are reportedly donning outrageous Monty Python–esque contraptions—from old fishing weights that accidentally fall down and out of a pant leg during board meetings to detached mouthpieces lifted from old trumpets, trombones, and tubas. (Blow jobs will just never be the same.)

One discovery that has definitely managed to quiet the sarcastic witch living inside me is the impressive electronic support system available to tuggers. Dwelling happily on the internet is a well-established cybercommunity where learned members share advice, helpful hints, and even personal photos of the restorative process. Savvy members are known to pepper their posts with the trademark signoff, "K.O.T." (Keep On Tuggin') or with special Tugger emoticons concocted and recognized by the group:

Uncircumcised====> Circumcised ====/> Restoring
(time)====/> R18 months Restored====>R

IT'S BEEN ALMOST a year since my husband began his quest for a foreskin. Aside from the occasional, "Not tonight, honey, I've got a dick ache," our sex life remains as healthy, active, and normal as ever. There is the occasional dash from sight to disassemble the foreskin machine, but I've grown accustomed to it.

I've also grown accustomed to him going through more medical tape than an ER and spending as much time in the bathroom as a prepubescent schoolgirl. I imagine that he, in turn, has grown accustomed to my occasional comments, like, "How's the slingshot this morning?" and "Could you unhinge your iron maiden so we can have sex?"

The only thing I'm not sure has grown, however, is his foreskin.

Although from my vantage point his penis appears exactly as it did when he started the project (he swears there's been marked progress), I do wonder what it will look like when the process is complete. Will I find its floppy little turtleneck of skin enticing? Will my husband have the wherewithal and dedication to see this day-in-day-out project through to completion—especially if he should have to begin working in an office away from home? What will happen if he decides to stop tugging mid-turtleneck?

Also, since circumcision continues to be a routine procedure, I can't help but wonder if tugging might eventually become a mainstream interest. Can we expect a full array of Tugger-related products? Tugger Brand Tape? Wear Your Device to Work Day? *Tugging for Dummies*?

Whatever happens, I'm confident that I'll be kept in the know through the regular consumption of men's group leaflets.

WHILE YOU ARE GONE

Stephen J. Lyons

I STAY UP LATE, past the eleven-o'clock news, *Letterman* and *Conan*, Black Entertainment Television and the Tae-Bo infomercial. The radio keeps company with the television, which, in turn, competes for airspace with the stereo. I might even dance with Bonnie Raitt. Well, not the actual Bonnie Raitt, because I'm faithful the entire time.

I shower less, but use up all the hot water. The bathroom door stays open. Without you to kiss and snuggle, some days I forget to brush my teeth or shave back the stubble. Sadly, you are not around to reassure me I'm not getting fat. As a result, I feel obese, which keeps me from walking around the house naked.

All the coffee is mine, and it's all gone by 10 A.M., but I still crave more even when I get that high-pitched pain in my chest. Since you left, my daily research has found that high doses of caffeine create the illusion of an exciting, productive morning. However, by noon all I have to show is an hour of what I believe is an excellent guitar practice featuring variations of one minor and three major chords. (I have accomplished this while still wearing my red flannel pajamas, the ones with the revealing snap-fly in the bottoms.)

To me, the guitar sounds like Leo Kottke. You might disagree, but you're not here. So I sing my favorite John Prine and Steve Goodman songs and pretend I'm at the Troubadour in Los Angeles and there are important people in black suits and modern eyeglasses favorably evaluating me. After I finish a rousing rendition of "City of New Orleans" that involves a complex finger-picking arrangement performed behind my back, I'm signed to a three-record deal, and as a signing bonus, the company publishes my long-awaited first book of poetry that I wrote in high school.

Food doesn't taste as good as when you make it. My grandmother once left my grandfather alone for several days, and because he could not read, he ate dog food. "Best stew I ever ate," he declared, wiping his mouth. Unlike Grandpa, I know how to cook (and read), but I'd rather not eat than eat alone. When I finally get hungry, I take my meals hunched over the sink or slouched in front of the television. Weird combinations emerge: cheeseburgers with red onions on cinnamon-raisin bagels. Pretzels and mints. Chicken fried in soy sauce. Saltines dipped in a yogurt-salsa mixture. I eat heavily salted crinkle-cut french fries with every meal.

Most of the time, though, I simply lack the energy to eat. Salads take too much time to prepare—all that washing, peeling, and slicing. Fruit now seems inedible, and I wonder if I'll get scurvy. Thank goodness for vitamins. So simple, so thorough, so clean. For some dinners, crackers and cheese and a giant bowl of wholesome, toasted whole-grain oat cereal might do the trick. The other night I got so absorbed in reading the back of the

Cheerios box that I almost swallowed a promotional gizmo from the movie *Toy Story*.

Did you know that Cheerios has its own website and email address? "Dear BigG@mail.genmills.com: Please stop producing those hideous blue plastic spoons that you place in specially marked boxes of Cheerios. I almost ate one by mistake. They are a wasteful and unnecessary use of our precious energy resources. By the way, I also found a thumb, an eyeball, and a ferret's head in the same box. Just kidding. There was no thumb."

I pay way too much attention to our cats. They are not as entertaining as when you are here. I note every twitch and physics trick performed to gain the upper hand. They pay too much attention to me through unwavering eye contact. They sense my moods and anticipate my every move. At dinnertime they perch and plead until I feed them. (Forgive me for occasionally snapping their tails.) They are hungry but have no intention of earning their meals.

For the first time I notice that Toby's kibble is shaped in the silhouette of a cat. Mickey's whiskers are a quarter-inch longer than Toby's. (I had the time, so I measured.) If I should die overnight from those espresso chest pains, I have no doubt the cats would tear into me within an hour. They see stuff I can't, jumping straight up into the air to grab ghost mice and conquer kingdoms of invisible winged insects.

Each morning I trudge downstairs to dig through their box for droppings. This was always your job. Instead of buried treasures, I find a week's worth of throw-up messes on the carpet.

Have the cats suddenly become bulimic? Are they placing their paws down their throats to show me up? Given the price of the gourmet cat food we buy, I estimate a cost of around 50 cents per vomit. I never wanted to think about any of this.

Different thought patterns emerge. My old self—the one you first fell in love with—returns. He comes in without knocking, carrying his old duffel bag filled with those two or three shiny tricks that brought him this far. We sit across the kitchen table from each other and watch the sunset in silence.

I look him over. At twenty pounds lighter, with a thirty-two-inch waist and only one chin, he looks better than I do. He always does, even with his body pierced in seven places and his newest tattoo, an illustrated history of surfing. Single, of course, but with plenty of recent, exciting experience that he's more than willing to share. He's been out in California, backpacking in the high Sierras, studying Zen masters, learning Spanish, and working on his long-range jump shot.

"How long is she gone this time?" he asks, putting his mud-caked cowboy boots up on the table and rolling a joint the size of Rhode Island.

"Look, I don't want any trouble this time," I answer, digging out an ashtray from the junk drawer and pulling down the shades. "I don't want to blow this relationship. Just stay long enough so I can remember who I was, or am, or whatever. And do you have to smoke that stuff in my house? Everyone on this street is a member of Block Watch."

"Still afraid I see," he says, squinting and inhaling half the joint in one loud toke. "Relax, I don't even exist. Anyway, I can't stay long. I've got a hot date with a little raven-haired senorita in El Paso. She and her sister have this certain game they like to play that involves hot oil. First, they slowly pull down—"

"Please, have mercy on me. My wife has been gone for three weeks. I'm a sexual camel, and I don't need to hear any narratives of your conquests."

"Suit yourself," he says, rolling another joint, spilling stems and seeds everywhere. I hear a siren in the distance.

"Man, I've got the munchies something bad. Do you have anything to eat, something salty or sweet? Got any Cap'n Crunch? What's with the cats? Don't you ever feed them? Their sides are sunk in. And do they have to stare at me like that? They're freaking me out, man."

"Cats are fine," I snap back. I give Mickey, who is obviously sucking in his cheeks for dramatic effect, my most evil human look. "Might have something to do with that cigar you're smoking."

He starts right in at me. "What happened to you? Remember when you first saw the Colorado Rockies, and that glorious fall weekend at the Highland Mary Lakes up above Silverton? Remember when everything you touched felt sacred and surreal? Remember all those chances you used to take—the time you walked back a mile into an abandoned mine shaft or rappelled into the cliff dwellings at Mesa Verde? I heard you now attend church and are even saving for retirement. How come you don't wear jeans anymore? Have you gained weight, or have you just given up?"

"Be nice," I tell him. "I'm trying to hold on here. I still have forty years of life left. I'm not eternal like you, and I'm not currently on an antidepressant. Besides, I like my modest life."

"Suit yourself," he answers, rummaging through the cupboards, finally settling on stale graham crackers and walnuts. "I'm going to crash on the couch. Where's the remote? Sure you don't want a hit of this weed? It's Garberville's best. You look tense."

"No thanks. I'll stick to coffee and jogging. Could you please take off your boots? God knows what you've stepped in."

"It's called earth, pal. Organic and sensual. Mother Earth. You might want to check her out sometime. Open those curtains. Take a good look. She's right outside that locked door." He lobs a few more sarcastic cracks my way, then fades off into the distance. The cats seem desperate to follow. As I watch him head south in the general direction of Texas, I reach for the air freshener and remember why I'm not the man I used to be.

Back in the kitchen, the large cast-iron frying pan, the one in which by accident I made blackened chicken, has been sitting on the stovetop for two days. Small pregnant insects are hovering above the mess. Just calculating the tremendous expense of elbow grease it will take to wash away that caked bird exhausts me.

With you gone, I have to make all these big decisions myself.

Do I watch *Frontline* or *Who Wants to Be a Millionaire?* Do I clean a little bit each day or do I wait until a day before you return and do one frenzied cleaning convulsion? Do I ski or take a nap? Should I do laundry or start a novel? Bathe or meditate?

In seven days you'll return. At first we'll be shy with each other. But the initial awkwardness will vanish with the first kiss. (How I look forward to that!) All the cellular subtleties will click into place—the comforting pheromonal smells, tastes, and touches that draw us to each other. Our thought patterns and emotions will shift back to the codependent way we've developed over the past five years.

I hope you will tell me I look thin, that I may have lost some weight. Your brown eyes will look prettier than ever. While we wait for the luggage, I'll tuck you in just beneath my shoulder, where you fit so perfectly.

I'll have our home sparkling in domestic tidiness: clean sheets and pillowcases, towels and washcloths. I'll even polish the wood. I may bake bread or cook my famous onion soup: equal parts butter to equal parts onions. I'll stock ample supplies of your favorites: fig bars and animal crackers. The toilet bowl will smell like an English garden. You will be able to see your reflection in the bathtub. The little hill of crumbs in front of the television will be vacuumed away. Dust balls destroyed. Cobwebs corralled. Litter box liberated. Plates and bowls will be so clean, you'll be able to eat off them.

Upon your arrival the cats will immediately calm down, but

still demand to be fed. You'll pick them up to see how much weight they have gained. They will try to tell you about the excessive tail snapping and the few (very few) times I sprayed water at them, but their meows will be incomprehensible. It will remain our little secret.

You won't unpack right away. This is always worrisome to me, as if you're reevaluating the situation. So I'll be on my best behavior and give you acres of space just in case. We'll start off slow, like we're courting—lots of hand-holding and close hugs. I will realize it's been a month since another human has embraced me.

You will have one of your hot relaxing baths, and I'll peek in to take a good look. I'll prepare the coffee for tomorrow. Mickey and Toby will eat again.

In just a couple of hours my entire orientation will go from solitude to grateful accommodation. That uninterrupted internal voice, so loud and persistent for the last four weeks, will speak a different language. And what is this language? When we speak it together, we are talking about our home, our simple life of books and birds, music and faith. A vocabulary of love. As you slip under the covers to join me in bed, the last thought I have will be, "I do okay alone, but I sure do better with you."

CRYSTAL IS THE CUSTOMARY GIFT—
I GOT DOG DROOL

Susan Musgrave

I SLIP OFF my wedding ring, which doesn't fit so snugly anymore, and add it to the plastic tray, along with two hand-carved silver bracelets and one of copper, a heavy metal belt, a brass watch with lizards curling around the band, and a necklace of flattened nails and vertebrae that a friend brought me back from Africa. I step through the metal detector.

On my wedding day, fifteen years ago today, I wore the same body armor, along with French garters, but that time I didn't take it off. I lit up the scanner's alert panel to the highest number: 10.

Stephen and I were married in a maximum-security prison. He had written a novel while finishing up a twenty-year sentence for bank robbery, and the manuscript landed on my desk when I was writer-in-residence at a Canadian university. I fell in love—with his writing on the first page, with him, before first sight. All I had left to do was to meet the man.

I wrote to Stephen, in my official writer capacity. My opinion was that his book should be published. I wrote later the same day, offering to work as his editor. I wrote a third letter, asking if he needed anything—books, paper, pens. In the last letter I sent that afternoon I wrote, "P.S. Will you marry me?"

I didn't get an immediate reply, so I wrote again the next day, apologizing for being so hasty. I got carried away, I wasn't serious. Just because he was a notorious outlaw (the FBI's wanted poster described him as bright, witty, a bon vivant) didn't mean he was going to fall for some woman who threw herself at him lock, stock, and Uzi barrel. He might, after all, be old-fashioned.

Stephen replied, finally. All thirteen letters had arrived on the same day. No one had asked him to marry her before, he said. He suggested we meet first. (I was right, he was old-school.)

I visited him behind bars for two years, in monitored rooms where we sat at square tables, at right angles according to regulations, working on his book, which grew to more than 400 pages, working on our love affair, which grew into an epic. When his book was published and he still didn't make parole, we set a wedding date.

The ceremony took place in the prison chapel, attended by my mother and sister and four of Stephen's friends from inside. Two guards stood watch over the cake knife as we exchanged vows.

As Stephen was escorted back to his cell to change out of the Armani suit I'd bought for him into his prison greens, I said good-bye to my mother and sister at the front gate, tossing my bouquet over the fourteen-foot perimeter fence topped with razor wire.

Then there was the honeymoon—a three-day affair in a house inside the prison walls allocated for Private Family Visits. They are conjugal visits, in the vernacular, but that makes it sounds as if it's only about sex. We cooked, read books, played Yahtzee, and watched *Late Night with David Letterman*. And when the phone rang, four times a day, we got dressed and went outside to be counted.

Not long after that, Stephen came home on full parole. We had a daughter two years later. Living together seemed easy. Unhappily, it was not forever after.

Our married life went into remission on June 9, 1999, the day my husband—disguised as a transvestite Barbie, and wired on heroin and cocaine—failed to rob the Royal Bank in peaceful Cook Street Village, in Victoria, British Columbia. Stephen, once the leader of the Stopwatch Gang (famous for making it in and out of a bank in under two minutes), spent four minutes withdrawing $100,000 of other people's money from the bank that day. "I could have taken out a loan in less time," he admitted later.

He remembers little of the car chase through the prim neighborhood park, or the shooting at police officers who pursued him. Both of us remember, only too well, the day six months later, when the judge sentenced him to eighteen years.

Stephen had fought a lifelong addiction to heroin, and the habit had won—this round, anyway. In an essay called "Junkie," just published in *Addicted: Notes from the Belly of the Beast*, Stephen wrote, "Prisons are about addictions. Most prisoners are casualties of their own habits. They have all created victims—some in cruel and callous ways—but almost to a man they have first practised that cruelty on themselves. Prison provides the loneliness that fuels addiction. It is the slaughterhouse for addicts, and all are eventually delivered to its gates."

My first visit to the medium-security institution where Stephen had been transferred was to coincide with our fifteenth wedding anniversary. It would be a family affair—including our daughter, who is twelve—and take place in the house designated for conjugal visits.

Once we are through the gates and metal detector, my daughter and I face a guard who pulls on a pair of black gloves to go through our personal effects, most of which I have itemized, as I've been told to do. My daughter has brought along her French homework and a suitcase the contents of which I have failed to list. The guard opens the bag and shuts it again—immediately. She must have a daughter who wears makeup, too.

My belongings are more problematic. The guard vetoes my pillow, citing enhanced security. I know better than to ask what this means—I have learned not to ask questions about prison policies. I assume that since September 11, prison administrators, like everyone else, have become even more security-conscious. Let one family member bring her pillow in, and the next thing you know, the whole family will be wanting to bring in pillows.

My pillow and I are bonded like Brinks guards; it has represented the very foundation of security for me ever since I was four years old and my mother threw my stuffed rabbit into the fire (they didn't have child psychology back then) because I kept crying for it in the night. I never leave home without my pillow. I won't sleep well—if at all—without it.

Now I have a choice to make: my security or my marriage. I stuff the pillow into a locker marked Private Family Visits, which smells of sweaty shoes and cigarette smoke. I remind myself that marriage involves sacrifice. Stephen doing eighteen years hard time is small beer compared to the three nights looming ahead of me, alone without my pillow, but I vow not to make him feel guilty about it. I start planning, instead, for our next family visit. A false-bottomed suitcase would be one solution, I think.

I realize as I relinquish my pillow that the guard is likely to bust a gut when she comes upon the Georgian silver flatware I spent the morning polishing. (I like family mealtimes to be a civilized affair.) Sure enough, she stands back from the "utensils," as she calls them, as if they could be weapons of mass destruction. They have to be locked up.

My insides reach a roiling boil. I never use stainless—"It leaves a taste," as my father always said—and just because I am going to prison, I don't see why I should be expected to lower my standards. The knives are bone-handled, passed down from William the Conqueror. And our table-napkin rings, with family crest and initials engraved on them . . . Oh, what's the use, I think, as I chuck my valuables into the vile-smelling locker. My values and my standards go with them—all of little consequence, I guess, where security is at stake.

Next she inspects my briefcase. Rules allow only one "reading book," which I will finish the first afternoon. Besides, I say, "I need different books for different moods, and who can predict what mood I'll be in by this evening, given I'll be . . ." the words *without my pillow* hang unspoken between us.

Even my daughter is beginning to look impatient. I narrow my choice down to *Getting the Love You Want,* then trek back to the locker with an armload of rejects while the guard homes in on my magazines. I've brought a new *Martha Stewart Living* (I was trying to be a good citizen and supported my daughter's school magazine drive) and two back issues of *Colors:* one devoted to war, the other to touch. The guard opens the latter, of course, perhaps because the cover features two naked men of different ethnic persuasions vigorously French-kissing.

Colors, I explain, is an art magazine. "Doesn't look therapeutic to me," she says, letting me know she views art, and private family visits, as therapy. She puts the magazine down and opens the *Martha Stewart.* My daughter looks at *Living* and says to the guard, "That's the really subversive one."

When we're repacked, we're told to stand side by side on two yellow dots in the middle of the floor. A black dog, trained to sniff out drugs, is led into the room; I pray my daughter has left at home the pot she grew for a school science project to impress her dad. It turns out I have nothing to worry about. The dog doesn't sit (as he's trained to do when he scores), and that evening, when her father and I bring up the subject of smuggling drugs into a prison, she says, with adolescent indignation, "Don't you two know anything? People come here to buy their weed, Dad."

(My husband wants to know what kind of people I have been letting our daughter associate with. This probably isn't the moment to enlighten him. Our Juliet has been sighted at the local hockey rink with the Romeo son of one of the police officers my husband peppered with birdshot.)

A van drives us to our cottage, where Stephen, who has already been transported from his unit, awaits us. His eyes meet mine, and when we climb out of the van he hugs our daughter first, and then hugs me—as if we are lovers who have been parted from one another for a long time, but not for the first time; lovers whose lives have become a familiar ritual of disruption and reconciliation.

Our daughter curls up with *Colors*—the Touch issue—while my husband and I unpack the supplies he's bought for three days of conjugal bliss. (He fills out a food order from the kitchen a month before our visit, and pays for the food from his account.) As he unpacks I remember that there was a good reason I used to be in charge of the grocery shopping when he was at home: if I asked him to buy flour, he'd come home with five twenty-five-pound bags. He was never one to live life—from robbing banks to grocery shopping—on anything but full throttle, and sure enough, we have enough food to feed the prison population until Christmas. In fact, we could probably do eighteen years locked up in this house with him, and not go hungry.

I hear our daughter's voice from the living room, where she's been engrossed in her magazine. "Mum, this is like totally sick. No wonder they didn't want you bringing it for Dad."

Her dad and I grab the magazine to see what we have been missing. If a twelve-year-old thinks it's sick, it has to be majorly disgusting.

We open to a man wearing black socks—you can't see his face because his head is in a pillory—and black underpants pulled naughtily down. A busty leather-clad dominatrix is lashing his red bottom with a whip. "When it starts to get intense," she says, "they wriggle and squirm, they use swear words occasionally, but they stay in place." I want to rush back to the front gate and explain to the guard, this is art, not pornography, and besides, I didn't know this photograph was there.

"What are they going to think of me?" I cry. "They'll think I'm some kind of pervert."

"They'll just think I perverted you," my husband sighs. "They think all inmates are criminals."

For the next three days and nights we live like a normal family, though nothing seems normal to me without my pillow. (I am definitely going through separation anxiety.) At the risk of being called a martyr, I decide it's important to make my husband aware of how much I have sacrificed to spend this quality time with him. When he stops laughing, he reminds me that I have crossed international borders with everything from an inflatable alligator (when I was nine) to emeralds (much later) concealed on my body. Now I am considering having a special suitcase made for my pillow?

I'm sorry I mentioned it, I say. Conjugal bliss is beginning to feel an awful lot like marriage.

In most respects, though, I adapt to family prison life quite easily. We have a panoramic view of the majestic razor wire surrounding our abode, and the phone only rings four times a day. It's never for me, it's for all of us. When we hear the phone ring, we have to get up, go outside, and be counted. Sometimes they call back right away, and we have to go out again for a recount. "How hard can it be," my daughter asks her dad, "to count to three?"

We cook, we read (I finish *Getting the Love You Want* the first afternoon), we play Scrabble on the floor. We watch movies about drug trafficking and prison escapes, which the public must find therapeutic—there seems to be one on every channel. In a drawer beside our bed I discover a Tupperware container full of condoms, lubricants, latex gloves, and dams, like the ones the dentist puts in your mouth (for safe oral sex, I suppose), and a miniature bottle of bleach—for those who somehow manage to smuggle in hypodermic needles. (It's a weird system: they'll bust your ass if they catch you bringing in drugs, but if you succeed, they help you use clean needles.) We conjugate, too. French verbs. For my daughter's French test on Monday.

On October 12, the day of our wedding anniversary (I remembered it as being the tenth, Stephen the fifteenth; I checked when I got home, and we were both wrong), we pack again and prepare to say our good-byes. But first we clean the house. We wash the floors, vacuum the rugs, and then rake them so that our footprints don't show. My husband has learned many new domestic skills since coming back to jail. These days, he says, he exchanges muffin recipes instead of tunnel plans out in the big yard.

My daughter and I will be picked up and driven to the front gate; my husband will accompany us that far. We have our bags waiting on the road outside our house when one van pulls up, followed by another. But now we're ordered back inside and told to line up in the living room, side by side, on the very spot where I made the word *innocent* in Scrabble last night and scored 15 points.

The same dog we met on the way in is led into the middle of my husband's newly raked carpet. He sniffs around us—not once, but four times. He noses our crotches and our behinds, leaving his drool. It's humiliating. Surely it's unnecessary. Definitely it is intimidating.

Then I think, Maybe my daughter is right. Maybe people do come here to buy drugs. It's evident that we're suspected of trying to smuggle something out of this place, and it clearly isn't my husband, who is staring at his shoes.

If I had tears left, I probably would weep, but instead I stand, shaken, angry, and, I admit, tired of it. (For a target search such as this, they have to be 99 percent certain they'll find drugs.) My daughter tells me later, when the dog doesn't sit and we're free to go, that she thinks the warden saw the bumper sticker on my car saying "Bad Cop, No Doughnut," and it was payback time.

The usual anniversary present for couples celebrating fifteen years of marriage is crystal, but trust Stephen to come up with something more romantic. At least I think it's romantic to get drooled on by a drug dog for your fifteenth wedding anniversary. (Which, I'm sure, is one reason our marriage has endured.)

Leaving is hard. At the front gate, 600 pounds of steel slams shut between his last heartbeat and my next one. I unlock the Private Family Visit locker and hug my pillow while my daughter applies another layer of makeup to face the world outside. And I think: If I can't have the love I want right now, right now I'm getting the love I'm meant to have.

MEATMARKET.COM

Heather Havrilesky

THE GOLDEN age of on-line dating is upon us. Just ask executives of Match.com, who last month reported a 195 percent increase in paid subscribers over the same quarter last year. Or look at Yahoo, where on-line personals have increased the company's revenues despite a decline in income from advertising. Or talk to any youngish single person in New York. When I asked a friend, who met her last boyfriend on-line, how many of her single friends had used or are currently using on-line dating services, she replied, "Pretty much all of them."

Look no further than the "Personals of the Day" you see pop up on Salon.com as well as the Onion and countless other sites, and you'll realize two things: One, on-line personals have become a major source of revenue for content sites, and two, there are some damn fine-looking young folks floating around out there. Unless Spring Street Networks, the source of those ads, has been inventing fictional singles with a crack team of models, stylists, marketers, and professional photographers, there appear to be a great many attractive people on-line these days, shamelessly hamming it up in the hopes of meeting that special anyone.

It's a far cry from the spring of 1996, when I attended a party

for Match.com that was populated primarily by computer pro-
grammers who looked like they hadn't left the server room of
their start-up offices in several months, their only contact with
other humans limited to those moments when they braved the
weak San Francisco sunlight to fetch a banana moon pie from the
company's vending machine, or to scuttle over to Cafe Centro for
a quadruple nonfat latte. That tall blond girl who worked there
sure was cute, but she was sort of mean!

Now that blond girl is prominently featured on the pages of
Match.com, pensively biting a manicured finger while lounging
across an unmade bed in her nightie under the moniker "sweet
'n' dirty."

So how did everything change so quickly, and why have people begun peddling themselves so shamelessly on-line?

The truth is, most young people see nothing the least bit embarrassing about on-line dating, or "man shopping," as one
woman referred to it in a recent *New York Times* article. Maybe
kids today are far less self-conscious about romance and love in
general, thanks to not having been exposed to *The Love Boat* during their formative years. The more likely explanation, though, is
that the anonymity of the medium, the prevalence of blogs, on-
line photo galleries, and personal websites, and the comfort most
of us feel in corresponding entirely through email have combined
to make on-line dating a perfectly acceptable means of meeting
new people.

Demand creates supply. When you think for a minute about

how inefficient and circuitous the traditional delivery system for meeting potential lovers is, it's not hard to see how we landed here. When your options are limited to getting set up by your friends, going out to parties, or visiting smoky bars in the hopes of getting drunk enough to knock over someone with a pulse, it's clear why shopping for a mate on-line has been embraced by mainstream America.

Imagine, if you will, trying to buy a food processor without a Best Buy, or a Macy's, or a Williams-Sonoma. Imagine if you had to go to crowded parties and other tedious functions and search the crowd for someone with an old Cuisinart at home that they might be willing to sell you. Furthermore, imagine if it were considered rude to bring up the Cuisinart straight off the bat—instead, you were expected to ask people about themselves, maybe buy them a drink, and feign interest in their rambling, self-involved banter, until finally, at the end of the night, loosened up by a few drinks, you could say what had been on your mind for hours:

"Um. I hope this doesn't sound too forward, but do you . . . process food?"

And despite all that effort, imagine that the person's face drops, and he or she replies politely, but in a clipped, uncomfortable tone, "No, I'm not really into that kind of thing," and then exits the party without even asking for your number in case he or she ever does get the urge to process.

Now that love has finally been commodified and booty has an

efficient distribution system, it makes sense that the branding strategies of those peddling their goods and services have become increasingly finessed.

Of course, it was only a matter of time before we gave up on classified ads and moved on to a more dynamic format. After all, how long could the same classy DWM, 50s, keep trumpeting his love for red wine and red roses and cuddling to any SWF who's both idle enough and disturbed enough to pore over that minuscule print? As Scott Bedbury, the marketing strategist who helped to launch campaigns for Nike and Starbucks, writes in his book *A New Brand World,* "The most innovative product line will grow stale in the minds of potential consumers if the marketing has become static, undifferentiated, or—even worse—irritating for lack of change."

A change has certainly come upon us. Browse the personals on Bust.com or Nerve.com, and you'll see for yourself: gone are the candlelit dinners and the long walks on the beach. Cooking and travel and nights by the fire sound as old and lame as that "Like a Rock" theme song that Chevy can't seem to leave behind.

We've entered a new era of self-branding, featuring tasty professional photographs and sales pitches feistier than those dreamt up by a skilled copywriter. Today's on-line love-seeker isn't looking for someone who's "sexy and sophisticated and fit," he's looking for "Someone to end my hedonistic ways—or someone to take me headlong deeper into them." You can almost hear Britney singing that bump-and-grind Pepsi theme song in the background: "The rrrride! Just enjoy the rrrrride! Don't need a reason why!"

That jingle doesn't actually include the word *Pepsi,* by the way—it's the natural evolution of ads that we move from an exhortation to consume the product ("Drink Pepsi!") to an invitation to enjoy a sensual experience that's only loosely (but inextricably) associated with the product ("Just enjoy the rrrride!"). Similarly, today's on-line ads are almost subliminal. What is he looking for? Not "a blue-eyed blond with a great rack." No! He's looking for "the connection, the compassion, the empathy and the acceptance we all seek." I had no idea Deepak Chopra was single!

In keeping with current advertising trends, today's on-line singles market themselves not by highlighting their best traits but by creating an imaginary self that's impressively snarky and carefree. Much like the recent spate of humorous TV ads for serious products like Washington Mutual or Budget Rent-a-Car, many personal ads use humor to draw in potential customers. For "Best (or worst) lie I've ever told," one guy wrote, "I never lie." And I found more than one straight man who listed *Deliverance* as the source of his favorite on-screen sex scene.

Of course, Spring Street Networks deserves at least some of the credit for provoking participants into offering up such original and zesty prose. When "self-deprecation" is listed next to cigarettes and booze under "my habits," and you're asked to answer whether you indulge in it "often, sometimes, or never," the mind starts working in self-conscious yet creative new ways.

And who can't help but get a little clever or provocative when asked to fill in the following: "(blank) is sexy; (blank) is sexier." For example: "Flexibility is sexy; focus is sexier." Why not just say "Good sex is sexy; great sex is sexier"? Or how about this zinger: "Appearance is sexy; attitude is sexier." Sounds like the next Sprite campaign.

You have to hand it to these on-line daters for the enthusiasm with which they commodify themselves. Most seem unabashedly honest in exposing themselves, and few appear to be unfamiliar with the value-add. As Bedbury asserts, it's important to "know that your advertising must create a proposition that your product or service delivers on, time and time again." Accordingly, chirpy love-seekers offer up their services with the enthusiasm of merchants at a street market: "I visit the beach or the canyons at least once a week!" "I'm easygoing and intense!" "I give great massages!" And then there's the more subtle: "I love cunnilingus!"

Furthermore, Bedbury explains, the great brands tell a story, like a great piece of mythology, "with the customer, not the company, as the story's main protagonist." Our on-line love-seekers seem to sense this intuitively: "[You're] not someone who thinks *Cathy* is funny, but someone who thinks *The Jerk* is funny." "You love who you are, but you want so much more." "You'll love my vegan pancakes in the morning!"

And since we've become products ourselves, it makes sense that we can only advertise ourselves by associating with other products. Indeed, each personal ad patches together an increasingly eclectic and romantic mélange of brands to create a signature brand: *The Anarchist Cookbook,* Moroccan Mint loose tea, Jack Russell terriers, *Naked* by David Sedaris, Tenacious D, Williams-Sonoma, *North by Northwest* starring Eva Marie Saint and Cary Grant, Vespas, late sixties Hanna-Barbera cartoons. The cultural references become dizzying after a while, with each brand standing on the shoulders of a million brands that came before it. Pepsi is Britney Spears is Marilyn Monroe is *Pleasantville* is the idealized 1950s. Chevy is Bob Seger is the American Farmer is Marlboros is Wrangler Jeans is *The Grapes of Wrath.*

But as on-line ads become more aggressive and clever and self-consciously crafted, what impact does that have on the human interactions that result from them? What does it mean to peddle yourself so effectively before you even meet your prospective partner? Can there possibly be any room left for the real, flawed, fragile human behind the ad?

And after buying into the suave vegan pancake-maker and cognac-sipping reader of Whitman, can you possibly accept the humble, nervous accountant who stands before you? With such a marketing blitz, followed by frisky, flirtatious instant messaging and countless e-mails, followed sometimes even by long midnight conversations and phone sex, is it remotely possible not to be disappointed with the real thing?

Like reading a book and then seeing the movie, you don't realize how much you've already painted a picture in your head until you see someone else's vision on the screen. Similarly, it's tough to know how much fantasy you're bringing to the table until you're sitting face to face, and you recognize suddenly that you'd ascribed a whole different set of verbal tics, affectations, and gestures to the person in your mind without even knowing it.

The smallest thing about the person can send you spiraling inward, thereby shutting you off from the experience. You felt sure, based on his emails, that he wasn't a mouth breather! It seemed obvious, given the flirtatious confidence with which she approached you on-line, that she didn't have a flabby ass!

In *A New Brand World*, Bedbury quotes University of Michigan business professors C. K. Prahalad and Venkatram Ramaswamy, who contend that a "product is no more than an artifact around which customers have experiences." Similarly, navigating today's on-line personals can feel more like an exercise in fantasy: We take the artifacts before us, and use our powers of imagination to create an idealized mate from these offerings.

Strange how easy and familiar this process is to us; but then, most relationships are at least 30 percent imagination. Without a fantasy-driven notion of themselves as a pair, most couples' relationships would collapse under the weight of years of compromise and self-sacrifice.

And besides, for as long as I've known her, my on-line dating friend in New York has been lamenting that she never meets any new men—ever! Now she meets them all the time. They're not all perfect, and sometimes she's built them up in her mind only to be disappointed. But now at least she's getting out there and hanging out with new people, and for better or for worse, she says she has a real feeling of possibility.

"I might have stayed involved with the last guy even though it wasn't working, because I would've thought, I'll never meet anyone else!" she says. "Now I know I can just go on-line and meet someone else tomorrow." That's right. There are always more brands on the shelf—I mean, fish in the sea.

IF AT FIRST

Diana O'Hehir

THE MAN on my doorstep is tall and muscled, healthily tan, and not the least bit bent. I'd been wondering if he'd be bent or stooped, his age showing; he's almost seventy.

I've been watching him now from my entry window. First while he stood, a little gawky and irresolute, on the other side of the street, then crossing the street, dawdling up the short path to my front porch. I recognize some things about him, height and body outline, tilt of the head. But not the hair; it's white now, and looks good. The way he clears the curb, in one big stride; I understand that. "Legs too long for my body," he used to say. Which wasn't true. He's always been well-proportioned. Handsome, in fact. I haven't seen him for thirty-five years. But I know him—correction, I used to know him—very well.

ONCE I WAS married to him. He's on my doorstep today by invitation. The doorbell rings; I pull the door open onto a treescape of northern California eucalyptus, the tarred smell of a residential road, my visitor. He wears a checked shirt and blue jeans. The word that presents itself, oddly appropriate, is *nice*.

"You look great."

We say this together, a chorus. We stare. We laugh.

I gesture him into my home in this academic town full of professors, writers, high vegetarian ideals, views of the bay. I bought my house here this year, after my divorce from my second husband.

Mel follows me into my living room, where the view is, alas, turned off; I bought this house because of its shimmering prospect of a green lagoon surrounded by cattails, but now the utility board has drained the water. "It used to be great," I announce, gesturing toward the expanse of asphalt bog, radiating heat like a Safeway parking lot.

He looks dubious. But he manages to be gallant. "You can see a bit of the bay," he suggests.

Well, yes you can, Mel, if you bend your head, crane your neck, and squint. The advantage of my disappeared view is that it gives us something to talk about. Talking is hard; of course it is, we've been apart for thirty-five years, half a lifetime. And for us there are also memories from before the separation, memories of silence and awkwardness. Of secrets. After all, we're ex-husband, ex-wife. We broke up, very painfully.

"The bay," he says, "that edge of blue. And that's got to be the Gate in there, right? But it's foggy," and I agree, "Sure, foggy," and he says, "I guess it's usually stacked up in that spot, huh?" and I'm all set to agree again when, thank God, he switches, turns from the window, smiling an expansive smile that I seem to remember.

"It took me two days to drive up here."

The normal driving time from Los Angeles to my house in Kensington is seven hours, maximum, unless you pull over at every McDonald's and rest stop and Road S-741 to ask yourself what on earth you're doing. We can both smile now.

"Were you scared, too?" he wants to know, and I say, "Sure. Of course." I start to add "scared spitless," but don't; that seems too revealing. I also don't tell him what a help his three letters have been.

He wrote congratulating me on my recent novel, generous words from an ex-husband. And then he wrote again. Those letters arrived during a dark time; my second marriage had finally collapsed, and I had stormed out of my own house. And sometime later I sat on the floor in a urinous Oakland motel room and tried to cry. And finally told myself, "So, okay, shut up and take your Xanax."

Against that background Mel's letters seemed like lights, stars, reminders of what the real world might be like, a world beyond me and my present angers, one where an ex-husband could make a sweet letter-writing gesture, and I could respond normally, decently. Like a regular human being.

So here we are, we're talking. I won't ask myself, how does it feel? I clunk a bottle of white wine out of the fridge; we settle down on the couch. And again we review his drive up here. (Did he do the pea soup restaurant? He did. Did he visit that rest stop whose name I love, Buttonwillow? Yes.) We reevaluate my novel, the decor of my house, the weather, the hike he has just taken through Tilden Park; we kill half the bottle. We start comparing notes on our son; unbelievably, he's almost forty now.

How can we have a grown son together and not have seen each other for thirty-five years? Well, we did that. With shared custody, too, summer visits to Daddy. Tears leaving, tears on arrival. But that's what airline stewardesses were for back in those days—the stewardess, the caretaker that you handed your child over to. Shepherdess of the commuting kid. Jesus, I think.

And what are you really thinking? I wonder. Men aren't sentimental, like women, I tell myself. They don't build stories, the way women do. I'm wrong in all that, of course. I know the fallacy even as I'm harboring it. I know also that Mel is separated from his wife, that his separation and mine occurred at exactly the same time.

We chat about possessions. He has an apartment on a Los Angeles beach; he has a car. The car is a Mustang, a '68.

"A '68 Mustang?" I inquire. "Terrific."

I'm faking here.

"You didn't use to know much about cars," he remarks correctly. We look at each other. There's recognition, recollection. And a touch of sadness, probably. We laugh. I'd forgotten about that straightforward laugh, with the eyes engaging you directly.

I'm aware of myself in my yellow dress, leaning against the couch back, balancing a wineglass. I've started feeling good. Simply and straightforwardly; here's someone who begins to make me feel healthy and younger. It's been a long time since I knew about that.

And it's been a long time since Mel and I laughed. The last time we were together, we didn't laugh. That was when we were saying good-bye. That is, I said good-bye; he hardly spoke.

IT'S NIGHT, September, balmy; we are outdoors on the grounds of our housing project in suburban Washington. The year is 1951. He and I sit rigidly on opposite edges of a small green sandbox, not talking, each clutching a corner of sandbox frame, each staring into a tiny prickly sandbox landscape decorated with broken plastic shovel handles.

It's dark; all of this illumined by the lights of our housing project. Albemarle Terrace is in the southeast section of the District of Columbia. The Albemarle builders intended their fake colonial brick boxes for young ordinary folk—that's how the Terrace was advertised—EX-SERVICEMEN! FAMILIES! But by some accident—nobody understands just how—the project got co-opted by Communists. By young ones, ex-serviceman ones, lower-middle-class ones. By us, in fact, who are almost what the builders intended, except for being Communists.

That's what we are—Communists. Both of us. Mel is more devoted and loyal than I am; he knows the Party can abolish unemployment, discrimination, war. We don't tell people who we are. Being Communists has made us different. Back in the good days, it made us serious and pious. And lately it has made us paranoid.

"Say something," I demand of my husband. But he doesn't respond, doesn't even budge, stares into the set of sand hills, his long dark face immobile.

Too handsome, that's what I thought when I first met him, the intense look too much like the second lead of a bad movie, the guy with the big frame and dark hair and eyebrows and mustache who dies at the end and sets the heroine free. But Mel isn't like that at all; he's gentle, stubborn, shy. Shyness can make you seem intense. He's loyal, awfully loyal.

Please stop looking that way. I try for a deep breath, my lungs feel locked shut. He's loyal to me. Loyal to the Party.

"I want," I say now, making my voice calm and flat, but louder than usual, "a divorce." He waits a beat. There's a noise in the distance—a plane. Finally he says, "Oh." No movement; nothing; I look at his shoulders, broad against the building lights, at his hands on the sandbox rim, no inflection. And then at last he says, "NO."

This is pretty awful, I think; I can't do it. Then I know that I can; here I am, doing it; I'll stick with it. Back inside the project, in one of the rooms above the sandbox, we have a two-year-old child, asleep, window open so we can hear him if he cries. I tell myself he's the reason I'm sitting here saying this, but also I think maybe that's a lie; maybe I'm just scared, the way the comrades have been saying to each other, passionately, every time there's a meeting of more than four people. "What are you—scared?" they say, or hiss, as if it were salacious.

Can you hiss a word like *scared?* I'm angry. And fiercely,

achingly sad. I won't go to jail and let my child be raised by his grandmother. Because that's what is threatened in this year of 1951. McCarthy has entered the headlines, and our Communist friends are getting arrested.

Mel hasn't spoken since his gut-wrenching NO. Light from a window hits the side of his face, contorting it into the mask of a Goya sufferer—there I go, standing aside and making artistic comments at myself, even when it hurts. Self-centered, the genuine me, always watching. Please, please.

Last week I sat in a parked car, down near the edge of this housing project, the car doors closed and the windows rolled up, hot and steamy and dense inside with B.O.; I sat there with three other Communists and a poor guy who was being brought up on charges.

Charges is what we call it when we have a kangaroo court like this one.

This man owns a little drugstore; that makes him a capitalist, a member of the ruling class, like Andrew Mellon. A capitalist, but also a CP member. He gave money, picketed, all that. And last week two thugs invaded his drugstore, tied up him and his wife, probably raped her (we haven't mentioned this; that's what I'm guessing; it goes with the story). They didn't kill the druggist and his wife, and by the next morning he got free and called the cops.

That's why we have him here now in this investigation. We're trying him on charges of siding with the oppressor. Of failing to support the true position of the Party. Because the invaders were Negro, and thus the Party's allies, and the cops are cops and of course the enemy, and he should not have called them. He gets lectured a whole lot and then gets expelled.

Probably he's glad to be expelled.

I sit there sweating and hating these proceedings, hating them and not saying so. I'm part of the judging committee. Judging this poor guy. What's wrong with us in the Party? What devious, destructive ailment has skewed our ideals, our love of the world, our loyalty to each other? I say nothing and look at the dirt pattern on the greasy car window and decide that this is it. The end. It's been seven years of the deepest personal and religious allegiance, and now it's over.

I haven't told Mel about this session in the car; he and I are in different Party cells and aren't supposed to discuss secrets with each other; that's how paranoid we're getting. Also I haven't told him because he and I don't talk to each other. About anything, anymore. Bit by bit, inch by inch, we've painted ourselves into the silent corner where you never say it. Don't talk, keep your distance. Freeze.

Three days later I move out of Albemarle Terrace with our baby. Mel is alternately amazed, furious, stubborn. He loves me and our child, but he also loves and is stalwartly faithful to the Communist Party; he won't see its faults. (There's no indication yet of the Mel who, five years later, will leave the Party and become, like me, "a socialist always, a joiner never again.") "Choose," he signals at me now. And I do. I settle into a new life; I get a job as an office worker and put our child in day care. I file for divorce.

AND NOW? Nineteen-eighty-five, in Kensington? Here's Mel in my living room; he smiles and fiddles with a wineglass; we have an hour of polite, tentative conversation, a couple of relieved laughs. He doesn't show social fear much, but I still know him well; I can guess what he's been thinking.

Closed, quiet, pulled back, that describes him. Qualities hard to recognize in so big and vigorous a man. And he's larger and more muscular now than he was back then. Back when.

We finish our wine; we start out toward his car. Once on the road, I'm hardly self-conscious at all about the wind blowing my hair and the two of us looking so fine in the white open-top car.

Mel the Mustang driver smiles at me and positions wide hands on the designer steering wheel. "Have you ever had an accident?" I ask, admiring his skillful negotiation of a complicated Berkeley intersection. "Accident?" he laughs. "Wow. Many, many times."

Yes; there's the Mel I knew; I feel a pull in the pit of my stomach. Doesn't brag, never admits to a special virtue. That sensation in my belly is okay; it feels good. But it bothers me, too. What did I expect from this encounter? This little foray into a distant past? Maybe a few days' relief from the agonies of recent divorce, perhaps a summer camp almost-romance, six days' flirtation with someone who used to like me once?

And if more, then more what? Pain, that's what Mel must

have thought, driving up here, stopping at every wildflower patch on the ugly flat north-south freeway, taking two days for a seven-hour trip. Hell, oh, hell.

SO WE'LL TALK about Berkeley. Do I know a lot of people here? he inquires neutrally. The town is pretty, he suggests. Land mines, even these innocent forays. It's too early for him to ask, these friends, are they good friends, were you happy with them; was it okay for you here until just before the end?

Pause. Turn a corner. "So, hey," he says, "you're looking really good."

I've chosen the restaurant because of nostalgic association. Maisie's specializes in crab cakes and flaunts a carefully vulgarian motto, MAISIE'S HAS CRABS. During our three years of marriage we lived in Baltimore and in Washington. And Baltimore is famous for its crab cakes. We heard a lot about crab cakes; not that we ate them much ourselves, we were too poor for that, but we knew all about them.

We settle down at the restaurant's best table, secluded in a nook with a view of a terrace. "Tell me about your magazine," I say. While I've spent my life teaching and writing, Mel has been publishing his magazine, a trade journal.

He shrugs. "I started it in my backyard garage; it supported my family. I had to be my own boss; I was blacklisted, y'know?"

Yes, I know. We're silent for a minute, remembering. I think at him, You never got arrested nor summoned before the House

Un-American Activities Committee. And neither did I. I remembered you during that time, Mel. I wrote poems about the two of us. I even put you in my novel.

"I want to talk about Mikey," Mel says.

Mikey. He used to call him that. How strange. Mikey, Diana, and Mel, the trio. Yes, I too want to talk about Mikey, our son, so sweet and gentle, with too many talents.

I ask for stories about the rest of Mel's family. He has a beautiful daughter, he says, she's a reformer; a nice son, also a reformer. "Those genes get passed on, maybe, huh?" He looks pleased. I talk about my youngest, Andrew, a writer, a reformer, a newspaperman.

I'm feeling something I can't express, that as we talk about the children, they begin to seem real; they're us and verge on being joint property.

I'm the first one to act out the impulse. I raise my glass with the tag end of my wine in it; then together we lift almost empty glasses. "A toast to our kids," I say. The sun makes a path across the uneven bricks of the terrace and hits the window in a bright assaulting splash.

"I'm drunk," I tell him on the way out. "I'm out of practice for drinking; let me hang on to you, don't go away now."

"Right. Count on me."

He doesn't mean it, of course; it's just something you say; he'd offer that to any lady who was wobbly and needed help. "Just count on me now." And yet, I tell myself, he does mean it, in a way. We're climbing into his convertible now; he says, "Thanks for the crab-cake dinner." "It was a good dinner." I lean back against the padded leather headrest. Summer is still with us, and darkness will come late; we'll drive back to Kensington through this elegant bright Berkeley sunset.

Real life is more convoluted than its outline, and it takes us six months of exploration, conversation, recollection ("I dreamed about us last night—you know, that Labor Day picnic?") before we make our decision. It happens at the top of a small mountain peak outside Los Angeles. (We've been taking turns commuting between Los Angeles and Kensington.)

At the summit, thirty-five Girl Scouts are squealing, pushing, giggling, and eating baloney sandwiches, but we circumvent them and scramble around the hill, where we hunker down over supermarket beer poured into plastic glasses.

We raise the glasses, touch, and stare solemnly. "Shall we?" And we agree that, yes, we will.

That was thirteen years ago, and we're still together. We have hope, taste, interest, enthusiasm in common. And we're in love. We think we always were.

LOST AND FOUND

Cara Klieger

SO IT'S TRUE: Everyone looks for his or her first love on the Web. We all do it. Mostly because we can. Then time passes, we start to browse, check stock quotes and news, and we forget to keep looking. I did. I couldn't find him at first, and I admit, I did not diligently keep trying. So imagine my surprise when I checked an email service that I rarely use, and there it was: a message from a screen name that I recognized instantly, sent to a screen name sufficiently different from my real one but, nevertheless, me.

Lo and behold, he had found me.

The message said, "I once knew a Cara Klieger—and that's an odd name. She used to live in Rockaway. Did you?" I opened my member profile immediately and rued the visibility of Cara Klieger, astonishing in its boldness. Why had I not created a sufficiently masking moniker, the way I had for my other email accounts? Was I in trouble? Oh, was I in trouble.

"Replique me, my baby." He met me on the street corner and grinned. Replique was one of the fragrances I wore back then. And then there was Femme, by the House of Rochas—who could forget that one? It sent him up the wall. We girls wore it, a veritable madam's *parfum,* only on weekend nights if we were lucky enough to score some—it would never do for schooldays.

Before our first date, I left my friend Lauren's house on a Friday afternoon to meet him, wearing Estée Lauder Super Cologne—it had just come on the market, and her sister had a bottle. We rode the train to the East Village to see the movie *Che,* about our idol Che Guevara and his girlfriend Tanya. Afterward we went to his "apartment," a suitably decrepit place in a walk-up firetrap on Sixth Street east of First Avenue. He was sixteen, I was fifteen. Not many sixteen-year-olds had apartments in the Village; it was quite a status symbol, and a reliable girl catcher as well, but of course it did not last too long.

Once school began in September, there was no apartment anymore; during that school year and part of the next I was to take two buses to his house every evening after dinner. (I didn't have to sing "Magic Bus"—even the bus knew it was magic.) The fact that we attended different high schools and lived miles from each other served only to underscore the preordained rightness of Andy and Cara as a couple.

Back then, you didn't date if you were hip—you hung out. So we did. On the street to socialize, but mostly in his room. Talking, kissing, loving each other beyond life and death, we said. Hushed and humbled, we sprawled together listening to Graham Nash sing, "Our bodies were a perfect fit, in afterglow we lay," subliminally aware that we were not the only tall, skinny boy and round, darker girl alive and in love. We celebrated anyway. Nearly every night we told each other, "This is one for the books," and meant it.

That is how we hung out most evenings, but not if there was a riot going on. If there was, we had to be there. We went to riots, peace marches, moratoriums, affinity groups, plenary sessions, you name it. We thrust our fists into the air and shouted, "Avenge Mark Clark! Avenge Fred Hampton!" after the Chicago cops broke into their house and killed two Black Panthers, one of whom I believe even now was sleeping when he was shot. And "Ho, Ho, Ho Chi Minh. NLF is gonna win!" Today I give myself 50-50 odds that I even knew what the initials NLF stood for at the time.

His parents were home in the evenings and entertained a great deal. They played Santana and the Moody Blues, which we scoffed at. The two of us disowned Santana shortly after he became too popular, but we liked to watch Andy's mother dance to "Black Magic Woman." I thought they played the album *Abbey Road* way too often, but hell! You were not about to walk into my parents' living room and hear *Abbey Road.* Their guests, a blend of academics and brats in their twenties, would loll around and discuss music and politics, envying us, we believed strongly, because we were on the front lines of the revolution. We were the youngest ones in the room, at a time when youth was the most valuable currency going.

When Andy was covered with chickenpox, I was allowed to visit because I had had the virus as a child. He looked just as beautiful that evening as at any other time. I brought him soda and told him not to scratch. His mother, Arlene, taught me how to cook the pasta called bucatini, and sometimes we played hearts or helped Andy's sister with her homework.

For Christmas, he gave me his old phonograph, and his father gave him money to take me to the pancake house. He liked crullers but couldn't remember their name. I spent $9 to get him Frank Zappa's *Hot Rats* and two Fugs albums.

For at least a decade, I walked around thinking that I had stopped being a virgin on the night after the New York Mets won the World Series. I thought this when they won it again in 1986 and I was living it up in Isla de los Ladrones, by then a true Mets fan. I thought so for an awfully long time and was more devoted to the team for having played a part in my coming of age. But I was wrong—it happened the night after they won the Division: "The Mets won the play-off!" he yelled on Wednesday, and that Thursday night, we did it. When I came home, I looked at my face in the mirror for ages to see how different, how womanly, I suddenly was. "Big girl," he said. "You're a big girl now." This occurred, of course, well before he began his numerical ranking system for the girls in his life or comparing the delights of our bodies in his notebook.

People say that the sixties were about sex, drugs, and rock 'n' roll, but they weren't, not really. Drugs were just something to have around, like incense and ashtrays (except acid, of course, which any earnest teenager had to take far more seriously than homework). Radical politics got us going, assured us that we were an invincible tribe with absolute beatitude on our side. Sex was the vehicle in which we traveled. There was no credibility in virginity; it was as ridiculous as, say, liking the music of Chicago Transit Authority or Blood, Sweat and Tears without Al Kooper as frontman: shameful and lame-o. And love was the petrol. After I finished messing about with one of his friends and causing a crisis to rival *Anna Karenina*, he wrote me a poem that ended, "Cara, I love you and I always will/The land lay flat before us/We've conquered the last hill." It wasn't his best work, but how profound for a sixteen-year-old boy, we agreed.

Thirty years ago, right now, I was carrying his baby. I wonder if he knows that. Is it something that he too would never forget? As he clicks the "Refresh" icon on his screen, checking his stock quotes and waiting for my response, does he remember how I snuck urine in a tightly closed jar, under a coat, from my house onto the subway train, all the way to the East Village free clinic? Or how he told me over the phone where to meet him? "Take the subway to DeKalb Avenue; I'll be at the front when you get off."

Does he remember how we plotted and schemed to get the paperwork done, and ate at a Blimpie near the hospital every time I had a doctor's appointment? The only way to do it was on "health of the mother" grounds. And the surest-fire way to present oneself as being unhealthy as possible was to threaten suicide, which I managed rather convincingly. But I prefer to remember having lunch together, eating for that other I would never see and laughing at Andy's jokes.

We had a good time before and after those hospital visits to see different psychiatrists for ten minutes at a clip, and oh, did we love Manhattan, wide open and exciting—spring in Spanish Harlem. Somehow, with minds honed at meetings of the high school student union, Andy and I plenary-sessioned until we had succeeded in hoodwinking both sets of parents into believing that I was going to Philadelphia for four days. When his father noticed that we were keeping the lights on in the bedroom more and more often, he said, "What's going on in there; are you two hatching an assassination plot?" We collapsed, smirking to ourselves, "If he only knew."

But keeping the lights on all those nights bore some pretty powerful results in strengthening us as a couple. We thought alike, and we began to look alike, too: my oval face became more heart-shaped, and his hazel eyes grew browner. "Derrrrh Igg Fuhrrrr Mouhddh." If he remembers, then he and I are the only ones in the world who understand that phrase. We went to the office of some local doctor we had heard about. I thought he was mean, and he refused to help me anyway, so when I ran out into the street, I burst into tears. Andy made me laugh by scrambling every last part of the doctor's name into phonetic oatmeal.

He was a good boyfriend all during that time; I think it was only later that year, when the sister of that other girl died in a car accident, that he relegated me to second place. I was asked to "share" while he spent a weekend on grief counseling, and probably pretty tender sex, if you think about it. I could not refuse because I knew that sharing was right—after all, the Jefferson

Airplane's "Triad" was one of the songs we loved best: "I don't really see why can't we go on as three," sang Grace Slick, pleading to be with both lovely men at the same time. Not only did I play along, I believed it too. Not once did it occur to my malleable mind to say, "Hey, wait a minute! I thought you were my boyfriend."

We decided to avoid hysteria, but really we were too hip to become hysterical. The facts were plain. In those days, Irish girls had babies, and Jewish girls did not. I was half each, but it was simply out of the question. I had nothing against kids; I just did not want any of our parents to find out. "If we were older," we kept reassuring each other, we would live in the country and name the baby Sandoz after the Swiss pharmaceutical firm. So I had to procure a phony ID showing I was eighteen years old, and by the time all these details were in place, months had passed, and the only solution available was the saline drip, the procedure that most closely resembles a full-term delivery, the only difference being that you don't go through all that hassle for a live, healthy baby, but for a dead one. It was too late to do anything else. I was four months along.

The hospital admission and consultations were so exquisitely dramatic that I could have been onstage. I was brave and excited when a rat scurried across the floor of my room; distinctly middle-class, I had never seen one before but thought it was high time I did. I kept the phony hospital ID bracelet as a souvenir. But then, maybe after I was in there three days, the curtains went up for good, and I had to quit thinking of myself as "Tanya in a hut."

We knew nothing about edema, so when my hand swelled to six times its size from the intravenous needle, we panicked. The labor pains were so unexpected, their intensity so off the chart, that I sent Andy away because I could not bear the terror in his face. He was not with me when I delivered the little thing in the bedpan by myself. (I woke up from a pain shot, and there it was. I no longer hurt. The bed did not have a call button, so I yelled for assistance, and they came and took it away.)

Is he caught up now in the rapture of downloading MP3s, maybe drinking a beer?

I heard once that Andy had married well. Yet I had gone him one better, upholding our earliest prejudice against our natal country and marrying foreign. I was an expatriate, carrying the same disdain for high school unity that we had shared as baby Weathermen—we who had scorned our proms and graduation ceremonies. That was the last I ever heard of him, until a week ago.

I have now lived twice as long as the age I was when I first knew Andy, and still I think of him in the purest terms, just as if these last two lifetimes had never been. He has tracked me down on the internet, a staggering event. Through all the years since I last saw him, well before there was such a thing as the internet, I simply figured that one day my secretary would buzz me on the good, old-fashioned interoffice communicator and say, "A Mr. Andy ———— to see you."

But no, he is on a screen before me in fonts I myself chose for their aesthetic appeal. He wants to know who and where I am.

What does one say after thirty years apart: "Where did you go to, my lovely?" or "Hello, it's me?" Do I tell him I am happily married with two kids? Tell him how grotesque I felt by the time I turned eighteen? Does this stranger prefer to hear that I have helped many people with AIDS or that I acquired the perfect tan? Which would matter more to him? "Yes, I live in Canada but winter offshore. I have an important meeting in Brussels next week, can't miss it, sure wish my sprained ankle would heal faster. And après-Bruxelles, well, Gerry Adams needs me." I can say anything at all. Design a life or reflect my real one.

Many times since he decreed that the other girl had won, I've thought that I'm not long for this world. Devoted parents, a decent education, and street smarts gave me thirty extra years, but I didn't really need them. What for—to make money? To bear two kids that Andy never knew? So I marveled at the beauty of Bali and the horror that is Bangladesh; I am not impressed, why should he be? I did most of what we said we would do—back then. Definitely a hip old girl, but her gait is slightly shambling—either a sprained ankle or the tardive dyskinesia of love. I didn't need all those years. You can have them back, Andy.

The abrupt end of my childhood is a little too sacrosanct to dally with, concomitant as it was, you might say, with the abrupt start of my womanhood. Which makes anything to do with him—thinking, remembering, even, God help me, contact—

"heavy." So I will probably respond quietly. I will not tell anyone, and then, late one night, I will send Andy a line from that most romantic of all morbidly romantic rock songs, "(Don't Fear) The Reaper": "The curtains flew and then he appeared."

See if he remembers. See what he does with that.

HUSTLING HORMONES

Carol Mithers

THERE WAS no avoiding the flash of drug déjà vu. Stand in line at the bank because the source wants more cash than you can get from an ATM; wonder what the teller's thinking as she counts out $600 in small bills; worry about getting robbed en route to the parking lot; drive to meet the connection, praying the stuff is good.

Fifteen years ago, I'd have been meeting the sleazoid would-be producer who paid his rent by selling party-time coke to my friends and me. Now it was a series of strangers, and expeditions that weren't about pleasure but desperation. The deals I made were for ampoules of human menopausal gonadotropin—brand name Pergonal—which, injected, would goad my ovaries into making masses of eggs each month, one of them good enough, I hoped, to produce a child.

I grew up on mind-altering street pharmaceuticals, but I reached a new appreciation of the surreal during the year I spent buying black-market fertility drugs.

Two forces got me there: generational mass delusion and capitalism. I was one of those women who considered the notion of the biological clock to be patriarchal hogwash. "I—I can't believe I forgot to have children!" proclaimed the T-shirt I actually wore proudly at twenty-six. It wasn't until I was just past forty, dazzled with love for my new daughter and motherhood—when my efforts to conceive another child were going absolutely nowhere—that I realized what a moron I'd been.

Enter the system: Yes, medical intervention might get me pregnant, but I'd have to pay through the nose for it. Even the relatively low-tech tactic of ovarian stimulation coupled with insemination cost more than $2,000 a try, and it rarely worked the first time. (In vitro fertilization, at ten grand a pop, wasn't even an option.) More than half the expense was drug related; pharmacy Pergonal ran $60 per amp, and a typical cycle required at least two dozen.

But one day, I noticed that my doctor's bulletin board had ads from women who were ending treatment and recouping costs by selling drugs they hadn't used. Secondhand Pergonal was going for as little as $15 a hit. Trading in prescription medication is illegal, not to mention that you can't be sure what you're getting. But with $1,000 a month at stake, who cared?

I actually recognized the first phone number I wrote down. It was that of the wife of an old friend, who, after four years of effort and maybe a dozen miscarriages, was about to deliver child no. 2. I called, made the deal, and two days later exchanged a handful of bills for a white paper bag full of drugs. They'd been purchased in central Mexico by the friend of a friend who had family there, then smuggled across the border. (Customs will allow small amounts of medication for "personal use," but she'd been stockpiling, and her original order was too big to qualify.)

I was thrilled at how easy this was. I now had a hefty supply of product for only $14 per amp, and the fact that it had come from someone who'd gotten pregnant seemed like a good omen. (Fervent belief in signs and portents is vital when you're infertile; otherwise you have nothing to cling to but the cold, immutable laws of biology.) Two months later, I'd shot it all up, popped over a dozen eggs, and been basted in sperm, but it hadn't worked. I was back on the phone.

Suddenly I was immersed in a sea of commerce and pain. I'm a journalist, used to intruding in strangers' lives, but I'd never before learned the state of someone's reproductive organs within five minutes of a meeting. "Here—I bought them for $60 each, but I'm only asking $20," said my next bulletin-board contact, an Indian immigrant in her late thirties, as she handed over the medication in her mid–Los Angeles living room. "My eggs are no good. I am waiting for a donor."

"We had to do IVF," cheerfully confessed a blond, clean-cut, and surfer-attractive husband with Pergonal bought in Tijuana, Mexico, to sell. "My wife's forty-two, and I have, uh, a count problem."

Maybe that part wasn't so strange, since just admitting we were part of this same awful world made us instantly intimate in a way we couldn't be even with friends. With someone else who'd been there, the mere sentence "Yep, trying for three years now" carried a weight of emotion and imagery—the needles, stirrups, plastic cups, hope, tears, regret, and sweaty, grunting sex giving way to something scheduled and grimly determined. And yet this profundity would be followed by the most banal social chat.

"Like my new patio cover?" asked the low-count man shortly after he gave me drugs and talked obsessively about his wife's successful medication regimen. (They'd hit the jackpot—she was eight months pregnant with twins.)

"Very much," I said truthfully. "We could use one just like it."

"Home Depot!" he answered immediately, offering aisle directions. The patio and yard, like the rest of the house, were frighteningly immaculate. I wondered if he and his wife knew what two little boys would do to the place.

Two more cycles, fourteen more eggs, still no baby. For my next buy, I followed directions to an expensive neighborhood at the top of the Hollywood Hills. Security cameras focused on me as I parked, catching, humiliatingly, my dirty, fifteen-year-old car. A maid opened the door. Inside, glass walls revealed a huge swimming pool and stunning views.

I walked down a hall, past a Diane Arbus print that looked real, to where my seller, a wan blond, sat in a light-filled bedroom nursing a very tiny girl. The baby had come a month early, the woman told me; sometimes that happened with older mothers.

"I'm forty-one. How old are you?" she asked. It was the question, in the doctor's waiting room, on the infertility bulletin boards I'd compulsively begun to cruise. I'd answer and sense mental gears spinning: She's even older than me! I've still got a chance!

Was I doing IVF, too? the woman continued in a dreamy voice. Too bad. Was I seeing the charismatic senior partner in the fertility clinic? He was fabulous, brilliant; it had taken several tries, but she couldn't have done this without him, and she was going to do it again, just as soon as she could. She showed me a box full of drugs she'd gotten from Europe—I had no idea how, but they looked legit. I counted out my money, resentfully this time. The house, the view, the $30,000 baby—couldn't she just give me the stuff in the name of barren-gal solidarity? Apparently not. She dropped the bills in a desk drawer, and the maid saw me to the door.

My upper-class drugs failed, too. As a new cycle began, the doctor scanned my ovaries to make sure they were healthy ($150) and asked if I needed a prescription for drugs. "I have my own," I told her. We'd gone through this before; the one time I mentioned what I was using, she replied, "I can't advise you to do this."

I got the same line from the nurses who had showed me how to take a one-and-one-half-inch needle and stab myself in the butt. It was a joke, considering that I was finding my illicit, used, cut-price foreign goods through this very office, and I wondered sometimes why my doctor and her partners, who operated a very prosperous, big-league clinic, didn't worry about being busted themselves. Instead, it was "Don't ask, don't tell," and I suspect the fiction allowed the doctors to feel they were "helping" patients by enabling them to save money. (Of course, it never occurred to them they also could do this by lowering their own prices.) Just like the desperate crowds in the doctor's waiting room, the number of notes on the bulletin board never seemed to decrease. "I WILL GIVE SOMEONE THESE LAST FEW AMPS FOR FREE—THEY WORKED!!!" announced one ad, but when I called, they were already gone. Instead, I bought from a forty-four-year-old Asian would-be screenwriter who lived near a notoriously violent West L.A. housing project and had just lucked into insurance coverage that would pay for future drugs. The house had bars on the windows and scripts on the floor. "I think sometimes, Why did I wait so long to have a baby?" she said, trying to smile. "But I can't remember."

I bought from an Iranian, in her early forties, whose face was haggard with stress and who would meet me only away from her home, in a café. "I give you these because I am done with it all," she said, handing over a brown paper bag.

"Does your husband help you in your effort to have a child? That's good. Mine did not. Never gave the shots. Never went to the doctors. He comes from a very traditional family; they told him that since I was barren, he should divorce me and marry a woman who was younger. He did not want to at first, but the trying wears you out. You stop making love. You feel like a failure. I gained thirty pounds and became unattractive. So now we are divorced, and he will find someone else. I have no husband and no child; this is not what I thought my life would be, and I am too tired to care."

I murmured my sympathies. "No," she insisted, "it doesn't matter. I really don't care." She reached out suddenly, hugged me, and kissed me on both cheeks. "I think these will work for you. You will get what you want. Tell me what happens." I left her outside the café, lighting a cigarette. When her drugs failed too, I couldn't bear to make the call.

I took some time off from the fertility game after that, and when I returned to the doctor's office, the for-sale notices had been cleared from the board. When I mentioned my intent to buy in nearby Tijuana, a nurse darkly warned against Mexican drugs, some of which, she said, were proving counterfeit.

In a year, I'd grown paranoid enough to listen. Instead, on a website, I found out about a Paris pharmacy that shipped product made in Spain. I faxed a prescription and credit card number, and two weeks later received a carton wrapped in brown paper, bearing the customs declaration "Produits de beauté." My youth potion.

Sometimes, when I snap the tips off the glass ampoules and mix the white powder inside with water, I wonder if the defeated Indian ever got her donor baby. Have two toddlers trashed that pristine house, and have their parents learned not to care? Did the screenwriter have a child, did the rich white girl manage another, has the brokenhearted Iranian put together a new life? Their phone numbers are gone, and I'll never know.

Instead, I shoot my new drugs—from Paris, city of lovers, a good omen, right?—and when the needle goes in, I get a high unlike any I've felt before. No euphoria or adrenaline rush, but I know that out of sight, my ovaries are charged up, flaring and, like some Fourth of July fireworks finale, sending up everything they've got before the show ends for good, and the sky goes dark.

REPRODUCTIVE AS A RABBIT, ABSTINENT AS A NUN

Jennifer Bingham Hull

IT'S A COOL Florida winter night. My husband has always had a certain cold-weather allure—a tall, lean fellow, Bill looks great in flannel pajamas and a terry-cloth bathrobe. And there he lies in both, available, appealing—and reading Penelope Leach on toilet training.

I'm reading about VBACs (short for vaginal birth after cesarean), trying to find a comfortable position for my bulging belly and feeling distracted. The next morning promises another wardrobe showdown with our two-year-old, Isabelle, and the book, *Toddler Taming,* that's sitting on my bedside table may be just what I need to ensure peace and tranquillity. But it's 11:30 P.M. We turn off the lights and crash.

Maybe tomorrow night, I think, I'll get to *Toddler Taming.*

My husband and I used to have sex on a regular, romantic basis. For years we weren't trying to make a baby. We would just be in the mood. One thing naturally led to another. I didn't even mark the event on my calendar.

Fertility treatments, pregnancy, and parenthood changed all that, putting us on a sexual roller coaster more unpredictable than anything I've experienced since adolescence. Lately, I'm having either too much sex or too little, as reproductive as a rabbit one month and as abstinent as a nun the next. Wildly fluctuating hormones and crash efforts at late-in-life reproduction explain some of this variation. Parenthood explains the rest. My husband may look fetching in flannel, but he's now the fellow I spar with over diaper duty, negotiate with over family finances, and meet with to schedule the painter, the plumber, and the roofer. The leap from logistics to lust can be a long one. And then to find a time when we are both in the mood and awake and able to be alone together—now that's timing.

It has become difficult to think of having sex for its own sake. Our fertility efforts put us on a strict monthly schedule: Every forty-eight hours. Every thirty-six hours. Every twenty-four hours. Ready, set, reproduce! For almost two years, sex was an item on my to-do list, along with grocery shopping and banking. No longer simply a woman with an appetite, I was suddenly a woman with a mission. Mood had little to do with anything. And humor, not lust, was the essential ingredient. What else can get you through when your man is holding a long needle filled with Pergonal, describing the shape of your butt over the phone to a medical assistant to ensure proper aim? "But you don't even cook!" I protested, laughing amid tears as he jabbed the needle in (with amazing dexterity, thank God).

When all that purposeful sex resulted in my first pregnancy, it seemed odd at first to even consider having an unscheduled romp. Why? What for? And what a relief not to! Hormones being what they are, that didn't last. Briefly, before my belly got too big and sex became more funny than sexy, Bill and I reverted to our old romantic ways. For a few months things were "normal," that is, sexy, sweet, and best of all, unplanned.

Then Isabelle arrived. Suddenly sex had to compete with the one thing we really couldn't get enough of: sleep. In those first months it wasn't even a contest. I chose sleep. This wasn't good. Newborns bring enough stress into a marriage without adding sexual tension to the combustible domestic mix. I'm sure Bill and I would have fought less as new parents had we made love more. But when you have to get up at 2 A.M. to feed the baby, having sex seems like the stupidest thing you could possibly do.

Yet after a year we were riding those roller-coaster heights again, trying for baby no. 2, using a formula a friend swore by, which consisted of having sex every thirty-six hours. I plotted out the month's sex schedule on my calendar. Prime time coincided with a law conference Bill had in Vermont, so Isabelle and I went with him. At first the prospects for a successful mission looked bleak. Then the session on international tax law adjourned, Isabelle napped, and—presto!—we launched baby no. 2, no doubt a little lawyer, now in utero.

If timing has proved one challenge to our sex life, geography has been another. Sex, once largely an exercise in seduction, after pregnancy involves a significant amount of damage control, and Bill has had to learn to negotiate unpredictable and treacherous terrain. There were those enlarged breasts from nursing, alluring to the eye, yes, but when it comes to caresses—ouch! There was that bright red C-section scar that ran across my lower abdomen, tender and about as inviting as a stretch of barbed wire. And now my belly rises like a large mogul on a ski slope, inviting a wipe-out. I'm not the woman I was two years ago—or even last week. I'm an obstacle course with ever-changing markers. One mis-aimed caress, and you're out. Bill learned this lesson one night when, to his astonishment, I burst out crying after a little inno-cent foreplay because—well, I just don't know why.

It's enough to make two adults in their forties feel like fum-bling adolescents. This isn't all bad, of course. There's more than one way to conquer the mountain, and I haven't enjoyed making out so much since high school. And after five years of marriage, it's nice to see my husband smirking like a teenage boy who has gotten away with something when things do work out.

Anyway, for now, maybe how much sex we have and how we have it aren't the point.

Recently, I started dreaming about seducing a fellow with thick, dark hair and full lips. The dreams all ended in frustration. Every time I got close to scoring, some relative or small child in-terrupted. I couldn't get my dream man alone.

Awaking from one of these dreams at 3 A.M., I felt frus-trated and restless. I considered waking up my husband. But Isabelle rises early, and during my pregnancy Bill has been getting up with her. He's tired. And now that my belly is the size of a beach ball, I wasn't quite sure what I would do with him, anyway.

But to be partnered and sexually frustrated—how ridiculous! Isn't convenient sex supposed to be one of the great boons of marriage? No need to dress up, find Mr. Right, and show him how to get down your particular set of slopes. This is worse than being single, I thought. I've got the guy, but I can't do a thing with him.

But hey, I do have the guy! My dream man may be unattainable for now, but he also happens to be old sugar lips sleeping right beside me—the man who does the morning shift and smells like exhaustion, the fellow who keeps asking me whether we should buy steel or aluminum hurricane shutters. I'd be lying if I said I always dream about Bill. The smell of baby spit-up can be a powerful antiaphrodisiac, and sometimes Liam Neeson makes for good fantasy fodder without the messy domestic complications. But mostly, I'm lusting after my mate, which sure beats chasing the fellow on the next barstool.

Perhaps it's the old saw: We women always want the guy we can't have. And in a neat catch-22, the domestic demands of parenting can incite lust by making one's spouse deliciously unattainable, even if those same demands make it more difficult to consummate the attraction. The fact that Bill is less available for a romp with me because he's getting up early to be with our daughter has a definite appeal to a lady now in her ninth month. When he bought new tires for the car this week, I fell in love all over again.

Who cares if we get to home base, as long as we get to the hospital?

WE BELIEVE CHILDREN AREN'T THE FUTURE

Lori Steele

I'M LUCKY my house is so quiet. At least, that's what an old college friend, whose four-year-old is testing upper octaves in the background, is telling me over the phone.

"I envy you," she says.

Envy? I have no idea how to respond, and the quiet in my house grows louder as she waits for me to say something. Anything. The pause is intentionally pregnant. I know she's waiting to hear the latest about my and my husband's tussle with infertility. But I somehow can't commit facts to words, again, as if speaking them will turn childlessness from a vague biological malfunction to a living emptiness. I do not want to conjure up unnamed ghosts.

I know she simply envies my empty airspace. I know that what she's hearing on my end of the line isn't quiet at all, but a reminiscence of her preparenting life. That time we were all young and lit by moonlight.

Instead of saying any of that, I change the subject, ask her about the new boat. It beats delivering the same tired response to the same covert question. My husband and I have been speaking the two words for years now: "We're trying." Each time I say this, the weight of colossal failure—among life's biggest, the inability to self-perpetuate—descends, a lactating Athena-size shroud of incompetence. My eggs do not play well with others. My husband's sperm is unfocused, not working up to its potential.

We are failed breeders, and having committed neither to accepting childlessness nor to enduring scary science feats or contemplating final-step adoption, we walk a no-mama's land. A no-papa's land. "My seed found no purchase," my husband says of our little savanna.

We still have a few years left in which to let low-tech fertility methods work. I take my temperature and eat zinc; he wears boxers and avoids bananas, per doctor's orders. But I foresee the years leading to a showdown with science as a surreal limbo, waiting to learn what the future holds and trying desperately not to care. We shrug, like Doris Day: "Que Sera Sera." What the hell. Doesn't matter anyway.

We play let's pretend. We tell each other we'd make surly parents anyway, now that we've had ten self-centered years together without having to relearn our numbers or synchronize our driving for soccer pickups. In fact, we've had so many years of living without tykes that we'd probably compete with them, bickering over whether to watch Bravo or Nickelodeon. I would hide the remote and taunt their undeveloped reasoning faculties. We'd urge them to emulate their peers on *South Park*.

They would be on their own. They'd learn to play with matches. Sleep in a pile under the stairs because we'd forget to give them a bedroom. Sell pencils for lunch money. We would beget *Lord of the Flies* children, savage hoodlums starved for love, direction, and daily grooming.

This is what we tell ourselves. My husband, meanwhile, serves our fourteen-year-old cat, the household princess, her water in a wine goblet and tells me "she likes it better that way." At a restaurant, he wraps his arm around our five-year-old nephew's shoulder and reads him everything on the menu. I hear them whispering to each other. "Are you sure?" my husband asks. Luke nods his head excitedly. "Okay, then." When the waitress arrives, the two of them look up toward her. My husband orders: "He'll have a thousand pancakes."

"Will that be all?"

"No. He'll also have an ocean of syrup."

I push away from the table quietly, praying no one sees as I head to a bathroom stall. Maternal urges have no manners. They wake up and howl at whim. They need to be carried out of the restaurant to avoid a public scene, soothed in the privacy of rest room cubicles.

What a beautiful, beautiful father. It hurts to see this. To think of the quiet in our home that could be filled with the sound of a spatula making a child a thousand pancakes.

"It seems so wrong," my mother laments later when I tell her about the pancakes.

To her, our infertility is a cosmic-size iniquity. We grow quiet. We are remembering the futility of arguing with science. At least,

I am. She, meanwhile, is measuring the world's injustices. Finding anecdotes with which to petition the Lord.

"I mean, look at Callie," she says. "She's a white-cat mother. How can that be right?"

Ah, the white-cat women. So many of them in the world. When I was eight years old, my family moved to a new blue house that had been unoccupied. A white cat had made her home in the basement, delivered a litter, and then abandoned the kittens. My mother nursed the tiny creatures with an eyedropper. Callie was like that white cat—a woman who forgot her children. Left them with a temperamental drunk who probably fed them microwaved pixie sticks for dinner.

By offering up this information about Callie, my mother is trying to negotiate with unseen forces. She mentions how I sing to our golden retriever and plant sunflowers with a squadron of neighbor children, how my husband can play Super Mario with a six-year-old cousin for hours—evidence of what she sees as superior humanity and parenting aptitude. Maybe, because of my mother's lawyering, Zeus and his clan will revisit the issue, and transfer Callie's offspring to us?

I try to cheer up my mother. I tell her I'm not a fit parent anyway. In fact, I'm a secret crack whore.

"You're not a crack whore."

"Pregnancy might kick-start a latent mental illness that makes me want to injure small children with forks."

"It won't."

"I would never wake up at 6 A.M."

"You would."

Nothing will pacify her. And so we talk about our prognosis, those embryo-defying topics. My mother finds hope where I see only obstacle. She believes, in her heart of hearts, the place where she believes God exists, that a baby will happen. She dreams of holding our baby.

Me, I can't go there. Hope is unthinkable because hope is a solid. It germinates and becomes a parallel-universe reality, something you can almost touch through the glass. My husband and I hesitate when we talk about babies. Sentences seem unfinished. It's as if we agreed, without saying, that to talk too loudly would conjure a dream that could break. A dream that, lost, could break us. We could summon a loss that would ask to be mourned.

It's much easier to be flip about children. When my husband and I meet people, it usually takes about three seconds after they give us the "you're a great couple" line for them to ask the inevitable question: "Why don't you have kids?" My husband has a pat answer. He says, "We don't believe that children are the future."

The pause that follows reminds me that people don't think anti-kid jokes are funny. These days, it's a form of blasphemy, much like mocking condoms or ridiculing recycling. Either that, or they see the edge of a lie in his eyes; they know that sarcasm usually masks pain, and they don't know how to respond. Laugh? Or flinch?

I know that feeling. Truth is, we do indeed believe children are the future—just maybe not our future. So saith the gods of fertility, anyway. It's much less painful to give a flip response—tell people that we were really, truly frightened by *Children of the Village of the Damned*—than to haul out the dreams deferred, the medical charts and other evidence stacked against us. Low motility? Check. Endometriosis? Yep. Bad karma from a previous life? Certainly.

The sins of our parents? One of my aunts thinks it has something to do with the hormones they fed cows in the 1960s. My grandmother felt it just wasn't time yet. Everyone has his or her theory about someone else's infertility. And everyone thinks it's okay to ask.

And we're just kind of ignoring it. Like a messy room that won't clean itself.

Either way—whether admitting we'd like to cradle a tot but can't, or expressing faux irreverence toward the children of today, tiny Buddhas all—we're outsiders in a baby-glorifying world, and we comfort ourselves by listening to the silence.

And I want to tell my friend on the phone that the silence she so envies would give her little peace. It is a quiet with its own growing vocabulary, a silence that howls at 4 A.M. I want to tell her about this silence, but I don't say a thing.

I MISS LESBIAN REPRODUCTIVE SEX

Laurie Essig

I HAVE TWO children. I will not be having any more. Not that I wouldn't like to, but my partner, a party pooper if ever there was one, has made it clear that if I have another child, I will be a single parent.

If I were my mother, I would just get pregnant anyway and then pretend it was an accident. But I am not my mother. For one thing, I am a bit less manipulative than she was. For another, I am a lesbian, and it's very difficult to explain an accidental pregnancy in a lesbian relationship.

I could try the "Oh, darling, I'm so sorry. You see, I just happened to be in the sperm bank and the lights went out and I tripped and stumbled and somehow, I'm not even sure how, I got pregnant" line, but I'm pretty sure it wouldn't fly. And so, now that my baby is no longer a baby, I am beginning to realize that I will never have another child.

This is sad in all the usual ways. I miss that baby smell and those little baby diapers and all that, but there's something else I miss too. I miss the reproductive sex.

I know, I know. Finding reproductive sex sexy is sick, perverse even. Reproductive sex is, by definition, the opposite of hot. There is something innately unattractive about the line,

"Honey, the stick is purple. We gotta do it, quick!!!" And yet, here I am, pining for reproductive sex.

Perhaps it is because there is something terribly naughty and titillating about two women in bed with a vial of disembodied sperm. In fact, the image of two women having reproductive sex is so naughty that it is nearly unmentionable. In popular culture, whether it's the children's book *Heather Has Two Mommies* or the sitcom *Friends,* lesbians do not have reproductive sex. Among the many lesbian couples I know, none of them had reproductive sex. They either did it the old-fashioned way (with a man) or took themselves to a doctor's office.

Perhaps it is because we as a society and we as lesbian mothers cannot conceive of creating a baby without a man present. The "man" takes the form either of a literal father or of a medical doctor, male or female, exercising control over the messiness of women's reproductive organs.

In the safety of a doctor's office, women in sanitary white gowns are allowed to reproduce with the aid of the doctor/father and the nearly surgical insertion of sperm. My partner and I tried the medical route once, sort of. With my legs in stirrups and a tube inserted into my o's, our feminist midwife handed my partner the syringe and told her to "Squirt away, stud muffin."

Then she suggested that I have an orgasm, since she believes orgasm aids in conception. But all this medicalization of reproduction was not a turn-on for me, and besides, I never could perform under pressure. After that, we decided to reproduce in the privacy of our own home. After all, this isn't brain surgery. It's reproductive sex. Even our parents managed to do it.

It wasn't exactly easy to make our babies at home. There were a lot of logistical problems. We had to transport the sperm home from the sperm bank. It was always terribly embarrassing to sit on the subway with a large metal tank with the words REPRO SPERM BANK painted on the side. Getting the sperm from the subway to the apartment was even more difficult. In my stoop-sitting, nosy neighborhood, more than one person asked me what I was carrying.

Once inside the apartment, my partner would become "Mr. Science." She would put on her nerdy glasses and carefully defrost the sperm to the exact temperature required. There was something frighteningly fatherlike about her. She was so in control and rational and practical all at the same time.

I remember the night we got pregnant with our first child. We had just sat through a rather long and not terribly good rendition of *The Magic Flute*. Four hours of opera had put me in a pessimistic mood. I didn't want to be inseminated, and I was sure it wouldn't work anyway. I began to cry. I insisted that we throw the sperm out and try again the next month.

My partner calmly explained that we had bought the damned sperm, and we were going to use it, whether I wanted to or not. I was angry and turned on all at the same time. I was angry because I didn't want Mr. Science, Mr. Rationality, and Mr. Control to tell me what to do. But I was turned on because I knew that once she removed her glasses and brought the sperm over to the bed, Mr. Science would disappear. Her role as the "father" would become ironic, distanced by her body (female) and her desire (lesbian). And I, always a sucker for a woman who knows what she wants, was enthralled by the idea that we would have reproductive sex whether I felt up to it or not.

Now that is hot. Sex and desire and reproduction, all too big and too important to be ignored or put off. Sex and desire and reproduction between two women—no doctor, no father.

I, for one, will always find lesbian reproductive sex sexy. And I will always feel a certain nostalgia and desire for the days of little purple sticks and large metal tanks and doing it whether we wanted to or not.

PICKING MR. RIGHT

Liza Weiman Hanks

SEVEN YEARS AGO, heart pounding, I told a story to a group of strangers at a storytelling class. It was about something so raw and personal that telling it was like drinking a straight shot of vodka. It made my eyes water and my hands shake. When I was finished, I felt flushed and free and slightly dizzy—even a little giddy.

The story went like this:

Every two months, a letter arrives for me in the mail. It isn't much to look at on the outside. Just a standard business envelope with a computer-generated label in the center and a rubber-stamped address at the top left corner.

Inside, there's one sheet of paper. It is gray. On it there's a photocopied list of about thirty lines. Each one reads about like this one:

234 YES Cauc/Eng/Dutch/Ital Grn/Brn 175 5'10" O+

Each line describes, in the most superficial way, a man. A man whom I know nothing about.

I don't know what he's like in the morning. Will he be mad if I want to read the comics first?

I don't know if he'll do the dishes when it isn't his turn.

I don't know how he shaves. Will he use shaving cream from a can? Or will he use that old-fashioned cake soap and a badger brush? Will he use a razor or an electric shaver? Maybe he has a beard.

What would he be like on a long car trip? Could he keep his sense of humor on the east side of the Sierra in the spring, as night falls and a dust storm kicks in and we have to stop for the night, but we can't find a hotel room because there's a marathon in Lone Pine the next day that we didn't know about?

What makes him happy? Would he laugh at *The Simpsons*?

What makes him cry? And how does he cry? Controlled single tears that trace a clean, straight line down his cheeks? Or huge, wracking, wretched sobs that make his back undulate like a wave?

Does he love his mother? Honor his father? Love his siblings?

Can I trust him to pick me up like he said he would, on a rainy dark night when I'm scared, and tired?

There's so much that I don't know about the men on that piece of paper. I'm not dating them. I won't be sharing dinner or spending the night, or the morning, with any of them. I'll never meet them at all.

But I will be sharing the rest of my life with part of them. I'll bear the child; my husband and I will love the child. It will be our child. And one of those men will be the biological father of that child.

How will we pick one from that list? How will we pick the father? These strangers offer us so much, but tell us so little.

When I wrote that story, choosing a sperm donor seemed like a momentous choice. A mystery. The list seemed like a talisman. An oracle. I studied it for clues. I saved the letters that came every other month. It seemed important to save them. I thought maybe if I found the right combination of letters and numbers, I'd know what to do, when to do it.

But it didn't work like that. Instead, after a few years, when we were done grieving for the child we would never make together, we just decided to make a baby. And, somewhat cavalierly, with a certain amount of "isn't this the weirdest thing" levity, we just picked three men off a list and went from there.

I wanted the donor who was part Dutch and part Japanese. I thought, "Why not go Pacific Rim? Sounds like he'd make beautiful children." We played haunted house with the dry ice the sperm came packed in. We enjoyed picking up the sperm in our tiny little icebox made for six-packs of beer. We joked that we'd tell our future child that we brought her home when she was "very little."

I came to look forward to waiting in the sperm bank lobby and meeting all the other proud and anxious women who were there to pick up their sperm too. We found ways to make using a syringe vaguely sensual. I heard myself tell my obstetrician that I wasn't a high-risk pregnancy—that we were just like any other couple, except we had to order takeout.

And now, our daughter is four. Everyone thinks she looks just like her dad. We decided early on to just say, "Isn't that amazing!"

and giggle at our own private joy that it is true. She's all ours—I recognized her elbows the moment she was born. Her dad's voice was the only one that stopped her infant cries; as I write this, she's curled around him on the couch like a vine, and they're both fast asleep. She gets our jokes. We get hers.

We're starting all over again—the tiny icebox, the dry ice, the phone calls, the testing, the timing, the waiting. We're using the same donor as last time, using sperm that has been stored on ice for five years.

We had to choose whether to have that option before our daughter was even born. I remember eating burgers, drinking beer, checking our savings account, and wondering whether we'd like the first kid, wondering whether it would be worth it to buy ahead and pay for storage. Five-year plans are just not part of our family's coping skills. It was quite a conceptual stretch, on every level.

I was right when I told the story of choosing Mr. Right to my storytelling class all those years ago. It is a mysterious choice, made with minimal information and monumental consequences. But I was wrong too. Picking the right donor wasn't really the point, because the child you get makes that choice "right" every time.

MY SEEDS ARE SPROUTING IN TWO WOMBS

Hank Pellissier

"HEY, HANK," whispers Rachel as she helps me set the table. "I understand 'phallus energy' now."

"Huh?!" I blush. "What do you mean?"

Rachel is my quirky, curly-haired lesbian friend. My wife Carol and I are feeding rock cod and tofu to her and her gal pal Monica tonight.

"I felt so studly, so powerful," she explains. "Sticking the syringe in Monica. I loved squirting your semen in her and knocking her up. Dang! I want to do it again!"

"It's a potent pleasure," I agree. "But doesn't Monica get to be 'phallic' next? We want YOU pregnant, too, Rachel."

Our tête-à-tête is interrupted by our corpulent partners, who enter the dining room, waddling arm-in-arm. My wife is a tall, blue-eyed WASP, while Monica is diminutive, raven-haired, and Jewish. Tonight they look identical because their T-shirts are both cinched up, exposing big bulbous watermelon-bellies.

"I'm fatter than you," remarks Carol. "But your boobs look bigger."

"What did the doctor say your due date was?" inquires Monica. "Mine is January first—a millennium boy-baby."

"December twenty-fifth," replies Carol. "Our daughter is the Antichrist."

Rachel and I escort our partners toward their chairs. We shove their portly frames toward their plates; we ladle them enormous quantities of third-trimester protein.

"Yummy!" burps my wife.

"Oink! Oink!" agrees Monica.

Sheepishly, I stare at the two happy fertility goddesses who are sprouting with my seed—my wife, inseminated by traditional calisthenics, and Monica, enlarged by semen that I wanked into a mayonnaise jar.

I feel like David Koresh.

"A toast!" crows Rachel. "To the tool who made this all possible!"

Carol and Monica hoist their teacups of neonatal brew. Materna tablets are poised on their lips, for swallowing.

"To our dear donor—'Uncle Wiggly'!" guffaws Monica.

"Polliwog Papa!" snickers Carol.

"How did you do it?" Rachel wonders. "What super-sperm food were you eating in March?"

"Cheetos?" I laugh. "Actually, I think we were all more fertile that month because we were filled with hatred, stress, and despair."

Carol and Monica were fighting viciously seven months ago—they were angry because their ovulation cycles were parallel for the very first time. When the procreation plan started, their cycles were two weeks apart; but a fertility drug ingested by Monica threw her off, directly into Carol's path.

A bitter struggle for sperm rights erupted on the phone; a screaming, hissing catfight for dominion of my dollops. Eventually, Carol slammed down the receiver and whirled on me. "I get you first, every day this entire week!" she snarled triumphantly. "You're my husband—she only gets what's left over."

Stupidly, I disagreed.

"Monica's older," I argued. "You're young, and she's forty—her eggs are getting astoundingly more brittle, every day. Besides, I promised my sperm to her before you were even interested in having a baby—therefore, she gets first dibs."

"You're insane!" snarled my headstrong spouse. "Your gunk IS MARRIED TO ME!"

"It's my body!" I hissed. "I own my fluids!"

Doors slammed; saucers and forks were tossed; sobs ensued.

"Okay, okay, okay," I conceded, forlornly. "It doesn't matter anyway."

After fifteen months of failing to inseminate either of them separately, my meager reservoir was suddenly supposed to simultaneously satisfy both thirsty uteri.

"I'm forty-six years old," I whined. "Double duty for five days? It's impossible. My tank will run dry."

Never, ever in my rather degrading life had I ever felt like such a loser. For fifteen months I had tossed my offerings into Monica's jars and Carol's loins without even a sprout to boast about. I ate icky health food, I slept immense hours, I exercised strenuously—but all the glue I grunted out desultorily refused to bond with their eggs.

My spunk IS alive—a sperm analysis verified this—but an emasculating curse had rendered my intimate maleness absolutely deficient. Perhaps my sperm was retarded—wandering lost in fallopian labyrinths. Perhaps its whipping tails were too puny to paddle up the pubic path. Perhaps its heads weren't pointy enough to pummel past the crust of the ovum.

To emotionally survive my special burden in March, I began furtively drinking beer with my "jogging" partner, Paul. I raced out my front door in warm-up sweats, to delude my wife. Three blocks away, at the Treat Street Pub, I guzzled ale with my chum, who also was in a procreating dilemma. Together we commiserated about the anguish of being sub-male. After an hour of jolly whining, we sprinkled water on our faces to impersonate sweat and strode home to our respective lairs, to drunkenly perform our testicular duties.

"That was a great one!" I lied to my wife, as I dramatically faked a gigantic, multispurting orgasm.

"Really?" she marveled. "There's a lot . . . coming out?"

"Pints!" I assured her. "Great gobs."

"Uh . . . what about Monica?" she asked. "Is there much for her, too?"

"Nope!" I chuckled. "She only gets a teensy-weensy speck."

"Oh honey," cooed Carol. "I love you!" My volume report regarding the lesbian drop-off was hideously, embarrassingly true. In my wife, I could bury my pitiful discharges out of view, but in Monica's glass mayonnaise jar . . .

"Where is it?" she asked, polite but ruffled.

"Can't you see it? Right there." I aimed my trembling finger at some shivering dampness in the corner.

"I'll get it!" grunted Rachel, her syringe poised aggressively. "Don't worry; it only takes one tadpole!"

Adroitly, she snagged the minuscule smudge as I hurried, crimson-faced, out of their home.

When my five days of stud service finally ended, I collapsed into an evil, despairing funk.

"This will never happen," I decided. "It's a fiasco, a joke. I'll never get Carol pregnant, or Monica, or Rachel" (who wants my semen when Monica's offspring is six months old; that way, their kids can be half-siblings).

My fantastic queer-friendly family plan seemed only a chimera; an illusionary dream impossible for a middle-aged man like me.

"Hank, my period's late," Carol told me three weeks later.

"Don't tease me!" I implored her. "Really, my ego can't take it."

Three days later, she came home with a pregnancy kit that she had purchased from a local Thrifty Drug store.

"I'm not splitting the cost of that," I grumbled. "What a waste of money."

Carefully, she urinated on the stick.

"If the lines appear with the same thickness," she said.

"Yeah, yeah, yeah."

Two minutes later, I heard her call out my name in a tremulous tone that I'd never heard before. I ran to the bathroom. I stared at the technological appliance that promised a miracle. We screamed.

"Ah gah ah ha ha ha! We did it! Ooowee! Yabba-dabba-doo!"

After shedding plenty of impending parent tears together, I remembered my other responsibility.

"This means," I blubbered obtusely, "that I can concentrate on Monica now, without interference."

"You're so rude," hissed my wife.

Sprinting to the phone, I dialed the gal pals.

"Guess what?" I gushed. "Carol's pregnant."

A pause.

"You're serious?" said Monica.

"So are we!!!" shrieked Rachel, in the background. "We're gonna have a baby!"

"Hooray! Hooray! Hooray!" I laughed.

"Hooray for all of us!" yelled Carol, grabbing the phone away from me for some serious girl talk.

"I'm finished!" I exulted. "No more sex chores! I don't have to ejaculate again for the rest of my life!"

I felt sorry for Monica when she got morning sickness, because of course I'm responsible. I felt annoyed when I found out that she was still drinking coffee—what's she trying to do, abort my son? I felt frustrated when she said she was "still in denial"—what's wrong? Is she embarrassed about the product of our chromosomal union?

Tonight, with the rock cod and tofu, is the first time that Carol and I have socially mingled with Rachel and Monica since the pregnancies ensued. Why? Well, one reason is because I'm afraid of appearing too interested. Or not interested enough. I'm confused, really, about how I feel. I'm glad, of course, that they're getting what they want. And, usually, I'm just focused on the daughter that Carol is carrying.

But when Monica's boy emerges, I'm worried. I know I'm going to bust loose with some wacky emotions. He's a boy?! Like me?! Will he look like me? Will he act like me? Will I love him? A son? Son? Is he really my son?

Monica and Rachel are embroiled now in a complex legal procedure that will allow Rachel to sign the birth document as the boy's "father." They need my signed consent for this, and they'll get it. I'm honest, and I've promised—no interference. The child is theirs. I won't have any parental rights whatsoever.

But still.

"Wouldn't it be fun?" proposes my excellent wife, who always vocalizes the secrets hidden inside everyone's minds. "Wouldn't it be wonderful if our children played together all the time, and got to know each other well? They're related, after all; they'll be half-brother and half-sister."

Rachel glows with happiness—a broad grin splits her round face. Monica's eyes soften; she's touched by Carol's profusion of friendship.

"Yes," Rachel says. "Yes."

"We can alternate baby-sitting," suggests Carol. "Or we can watch them together. We can celebrate their birthdays together. It takes 'community' to raise happy children, and the four of us together have a natural bond."

"Let's do it," whispers Monica.

The talk turns now to names. Carol and I are going to call our daughter Tallulah Elizabeth, but Rachel and Monica are undecided.

"An Old Testament name, because you're both Jewish?" I guess.

"Yes," Rachel agrees. "Maybe Ezekiel, or Jeroboam, or Abimelech, or Zechariah."

"You could name him 'Onan,' after his masturbating papalineage," I cackle. "Har har, har har har!"

No one else laughs.

"Maybe Amos, or Obidiah," suggests Monica. "Or Nehemiah, or Ephraim."

"Those are all excellent names," I lie. As a neo-pagan I've got ornery opinions on the subject, but I don't say anything. He's not my son, after all. He's not my son, he's not my son.

Then again, he is, at least sort of, and hard as I try, I can't stop the horrible and sweet emotions bubbling inside me already about this tiny life—these tiny lives—coming into the world.

POST-NUCLEAR FAMILY LIFE

LOVE ME, LOVE MY GUNS

Susan Straight

I NEVER SAW a gun until I was twenty-four. I didn't grow up in Mayberry; I grew up in southern California. In my old neighborhood, drugs and alcohol fueled many parties and fights. One night, my younger brother and his friends had an altercation at the end of the street; from my bedroom windowsill, I watched them run home. A boy named Sammy had a knife; someone hit him in the head with a baseball bat. He was killed.

In junior high, where I met my future husband, Dwayne, we witnessed mass fights and riots. I saw girls with razors in their hair and boys with fists. There were more riots in high school; boys fought viciously, one with a tire iron. Fights could be brutal; our friend B. D. got his jaw broken over a quarter in a parking-lot craps game. But no one was killed in school, and no one had guns.

Dwayne had seen guns in his neighborhood. Many fathers there, originally from the South, still hunted. On New Year's, they fired guns in celebration.

But Dwayne never had a gun. When we were newly married, hanging out at my longtime girlfriend's house as drugs really exploded in our city, Dwayne was terrified when my girlfriend's husband pulled out a semiautomatic pistol from under the couch. A potential customer, or killer, had knocked. I was upstairs with my friend and her new baby.

Later in the car, Dwayne told me we couldn't visit them again. "He pulled out a piece. We can't take that chance," he said. "Could be the cops. We could get caught in a shootout." He shivered, I remember clearly, and said, "I heard him cock that baby. Click, click."

Thirteen years later, a shotgun fell on my head as I searched the closet for baby clothes, and my heart leaped in fear, like a small animal tethered to my breastbone. Dwayne hadn't told me about the shotgun, never mentioned we were armed. I suddenly imagined him holding the gun, cocking that baby. *Shuck, shuck.*

Since college, Dwayne had been working with juvenile offenders at a correctional facility. Many of their crimes involved guns. When I was five months pregnant with our first child, Dwayne worked graveyard shift. One night, a juvenile pretended to take an overdose of stashed pills, and Dwayne had to escort him to the hospital. A man jumped from the bushes and shot Dwayne in the chest with a Taser stun gun. Dwayne staggered, but his size, his sheepskin jacket, and his bravery blunted the shock. He punched the man, knocking him down, and ran after the hobbling juvenile headed for a van. Then another man emerged from the van, pointing a .38 at Dwayne's face. Dwayne had no choice; he had to back away.

He didn't tell me. He didn't want me to faint, to upset the baby. But I read about the escape in the paper, and then I saw the burn marks on his jacket. When he described what had happened—to me and later to the court during trial—I heard what bothered him most: the unfairness of the gun. Bravery and size and loyalty don't match up with bullets.

I confronted him about the shotgun, after gingerly laying it on the floor. I knew nothing about bullets or shells or what the heavy black weapon might do. Dwayne sighed. He said our city had become increasingly unsafe, with carjackings and drive-by shootings and random violence. He'd gotten the shotgun for protection, for the intruder that might break into our house. He would be ready to protect us—his little family. He would be a good husband and father; repelling evil was his job.

But I saw him fall in love with the guns themselves, the seduction of the barrels and oil and wooden stocks with carving, the power of caliber. He bought a handgun, then another, and spent hours comparing weapons with our next-door neighbor and my brother. Our neighbor, a very conservative guy, had gleefully told us that he thought a burglar had tested his bedroom window one night. "All he has to do is put a finger over the sill, and he's inside the threshold of my property. I can blow his ass away. It's my right."

My brother acquired his first gun when he was very young, from a recently fled drug dealer's residence. Now he lived in a rural orange-grove area, and he shot at coyotes who killed his animals, and at drug runners who used the groves for transport. Sometimes he joked that he only shot what moved.

Dwayne began shooting at the range, and shooting in the groves with my brother. Even my brother was impressed when my husband bought a Chinese-made SKS assault rifle. "How many rounds would it take to kill a possum in the yard?" I joked. But I was scared. I didn't want anyone pushing on my window screens, but neither did I want the burden of a dead person lying across the sill.

The guns themselves fascinated me for a short time, but underneath my curiosity I was terrified. I never learned to shoot them like the neighbors' wives, who went to the range. Instead, I opened the oven, and there they were, baking at a low temperature as part of the cleaning process: a 9mm handgun, the shotgun.

Dwayne spent hours in the garage cleaning and oiling them and making his own ammunition with a reloader. He spent hundreds of dollars on weapons, bullets, and accessories. Hobbies are expensive. But these were weapons. Not for play—they could only shred targets or skin and bone.

"Only a shotgun, for intruders, and the shells are somewhere else," I'd been told that day, after the closet. But then I found a handgun on the dresser under a knit cap, within easy reach of our daughters. There was a gun in the camper when we took vacations, a gun in the glove compartment of the car. All those years, I'd been afraid of the police stopping Dwayne, a black man, and now I was even more scared; what if they saw a gun in the glove compartment?

Every night, while I graded papers, Dwayne was in the garage making shells or sorting bullets or oiling a gun barrel. I watched him, I asked him about the guns, and I wrote about them in my last novel. I imagined being a teenage boy, surrounded by gangs and death, who falls in love with weapons as defense; who cannot kill but who cleans and stores and loads the guns to protect his own sanity. But my imagination was still afraid, and when I knocked on the closed wooden door, very late, my husband answered wearing his 9mm in a shoulder holster. Who was I? Was I on the threshold?

We had three children, and suddenly he had ten guns. I didn't feel protected. I felt like I was living with a different man, one who didn't play basketball and read *Sports Illustrated* like before, one who baked his guns clean and read *Guns & Ammo*. Our house and garage and vehicle, my spouse, carried instruments of death. The 9mm handgun on the dresser, shockingly heavy to me, could have been picked up, dropped, fired, by fingers smaller than mine. And I couldn't forgive that.

When we visited our old neighborhoods, drugs and guns were everywhere. Our girls approached the car of a childhood friend, and I saw an Uzi on his front seat. The stubby barrel was barely hidden. I nearly screamed. A relative had a derringer, tiny and palm-sized, in his car. When I finally told Dwayne I didn't want to live like this, he replied, "This is real life." But I didn't want it to be my life, my children's lives. Guns and his work and this real life had engendered a paranoia, a mistrust, a secrecy, and a fatalism that I couldn't share.

On our last walk together, without the kids, we took a trail in the nearby river bottom, a place we'd explored as children. Stepping down a narrow path through fall-browned brush and wild grapevines fallow for winter, we saw in the tall bamboo a homeless encampment where dogs barked at us from the entrance. Then we were in a clearing near the water, and a huge snort came from the arundo cane. Feral pigs lived there, though we'd never actually seen one. They can weigh two hundred pounds, tusks included, and they've charged riders on horseback.

Dwayne pulled a 9mm handgun from his back waistband and aimed toward the cane. I was amazed. "Back up," he whispered. We both did. The snorting was grumpy, not enraged, and then the cane trembled as the pig crashed the other way.

I stared at the gun. "So you were gonna shoot the pig?" I said, and Dwayne tucked the gun under his shirt. "And when that pissed him off, he was gonna charge the littlest person—me."

"I didn't bring this for wild pigs," he said unapologetically, as we walked back. "I brought it for wild people."

I know he's right—the wild people are out there—but inside my house, there are no wild people. My daughters hate guns. They hate seeing guns in constant advertisements for movies, and on TV news, which in southern California often consists of freeway chases ending with drawn guns, or videotape of convenience-store robberies where people wave guns. They hate their uncles' guns, and they hate their father's guns.

Is this because I've told them to? Because they're girls? No. It's instinctive fear. I'll never forget volunteering in a kindergarten class, sitting near the circle of children while they talked about a book. Then a boy said his dad's gun could have killed the monster. The teacher said, "Guns are scary." She looked shocked. "How many people in here have seen guns?"

I drew a quick breath when my middle daughter Delphine raised her hand, along with nine or ten other kids, and said, "My dad has a gun in his car."

"Mine does, too," the first boy said. "It sits on the seat next to me."

The teacher glanced at me, incredulous, and I was ashamed. For all of us.

My daughters are afraid of pit bulls, of the stranger waiting to kidnap them. I was afraid of those things; I still am. But my kids are truly afraid of guns, of their presence everywhere.

This breaks my heart: that they are so young and know too much. I have a desk drawer full of bullets. Yes. I have found spent ammunition on my sidewalk, and several years ago a teacher at the girls' former preschool poured ten bullets into my cupped hand, her eyes full of tears. She said her ten-year-old son was given the bullets in their apartment complex, encouraged to get a gun. She moved to North Carolina soon after that.

I have ten of Dwayne's bullets in the drawer, too. He lives a short distance from us. One night at dinner my youngest, then two years old, mentioned the gun she'd found under the couch at Daddy's house, and then Delphine frowned and mentioned the two she'd seen under the bed. They'd been playing hide-and-seek.

I felt twinges of pain between my hipbones, where my babies rested inside me, where fear always circles for me now. "It was only a BB gun," Dwayne said when I called him, immediately, angrily, incredulous. "And the rifles were in a case."

"Well, okay, and I'm glad she has that third eye in her forehead for when the other one gets shot out," I said.

For me, saying, "You'll shoot your eye out with that thing" is not a joke. I know a woman blind in one eye from BBs shot by siblings. On the phone, I went ballistic. I went postal. Gun phrases, now an integral part of our culture.

I told him the kids couldn't visit under these circumstances, and we argued for days. I said I didn't care if the guns had only been stored under furniture temporarily. I still remembered the dresser, the glove compartment. And now, a year later, the guns were stored in a locker at the foot of his bed. The girls whisper to me that they hate sitting on the blanket-covered metal chest. "It's scary to sit on the guns. They're in there."

The shotgun, the same one that clunked me on the head, is hidden in my house—the one that started this whole thing, the one Dwayne left behind when he moved out. "So you can protect yourself," he said when I called him about it. (A year after he left, I got on a ladder to vacuum the moldings and found more than thirty cartridges stored around the room, beneath the ceiling, where he could easily reach them.) I haven't loaded it; I don't want to know how. I have held it, looked at it in the mirror, made that *shuck-shuck* sound, put it away.

My children are my life. I don't want scars anywhere on their bodies, or in their brains and hearts. The way parents were afraid of polio in the 1950s, scared of public pools and free-floating germs, I am afraid of guns. I picture anonymous gun barrels while I wait outside the chain-link fence at school, while I walk across the store parking lot where someone was shot a few years ago.

Was my mother ever afraid of bombs like this, after surviving World War II in Switzerland? Was my father-in-law afraid after surviving depression life in Oklahoma?

All his relatives had guns. I remember watching westerns with him years ago. "There's the Colt .45," someone would say with reverence. "The peacemaker," someone else would chime in. "Tamed the Wild West." But Dwayne's father would reply, "All we ever shot in Oklahoma was dinner squirrel or rabbit." He never had a gun, other than an ancient hunting rifle, which Dwayne keeps in his collection.

People hunt people now. That's the difference. That's what Dwayne was trying to say, over and over, to me. How did we come to this, all of us?

I am afraid of the wild people, just as he is. And when I think about a wild stranger touching my children, I even wish, briefly, for a handgun. On our strolls to 7-Eleven for Slurpees, I watch everyone passing us on the busy street, on the eucalyptus-lined sidewalks. I plan what I will do to a possible attacker. I admit it— I visualize "the great equalizer," the peacemaker, the one thing that would make me, five-foot-four and 105 pounds, able to repel anyone who tried to hurt my girls.

Then do I understand how Dwayne feels? Do I understand how any of them feel—husbands with guns or boys like the two I saw outside my living-room window, comparing handguns and then tucking them into their waistbands before getting back on their bikes? A gun gives anyone all the power in the world. Here in America, the most powerful country in the world, we have the most guns of all. And we are all, almost all of us, afraid of each other.

In my bedroom, perched high in the moldings, there are probably stray green shotgun cartridges. Somewhere in my house, tucked away, is a shotgun. I don't think of them as protection; they don't provide any relief. I think the gun was one of my ex-husband's favorites, left behind as a phantom guard in his absence.

Maybe it makes him feel safe.

Callie Milton

IRRESPONSIBLE behavior runs in my family. But so does redemption.

A couple of months ago, I went to the funeral of my ninety-year-old great-uncle, Henry Washington, and was amused to hear the preacher describe old Uncle Henry as almost perfect in his virtue, referring to him as "a saint, the sweetest old man you'd ever want to know."

Was this the same guy who had a rep for chasing the ladies, for whoring around? Or as my cousin put it, who "couldn't keep his dick in his pants?" Was this the same guy who kept trashy magazines in his desk at work, who got divorced back in the days when nobody got divorced? Yes, it was.

I'd seen those old black-and-white photos of Uncle Henry decked out in a white double-breasted suit, standing bowlegged next to a black sedan, his fedora cocked over to one side like a pimp's. Uncle Henry was a randy son of a bitch, as rowdy as they come.

Then something changed. Maybe he just outlived his old self, but he became a model citizen long enough to earn a preacher's sincere praise at his death.

And then there is my cousin Teddy, a maniac from the time he was able to walk until his late thirties. Once he overdosed on LSD, kicked the windows out of his dad's house, and was hospitalized. He was drunk or drugged every waking minute I knew him. But then something happened. He gradually became domesticated enough to allow himself to be elected a deacon in the First Baptist Church. And he meant it.

In my family, when you swing back, you swing back hard. One of my brothers, who drank himself into living at the Salvation Army and then out of the Salvation Army to a clump of trees behind a 7-Eleven, is finishing up his master's degree and working as a counselor at a world-renowned treatment center.

I thought of these family histories the other day when Silas, my oldest son, came home talking nonstop about *Chicken Soup for the Kid's Soul,* a book his teacher has been reading to his class. He told me about a character named Kel Mitchell who escaped a life of gang violence and went on to become a successful actor on the TV show *All That.*

My son was visibly excited by this stranger's tale of rebellion and redemption, which I thought mild compared to mine. As he spoke, I wondered how much family history my kids need to know.

I believe in the power of cautionary tales; in fact I told Silas one the other day after he decided to get into a shouting match with rock-throwing teens. Tired of repeating my maxim, "Don't mess with strangers," I finally broke out the story of my wayward brother. "Your Uncle Walt," I said, "decided to get into an argument with a man he didn't know. The man broke the beer bottle he was holding and slashed your uncle's neck. Look at his scar the next time he visits. He's lucky to be alive." My son stopped doing his warrior dance, finally able to get the message.

But what about my experiences with the dark side? Do I need to tell my kids about the time I woke up hung over in a jail in Daytona Beach with no memory of how I got there? My ankle was so sore, I couldn't stand on it, and I had scratches all over my body. When the sheriff walked by the cell, he leaned close to the bars and said, "How you feeling today, Rabbit?"

Later that morning I sat numbly in court, scared to death of what the judge was going to say. Had I killed someone? Had I wrecked the car? Had I robbed a bank? I sat next to a bedraggled, six-foot-three drag queen who wore the biggest pair of black patent pumps I'd ever seen. I focused on those shiny black canoes of leather as I waited to hear my fate.

It turns out that I hadn't killed anyone, but I very easily could've. I had driven in a drunken blackout from Orlando to Daytona Beach. At some point during the night, I turned my headlights off and a sheriff pulled me over. When he saw that I was drunk as a coot, he tried to arrest me, and I tried to run. Hence the twisted ankle and the nickname "Rabbit."

This wasn't my first experience with being arrested, but it was to be my last. At the time of that arrest, I was waiting to be sentenced for an earlier DWI as well as a charge of resisting arrest. The judge in that case had warned me to stay out of trouble.

Needless to say, when I appeared in his court the following month, and he asked me whether I had stayed out of trouble, I had to say no. I had gotten arrested in Daytona. My attorney, an overworked public defender who hadn't even thought to ask me himself, winced. We were both a couple of losers. The judge sentenced me to six months in jail.

Altogether I spent a hundred days in jail, surrounded by women who had done everything from murdering their children and lovers to writing bad checks. I didn't feel like I fit in. I'd never felt like I fit in. For God's sake, when I was fifteen the American Legion picked me out of a pack of other teenage girls on the basis of an essay I wrote, and sent me to Girls' State, a week-long course in government designed to instill leadership skills. Ha, I thought. Secretly, I was an anarchist who admired people like Abbie Hoffman. I was smart enough to appreciate the irony of my being chosen. The other Girls' Staters arrived at the gates of Florida State University with their parents; I rolled up in a dented Dodge Dart with my boyfriend and a bag of reefer. I spent all my free moments drinking wine coolers in a restaurant across the street from our dorm. I was just a good girl out to be bad. I didn't want to kill anyone. Except perhaps, myself.

I had always been a thrill seeker, intent on experiencing the world head-on without a thought to the consequences of my behavior. I wrecked everything from tricycles to motorcycles. I almost crashed a single-engine Cessna one day when it was way too windy for a novice like myself to be out flying. Luckily, I bounced down the runway, unharmed.

I wasn't so lucky when it came to drugs.

When I was twenty-one, my mother was killed in an accident, and my siblings and I got some money. It wasn't much, but it was enough for me to invest in an ounce or two of cocaine. Needless to say, I wasn't much of a salesperson. I got into the goods, snorting my profits. I did sell enough to break even some of the time, but there came a point when I thought selling coke was a waste of a good thing. The same with snorting it. I began shooting up.

For almost two years, I shot up at least two or three days a week, stopping only when I ran out of cash. Things got bad. Needles were shared. Veins collapsed. Once, when my power got turned off, I sat in the dark by the apartment window, desperately trying to catch enough light from the streetlamp outside so I could see to hit my vein.

I knew I had to do something, or I was going to die. I moved to Orlando to live with my sister and brother. There's a picture of me at Disney World wearing a National Organization for the Reform of Marijuana Laws T-shirt. My wavy black hair hangs to my shoulders. Needle tracks are visible as purple bruises on my arms.

Shortly after that photo was taken, I made my ill-fated drive to Daytona. I still don't know why I was headed to Daytona. But that short ride got me to where I'm at now. I needed those hundred days in jail to show me that I wasn't as hip and smart as I thought I was. I needed to be surrounded by some stupid people. I needed to meet the woman who shot her little girl and left her for dead in the woods. I needed to meet the woman who poisoned her husband, and the woman who pounded her fingers with a hammer to get painkillers from her doctor. I needed to meet the prostitutes who risked their lives every time they climbed into some yokel's car. Jesus.

I really needed to meet Lee, an ex-bartender from Greenwich Village who voluntarily came to the jail to tell us stories about her own drunken debaucheries, and how she got sober. When she told the story of waking up on the subway in New York being humped by a strange man, or the story about riding her motorcycle into a bar, I thought, here's a kindred spirit. Her tales caught my attention. She was wild. She was crazy. She was clean and sober. And she helped steer me in that direction when I got out of jail. It took a while. In spite of just having served a hundred days in jail, I needed to shoot up a few more times before I was beat. But I finally made it, and I've been clean for about sixteen years.

My children don't know the person I was before I got clean. I'm not sure how they would react to news that their mother used to sell cocaine and reefer, that she once got arrested five times in one month, or that she spent time behind bars. They only know me as who I am now, their mother, a writer with a Ph.D. in English who has taught at a small community college since before they were born. I'm the person who takes them out into the woods to look for turtle shells and pottery. I help them set up their lemonade stand. The most illicit thing they've seen me do is let them sit in my lap and drive down a few long, orange-clay roads.

Clearly, now is not the time to tarnish their image of me. My ten-year-old can't bear the thought that I used to smoke cigarettes. (I still do, but only at night when he's asleep.) My four-year-old can't conceive of my having had a life without him; and my sixteen-month-old—well, he just wants a Popsicle to soothe his aching gums. But if these boys ever need a dose of reality, a head-spinning cautionary tale, I have a few I can whip out.

ON BEING KEN

Tim Cornwell

THE QUEEN of China is knocking at the door, tall and stately in a red velvet robe, which is offset by hair the color of tomato soup. Ken is scurrying about, getting the family ready. "Quick, the queen is coming! The girls must have their dresses on! They must take their seats facing the door!" Whitney, the youngest, is trouble as usual, jumping up and down on her jointed legs, flouncing her long frizzy hair, whining, and generally giving Ken hell.

Ken is nice, but stupid. The queen takes off her robe. She's an orphan girl with no home. Ken offers her some dinner—she must be starving—and Whitney's bed for the night. She tells him her name is Ariel, and asks, "Can I call you Dad?" Ariel finds her long-lost mother. But the children are jealous. Whitney throws a tantrum, then tries—literally—to kick Ariel out of the house. Ken does his ineffectual best to keep the peace.

We never wanted Barbies in our house. But they infiltrated our family as ruthlessly as ninjas, smuggled in as birthday gifts from less discerning friends. We acquired a neighing Barbie horse, then were loaned a Barbie car. (I lost my fear of Barbies on a camping trip, when it became a prime sport for my two young daughters to hurl them up a steep rock face and watch them scrape and slither down.)

Our Barbie family begins with three brunet babes, indistinguishable chorus players whose characters and names rotate. Mostly, they play the role of sisters, good or bad, to Ariel, the Little Mermaid, and the looker of the family. She has—for the uninitiated—bright red hair, wide sparkling blue eyes, and a perky white smile. I couldn't tell you if she's the genuine Barbie or a Disney offshoot.

Then there's Michelle, a blond punk, her hair shorn off one experimental day with a pair of scissors. Whitney, the angry little sister, arrived in a purple helmet on a bicycle. Ken drifted in, I don't know when, as a hand-me-down from the older sister of a school friend.

With the arrival of Ken, a wussy Malibu type not at all like the British action men of my youth, I have been much in demand on the Barbie front. For our four-year-old daughter Eliza, there is something indescribably attractive about a grown man playing Barbies—and in particular, there is great attraction for me in playing Ken.

I read somewhere that a child needs just twenty minutes a day of personal parental time, on the game of his or her choice, to grow into a well-rounded American adult. I reckon I can Barbie for an hour.

True, I often groan inwardly when they bob their little heads, clutched in my daughter's hands, imploring me to join the party. The mere prospect of the game can induce a heavy urge to go to sleep, surf the Web, or reach reflexively for the liquor cabinet. I will ask to play cards or a board game, anything but Bar . . . then pinch myself awake, summoning my daddy conscience. This is, after all, a passing moment of childhood, one I should cherish. In years to come, utters my better self, I will long for the days when a little voice cried out for me to play Barbies.

And on occasion, a kind of magic ensues, and the little plastic faces come alive for both of us, laughing, crying, snorting in anger. They are contract players in a studio where we pull all the strings, Eliza as director and screenwriter, while I manage the talent. She sets the parameters for the play, selects a part and a premise, and then calls for action.

Enter, Ken.

Now I realize that the game carries a particular responsibility. Here, I am defining for my daughter the relationship between *homme* and *femme*. It is, of course, part of the father's broader job description to cultivate a healthy relationship with his daughter, to lay a steady groundwork for her future relationships with men.

So I play my part with a mind to showing her how to get along with a guy, with perhaps some subtle indication of the kind of guy she might want to get along with. This amounts to making women equal, even dominant, partners in the scheme of things. In the Barbie world, the women must be able to tell a man what to do.

So my Ken is, by popular and persistent demand, nice, but stupid.

Sure, he has $20 good looks, but his cheek has two inky scars from an instant marker, and his forelock, after many washings,

shoots straight up off his head, giving him a permanently surprised look. He's got hunky shoulders, but he moves stiffly,
stoopingly, stupidly.

Nice, but stupid. I tend to defend Ken as well-meaning, but
overloaded; well-intentioned, but a little goofy. For Eliza he's simply nice, but stupid. Sometimes he is straightforwardly a bump-
kin, a clown. The children run circles around him. He is made
speechless by beautiful women and is apt to take refuge in the
kitchen.

He's a man in a woman's world, constantly surrounded by at
least four or five of them, with busts and buns of exceptional di-
mensions. He loses his trousers and finds himself naked in public
places—in fact, he lost them long ago, somewhere in the back of
the toy cupboard.

Our early stories were borrowed from movie scripts. The Barbies ran shrieking from dinosaurs, then challenged the beasts,
mostly by bonking their heads with a small toy drum. But lately
our scenarios are family dramas, featuring the kind of dysfunctional families long cherished by the best storytellers, from Roald
Dahl to the Brothers Grimm.

In a recent fit of pique, Whitney moved all her plastic animals—
an entire zoo—into the dollhouse, backed up by Ariel, over Ken's
desperate protests. Ariel, meanwhile, is frequently an adopted
daughter with a mysterious past. She arrives at the door, pursued
by taunting, invisible boys who shout, "Redhead! Redhead!" Ken
runs to the rescue and shoos them away.

She recently urged her parents to put salt in the backyard pool, but she won't go swimming with her sisters. Instead, she sits demurely at the side. Played by Eliza, Ariel is silent and elusive, righteous and well-behaved. And she has a stunning secret. At the beach one day, Ken stumbles upon his daughter swimming; it turns out she's a mermaid, with a fishy tail. Her sisters know her story, but when Ken tells his wife, she doesn't believe a word of it. He falls in the sea and begins to cough and drown. Ariel saves him.

At one point, Ken is encouraged to break all the rules of a civilized family and tell Ariel that she's more beautiful than the rest of his daughters. The family erupts; Whitney is in an absolute fury, and so are her siblings. But my Ken is never, never tough on his daughters. Once, he sent Whitney to her room when, by common consent, she was being particularly bad. On rare occasions, he rises to a challenge and asserts himself as head of the family; at times, he's a calming influence.

The ruling authority in my childhood, as our parents divorced and added two half-brothers, was my mother. She didn't kick a ball around with us; I remember her, perhaps mistakenly, as determinedly unathletic. But I loved to cook with my mother, and I love to have my daughters cook with me in the old-fashioned way, baking hot, buttery English dishes in a California kitchen.

So Ken, in one of our better stories, is a baker. A busy but gifted chef whom the queen calls upon every morning for fresh croissants. Two sisters of ravishing beauty move in upstairs. Ken, unable to express himself in words, delivers gifts of bread and coffee cake, but starts to get his orders mixed up.

And then life starts to get on top of him. The queen orders a chocolate cake, a great honor, but it must be ready for tonight, or she'll cut off his head. Ken's mother, Michelle (with the shorn head), pays a visit and announces she has sold her house. She's moving in, and she'll take Ken's bedroom, thank you. He'll sleep in the bakery. Ken's mother declares her love for Ariel; Ken nervously puts a stop to the plot line.

These days, Ken has been sitting around with the stuffed animals, listening to show tunes. He's found something to wear: an old bra, wrapped around him like a toga.

Just the other day, he actually got to be king, attired for the first time ever in a green, fur-lined robe. Eliza's older sister stepped in, prepared to be Ken. "No," said Eliza. "Dad's Ken, because he's stupid."

I am presuming that she meant that my stupid Ken is the best Ken of all. After all, not everyone can do Hamlet, either.

HE AIN'T HEAVY

Lisa Zeidner

"YOU'RE going to die," our son announced.

He was five years old. Our wills were in order. We wrote them ourselves, with Family Lawyer for Windows. Maybe we should have hired a real lawyer, even if it cost more than the flight for our first jaunt away from our son. We also could have taken separate planes. We know people who actually do this, routinely. When childless, we'd mocked them. Suddenly it seemed like a sensible idea. If we cared about his future, if we didn't want to destroy his life, would it be so very terrible to stagger our departures from New Jersey?

"We're not going to die," we promised him, and we mostly believed this to be true. Odds were that the 747's engines would not explode; no terrorists would board; we would not even get crushed by a double-decker bus when we looked the wrong way crossing the street in London. We simply couldn't die, because we have no satisfying choice of recipients for our most precious possession—the fruit of our loins.

Neither, by the way, do any of the other parents I know.

Show me a photo of a doleful Romanian orphan or a disoriented Ethiopian toddler with flies on his eyelashes, propped up by his dying mother, and I will get teary-eyed immediately.

Maybe all parents do. No doubt that becoming a parent changes—and intensifies—your fears about your own mortality. It also introduces some thorny logistical decisions that are different, I believe, for our generation than for our parents'.

My husband's parents are dead. My parents are seventy-two. They can survive (just) a week baby-sitting, but they are not good long-range prospects as guardians. My sister in North Carolina now has a toddler of her own, so she might rally herself to more enthusiasm about inheriting my son than she did on the occasion of that fateful first separation, three years ago. At that point she said, somewhat vaguely, "Maybe you'd better ask Russell."

So if we die, our son Nicolas—and the life-insurance money—will go to my brother in San Francisco, who is, despite the tattoos and earrings, a kind, reliable adult.

Or so I thought.

"How much money do I get?" Russell asked, when we rubber-stamped the arrangements for the will.

A million, give or take. Probably, we told him, enough for college.

"Cool!" Russell said. "Forget college. Nick and I are going to Tahiti."

He was kidding, I think.

Nick's first reaction to the prospect of life with Uncle Russell was enthusiastic. "We'll get a lot of pizzas," he said, "and throw them at each other, and throw ice cream, too." But then he began to worry. "How will I get to San Francisco?" he wanted to know.

How would he know we were dead? If we didn't pick him up at school, would they just leave him locked up there in the dark? And who was Russell's wife? Did he have one? Did she want children?

An uncanny question, since Russell's girlfriend would rather have head lice than children.

Of course it is family to whom you are supposed to turn in a crisis, to the rock-steady obligation of blood ties. But family no longer seems to have the same societal weight. While I'm lucky to be close to my siblings, many people I know only speak to theirs, grudgingly, at Thanksgiving and Christmas.

It's hard to imagine that, if all members of my immediate family got struck by lightning, a cousin in a distant port could be sent a telegram saying, "You're all he has left," old-novel-style, and feel any moral compunction to rise to the occasion. I thought of this, repeatedly, during the heartbreaking Turkish earthquake. If buildings collapse on us, believe me, no caravans of concerned second and third cousins are going to be braving the jammed New Jersey Turnpike with their own generators in tow to rescue us.

My son barely knows his aunt and uncle, much less his extended family. Now that people don't regularly stay put and die in their hometowns, it's more difficult to foster the close, daily relationships that might allow people to comfortably embrace a child not their own.

Even the simple fact that people marry and procreate later

changes things radically. My parents should not be so old in relation to their grandchild (though I thank them for not noting this more regularly during my dating years). If we'd started a family earlier, we might have had time for more than the one little tyke, which in movies, at least, seems to make orphanhood more bearable.

An old friend and his wife asked her sister to take their two boys in the event of their death. The sister said, curtly, "I don't really like any kids other than my own." So the winner is—his seventy-year-old parents. (Hers are bitterly divorced, and anyhow her father and his third wife have their hands full with a toddler of their own.)

"Well, we'll take your boys," I offered, at a rare dinner. We've known them for almost a quarter of a century, but we live a thousand miles apart; I see them once, twice a year.

"And we'll take yours!" they agreed.

We clinked glasses to jocularly seal the deal.

Surely we must have better options. What about my local friends? Shouldn't I have friends whose children are the same age as my children, whom I see regularly, who will take my son in for an afternoon if I need a couple of hours by myself for, say, root-canal work? Well, I don't. We barely see our friends. Most of them can't make room for lunch, much less a grief-stricken orphan.

One of these friends spent weeks trying to get off work for a mammogram. Her frantic schedule was not the only problem. She was terrified. "I can't die," she said. "I can't die now. It is out of the question. I have kids."

This line made me churlish. Would dying be peachy if she were childless? Are Americans so unable to admit to any personal longings that even a desire to live must be deemed selfish unless wrapped in the flag of Family Values?

I thought of the warped, silly sentimentality of *Titanic*—the bad guy grabbing the baby so he could get the last seat on the lifeboat. What a cur! Yet if Kate Winslet had simply boarded the goddamn lifeboat when she was supposed to, Leonardo DiCaprio would not have had to give her his seat on the piece of flotsam, and he would have lived. If that's generous love, give me selfishness. It's okay to want to live, even without children.

True to my friend's wildest fears, the mammogram turned up something suspicious. She had a biopsy, the news was good, and she was told that she was in no danger. The last couple of developments happen much quicker on the page than they did in life, and I don't want to belittle her panic—I'd gone through it myself—but this friend acted, every step of the way, as if it were time to pick out her headstone. She simply knew she was going to die.

"Cut them off!" she begged her doctor, in re her breasts. "My kids need me!" Another woman I know remains convinced, despite the reassurances of several doctors, that she is at extremely high risk for breast cancer. She also worries about brain tumors from living too close to high-tension wires. And toxic mold. This is less fear for their children than, in my utterly unqualified psychiatric opinion, a plea for attention and appreciation. These women had been so buried in the relentless needs of their families that they feel invisible, even to themselves. And being too generous, too other-directed, to complain, they unconsciously seize on an opportunity to set the score straight. It's the grown-up version of a game we all play when we're little: "Won't you all miss me when I'm gone. And boy, will you be sorry."

Now that my son is eight, he's quite capable of wishing me dead if I, say, make him do his homework. He understands about the insurance money. He has let it be known that in the event of my death he would like to be able to spend it at his discretion, without an intermediary. There are certain Pokémon cards he would like to buy, on Ebay. He would like a new bike with— "Wheelies"? "Poppers"? He would also like to visit the surfing beach in Australia that he saw in *Endless Summer*.

We have explained that the money is for college. "Why would I need to go to college," he retorts, "if I'm a millionaire?" He has now met Russell's girlfriend; he even liked her. But of course he cannot really conceive of losing us.

We all want to bequeath our children the dependable yet twinkling goodwill of Jimmy Stewart in Bedford Falls. But it's not as if *It's a Wonderful Life* was a piece of social realism in 1946. Every orphan is an orphan out of Dickens. For all our careful nest feathering, our son is about as buffered against ugly contingency as a passenger wearing a safety belt during a plane crash.

My brother Russell, it turns out, is on many parents' approved-guardian lists. In fact, he has agreed to take five little boys in addition to my own. This disturbed me at first, but now I try to look on the bright side: half-a-dozen screaming boy-children in a one-bedroom, one-bath house on Potrero Hill might rouse themselves to some amusing food fights.

My brother and his girlfriend, who are heavily involved with virtual reality R&D, don't do Christmas, but I hear they have a really good homeopath. It's a charmingly high-concept extended family—not a wonderful life, perhaps, but it will have to be good enough.

DYR MOM: WY R YOU SO LAVEABL?

Gayle Brandeis

A FEW MONTHS ago, I bought some sugar cookies shaped like the letters of the alphabet. When Jewish children begin to study Torah, rabbis often give them a spoonful of honey so they will always associate learning with sweetness. I figured the cookies would provide a most delicious reading lesson for my five-year-old daughter. I could picture us at the table together, spelling *cat* and *love* and *apple* on paper plates, our mouths full of shortbread and sugar and the lingering sweetness of words.

When I got home, though, I discovered my daughter had already created her own movable feast. Hannah had been sent to her room for some minor infraction while I was out, and she was not happy about it. Did she whine? Maybe. Did she cry? Most likely. I wasn't there to hear her protests. She did leave some evidence behind, though. She wrote.

Hannah had never written anything all on her own before, other than her own name and the names of our family members. She had never constructed a sentence, never sat down with the intention of getting her thoughts on paper. In the hour that I was gone, though, she essentially figured out the whole writing process.

As I walked through her door, Hannah handed me a piece of paper.

"DYR MOM," it said. "DED IS ALWYS MEYN."

Rough drafts of the letter were scattered around her room: "DRY MOM," one began. "DYR MAM" read another.

I was blown away. Not only had Hannah written a sentence for the first time, she had edited her own work! After years as a writer, I have only recently made friends with the revision process. Hannah shook hands with it her first time out. My heart filled to bursting—my little girl, a writer!

My husband was amazed, too, although he was not completely thrilled to be the villain of her first literary undertaking. This gave us a little peek into what it must feel like to read a daughter's tell-all memoir. Wait, the author's parents must want to say, that's not the whole story! We're not bad people! We bought her a Sno-Cone from the ice-cream truck just minutes before the alleged incident! And, you know, she never would have been sent to her room if she hadn't thrown a stick at her brother's head!

Before we could get too worked up about her initial angry outpouring of words, though, Hannah began another series of letters, sweet as any sugar cookie.

"DYR PYPIL," she wrote. "I LAV AVRYWON."

"DYR IDAHO," another said. "I WD LIK TO GO THAR."

It didn't take long for her to return to her writergrrl roots, though. In a little heart-covered, pastel-papered notebook, she wrote more scathing critiques of her dad, and even more of her brother. So far, I've managed to escape her writerly wrath. "MOM," she wrote in her journal. "WY R YOU SO LAVEABL?" I know I won't be immune to her poison pen forever, but for now, I enjoy being the subject of her little tributes. Who needs good reviews when your own daughter writes "THAT DANS WS GROOVY" and "MI MOM IS A POET. YOU CN TEL BCS OF HR BUKS"?

Hannah often sits on the couch, one leg crossed over the other like a stenographer from a 1940s movie, pencil and note-book in hand. She loves to write lists—"LOBSDR, FISH, SHRIMP, SHRK"; "CHIKIN, TRKY, DAK, ROOSDR"—little inventories of the world she knows. She has her own "dictionary of bad words," which right now reads "ASS ASS ASS HL." She seems to know that writing is a safe place to explore the taboo, to delve into rage and joy and the enchantment of the ordinary.

"I have my own way of spelling," Hannah says excitedly, like she's created her own civilization. When she asks me how to spell something correctly, I tell her, but I love the playful, fluid way she chooses to spell words. I want to give her some more time to swim around in her own language before she has to worry about spelling tests and red pencils, marks and grammar and precision. That will come soon enough.

I think of Margaret Atwood's poem "Spelling," which opens: "My daughter plays on the floor with plastic letters, red, blue & hard yellow, learning how to spell, spelling, how to make spells."

Hannah is learning how to make spells. Her own spells. Her own magic.

Hannah and I never did have our sugar-cookie spelling lesson. Our family polished off the container of treats like speed readers, spilling spelling crumbs everywhere, before we had a chance to act out my plan. Hannah taught herself more than those cookies ever could, though.

The very last page of Hannah's heart notebook reads, in large letters, "I AM JIST FYN." Isn't that, ultimately, what we all try to say when we write? Aren't we all trying to convince our readers and, even more so, ourselves, that we are just fine? That our words are valid? That we deserve to be heard?

Atwood writes later in the same poem, "A word after a word/ after a word is power." It is very cool for me, as a writer and a woman, to watch my daughter discover that power inside her. She helps me remember my own power as well: words sweet and biting, pungent and nourishing, in all of our fingers, on both of our tongues.

THE NEW DAD

Jonathan Kronstadt

WHEN I LOOK into my father's eyes, I see a man I don't know very well. I don't know him because he wasn't around much when we lived in the same house, and neither of us has made much of an effort since. Now we're both fathers, but our experiences as fathers are as different as Prozac and Pez. In just one generation the role has changed into something he couldn't possibly recognize.

My father is an immigrant who didn't finish high school until he was in his sixties. As a young man he built a business and married a woman with a prominent Jewish last name and a master's degree in education. Then he did the only thing that made sense at the time—worked his ass off and left the child rearing to his wife. He did what was expected of him, not knowing that by working to make our lives better, he'd lost his chance to be a part of them.

My life is different. My father worked hard so I didn't have to, and believe me, I didn't. This pampered childhood led to a lazy adulthood and an antipathy for authority figures that plagued me through my twenties and most of my thirties. Then I got lucky and found a woman who not only put up with my bullshit but found it amusing.

Then, on or about June 29, 1994, my wife went back to work and agreed to leave me alone with our three-month-old daughter— my own little independence day. I got to shitcan my lousy job and turn to a career with a future. I had finally found my calling— as a dad.

But what does that mean anymore, anyway? Who's my role model? Hugh Beaumont? Robert Young? Neil Young? Full-time fathers are everywhere and nowhere at the same time. We're there on the playground (at least I am), but the gaggle of women deconstructing mommy minutiae over by the swing set doesn't know what to do with me/us, so they do nothing.

How stupid is this? I'm there, obviously an enlightened penis bearer, a veritable fountain of male perspective, and I'm a one-man no-fly zone. I know what they're thinking: either I'm unemployed, which renders me pathetic, or I chose to stay home, which renders me threatening. And if they let me into the conversation coven, they won't feel free to bitch about cracked nipples and how their husbands won't go down on them anymore.

It's like some painful junior high school dance—except I'm on the boys' side of the gym all by myself. I've made lame attempts to infiltrate their ranks, but I don't need to relive that kind of awkwardness. (To be fair, in one-on-one situations most women get positively giddy when they hear that I stay home, and making women giddy is damn good fun.)

Men don't really know what to think of men who stay home, either. Lots of them, when they hear what I do, strike a wistful pose and offer an earnest, "Man, I wish I could do that," which rings as hollow as a chocolate Santa. The fact is that while women have been legitimately complaining for years that they can't have it all, men's claims are every bit as legitimate, if not as time-honored.

If we stay home, we're outcasts, flung from our "natural" role as provider and alpha dog. Less than 1 percent of fathers stay home with their kids, compared with 21 percent of mothers. If we consider, for a moment even, my father's approach, we are cast, quite fairly, as Neanderthals. And if we try to split the difference, we never make full partner at work or at home. We find out what women have known for decades: you can't truly be a star at work if you're truly serious about being there for your kids as often as they need you. There will always be some hotshot who's willing to give up more to get where you could go if not for what you need to do at home.

And at home most fathers take their child-care cues from the mommies, as if possession of a uterus automatically makes you a better parent. Women are typically better parents, but more because of driver's-seat experience than biology. Men are often either reactive or overreactive parents, coming in as a backup to the primary caregiver or as a misdirected disciplinarian, kicking ass and taking names because, well, that's what we can do.

And if by some miracle we do manage to satisfy the scrotum-shriveling demands of husband, father, and breadwinner, there's nothing left that's only for us: no time for the ridiculous but cherished rituals of American manhood, things like playing poker with the boys, watching Australian Rules Football with the boys, and picking nits from one another's scalps.

I realize that it's unseemly for a man to bitch about something that women have been dealing with for decades. I understand that the two-thousand-year-old grip white males have had on world dominance is slipping, and I'm okay with that. It's like Willem Dafoe said in *Platoon*: "We've been kicking other people's asses for so long I figured it's time we got ours kicked." He was talking about the U.S. military, but the analogy holds.

The problem for American fathers is that there's no blueprint for what comes next, at least none that is reality based. Looking to television for a reality reflection is absurd in the extreme, but its prism is especially whacked when it comes to poppas. TV loves single fathers, so much so that fifty-one shows in the 1990s had primary characters who were single male heads of households, a group that in the real world shows up in a full 4 percent of families.

Blend this with the fact that fathers show up as central characters in only about 15 percent of network prime-time shows anyway, add in shlubs like Homer Simpson and Ray Romano, and it's no wonder we watch sports all the time. That's where all the good father role models are, right?

Men's groups are obviously on the rise, and though some got started and are fueled by bitterness over America's divorce laws, many seem to be good ideas. Anything that gets my brethren to open up about anything is a good thing, however messy it will inevitably be. And it will be messy, because you don't wake up from thousands of years of emotional hibernation looking good.

But maybe that's the best reason of all to cannonball into the whirlpool of active, involved fathering. Kids have big, brightly colored emotional buttons that scream: "Deal with me!" And you can't deal with their emotions effectively without casting a passing glance at your own, which is a much closer examination than most men have given their emotions since the junior prom.

A generation of emotionally reawakened fathers would be the best thing to happen to American children since *Sesame Street*. But as with anything else, we're in a partnership. Changing roles have confused everybody, and if fathers are going to take the bold step of defining and then mastering their new role, then mothers need to be part of the solution.

Mothers need to be less judgmental—an ounce of shutting up at the right time can build pounds of fatherly confidence—and realize that different parenting isn't necessarily inferior parenting. When women complain that there are no good men out there, I always respond, "Well, who the hell raised them to be such assholes?" and then I duck. Egos need to be checked at the door, and fathers need the freedom to commit dozens of well-intentioned screwups.

And men need to quit being so passive when it comes to their own children. It's an annoying cliché, but it's true: nothing you do in life will be as terrifying, as rewarding, or as important as being a father. Learn what you need to learn from your partner or your kids—hell, read parenting books. (Or do as I do and have your wife summarize them for you.) Just don't whine about it.

It's about choices. My father didn't have many—most of us do. If you've made the choice to create lives, take the next logical step—be in them. Yes, it's hard, and at times you'll be worse at it than at anything you've ever tried. But it's the best thing I've ever done, and what's second isn't even on the screen.

Being a father in the new millenium is an opportunity to be wrong almost incessantly, to have your guts yanked out and stepped on by people wearing Teletubbies sandals, to feel inadequate in nearly every arena of your life and so much more. But it's an opportunity you can't pass up, because the regrets aren't ones you can handle. Just ask my dad.

EVERYTHING FALLS

Jill Ketterer

MY FATHER'S sitting on the cold radiator across from the sink I'm standing near. There's a table between us, a home to four empty chairs. I'm examining the sloped floor. I'm perched at the higher end, and it's as if my father's gaze is desperately trying to climb up to me, only to slide back down in the landslide that is our kitchen floor. This home is crooked. It was like this when we moved here. It needs books or something to prop up my father's end, to level everything out.

The sun is shining behind him, giving him a glorious burning head like Lucifer before he fell. My father's face is a shadow, a black hole inside that mane of fire. His pants are greasy and way too big for him, and the red, stained Hanes shirt he's wearing has a hole near its flimsy little pocket. He's a peasant. He's a martyr, sitting as if on trial before Judas, his daughter.

I'm holding a basketball, twirling it in my hands, thinking it's the most interesting thing in the world. This rubber ball does just what I want it to—I throw it down, it bounces back. It has bounced off cars, hoops, me, my boyfriend, the gravel, the walls of my house, and even once, by accident, the neighbor's dog. And it's still here.

My father's smoking Marlboro Lights from the hard pack, which he sticks in the pocket of his sweaty T-shirt. He does this not so much to resemble the Marlboro Man or Jack Kerouac, but because it's accessible and convenient. His cancer stick is his sword of fire. As long as that one addiction is indulged, he can fend himself against all other transgressions. They float up with the spindly, translucent smoke.

His coughs come out like words. They say he's uncomfortable. He's getting tired of waiting for me to speak. He's restless. He's getting sick of watching me play with my basketball, he's kind of phlegmatic, and that's because he'd like to go for some goddamn coffee instead of sitting here in my mother's kitchen saying nothing.

This kitchen hasn't been remodeled yet. The walls are a sickly yellow covered with grime like shaded pencil, the floor a cracked linoleum substitute. Off-white. Peeling. When we moved here six years ago, there were plans to tear this crooked place down and build a better home in the backyard. It never happened. This is the same crummy, dilapidated place it used to be.

It's September of 1996. I'm fourteen, and every bit as awkward as one imagines high school sophomores are—not a freshman anymore, not a senior yet, still at the bottom of the food chain but not low enough to see the beauty in all of it. I'm still a basketball player. The mayor still lives two doors down in our black-and-white little coal town. Bill Clinton is still president, but hasn't been impeached yet. He hasn't been caught yet. My father, however, has been caught. My sister and I realized what was going on while we were playing darts in her garage two days before.

"Well, what do you think he could've meant by 'Your suspicions are probably correct'?" She tossed a dart. *Bonk. Pluck.* Not quite.

"I don't know," I said. "I have no suspicions. I just know he's leaving Mom." *Sloosh. Bonk.*

"Well, I don't know either." *Pluck. Sloosh. Bonk.* We were silent for a while, trying to put the facts together. My parents had never been happy. My father had always slept on the couch. What was different now, after fifteen years, to make him leave?

The answer hung over us like fog. It wrapped around us so closely, we couldn't see it. *Pluck. Sloosh.* And then, suddenly, someone turned the fog lights on. *Bonk. Sloooosh . . .*

"You don't think . . ."

"He's cheating on Mom . . ."

"With who . . . no way . . ."

"Janine . . ."

"Aww, Christ . . ."

Bull's-eye.

He was fucking a young married woman from our church. A

woman I played Nintendo with on Sunday afternoons. A woman whose children I baby-sat.

And now he is in my mother's kitchen. On the radiator. I'm twirling my orange globe. He scratches his balls from time to time. I've lost the ability to be courteous, and I tell him to stop, it's disgusting. Well, he says, he's got jock itch. He coughs. I say that it's even more disgusting, then. Well, he replies while puffing himself up, I shouldn't be disgusted by my father. Daughters should respect their fathers. I ask him if daughters deserve respect too, and he says yes, and he respects me as a father should, with discipline.

Then why've you been sleeping with my friend? What are you trying to teach me now? He never answers. He just sits there, bruised and battered like a martyr pelted with stones. And I'm his Judas. I utter the condemning words. I throw the final stone.

A jingling sound announces that my dog is entering the room. I'm petting her, loving her for her loyalty, for her precious eyes and the way she understands right and wrong. For the way she knows to lower her head and slink away if she messes up the carpet. I'm remembering that she is Holly the Christmas Dog, the runt of the litter who nudged my hand six years ago, with her red collar and meek little grin. My father is calling her, but she's staying with me. And he calls and he calls, and he snaps his fingers. And she won't come.

He's leaving. He's got to take a load of his stuff to his new home. Light is following him out the door, illuminating his golden head. The radiator is still cold. The sun, still a glowing peach in the sky. I feel so righteous I could pluck it from its place in the heavens and take a bite. I'm seeing freedom in his every step. I'm watching the fall of Lucifer from my spot near the sink. I'm bouncing my basketball one time for each lock of his burning hair that's going sizzle, sizzle, and turning to dust.

Chris Colin

BACK EAST, high school students have sex on the backseat leather of my parents' new Honda. The driver, my younger brother, delivers the news with manufactured disgust, guarded pride.

"They held up the condom," he whispers in our weekly phone call. I hear the preparation of dinner in the background.

Kevin is a senior in high school. Kevin is not his real name—the pseudonym is but one of many extravagant protections I confer upon my brother. In fact, I have saved him all my life. As a child, I held watch for bullies, placed my body between his head and kitchen counters. Summers at the neighborhood pool, I kept one eye on him, long after he was the better swimmer. Even in our backyard tussles, I'd make a preliminary sweep for rocks or sticks before bending his arms behind his back and buckling his knees to the dirt.

Now he chauffeurs the sexually active. Now I need to perform a new kind of rescue. The sex happened on homecoming night, I'm told, a car full of drunk seniors skidding from dance to party. Kevin did not drink, though maybe he was tempted—these friends of his are new, and new friends are often the ones who get people to drink or smoke or jump off the wrong things.

On the big night, as neckties were pulled from teenage collars, I sipped a sipping drink on the other coast. While the young exhibitionists fiddled with buttons, I chatted with a friend about the fact that it was raining. It was fine, but we did not disrobe. By the time the East Coast condom had been flung against the curb in front of the party, my friend and I had waved and said we should do this more often.

I live helplessly in the West. I take the news of Kevin's exploits like a tied man, held hostage by the intervening miles. I'm the one who's supposed to be intervening. I should be over his shoulder, at his doorway, in front of his eyes. I should be keeping back the backseat drunken overstated solecism that has no business, yet, among his unruined affairs.

In the past, these responsibilities left me triumphantly spent. Picture Atlas, hoisting a seeing-eye dog that is leading a guardian angel who is whispering into the ear of a bodyguard. I am these and more, and yet, these days, the net result of my brilliant guidance is attended by a sense of falling short: the paraded condom, and Kevin's subsequent muffled awe, worry me.

In my weaker moments, I'm a dick. The words for what I am take the wind out of me: meddling, protective, scared. "How often do you get high?" I heard myself ask recently. I tried to make it sound like idle chatter, like I wanted to know his taste in tennis shoes. He won't ever be fooled by these ploys, but with any luck they'll work on me. I will believe that I am not an uptight, overprotective, busybody asshole. Goodness. I need to mellow out. I should probably smoke more pot.

The appropriate metaphor here is that of a coin: On one side is the debauchery encroaching on Kevin's universe. On the other is just me, aging me, increasingly boring me, civilized me. Is the world getting hotter and heavier, or am I becoming a sissy? "Wherein lies the true problem?" the coin asks in that stuffy way coins talk. The problem with the coin metaphor is that it's just a metaphor, and metaphors don't stop people from stripping in my family's car.

I remember this: The night of Kevin's homecoming, a freight train woke me just before dawn. I opened an eye and was too sleepy to know anything. I didn't know what was under my head. It was a pillow. I asked myself, what is this? It was soft and under my head. My second eye opened, and I floated nicely in space for another minute before things made sense again. The next day, I told friends the pillow news. It seemed like a very good story. It had: (1) a pillow, (2) disorientation, (3) nighttime, (4) reconciliation. My friends let me finish the story, did not complain afterward. Their lives are as dull as mine.

One is inclined to take stock at junctures like this. I am in my mid-twenties. I work in an office, and there is a Rolodex on my desk. Also I tuck certain shirts in, avoid hard drugs, shoo the cats out of the rhododendron, eat cottage cheese, consider gas mileage, have one of those stupid patches of hair under my lower lip even though those patches are stupid. I don't own a toaster oven, but that could change.

I still go to parties, like Kevin, but mine seem to end earlier.

Maybe I break a glass, maybe not. Halfway through I put in some extra-large fake teeth and want the music/talking to be louder. When it's over, I say good-bye. Back at home I lie around with my roommates or look for thread to fix the hole in my pants.

No room for decadence in this new life of mine. I'm not a prude—I offer "damn," "shit," and "fuck"—but I can't deny the recent emergence of rules in my head: I do not think people should have sex in the back seat of my family's car, or really, in any kind of vehicle my brother is operating. They should get in a bed. Also, no holding up of condoms.

My life happens three time zones from my brother's. We talk when we can, do so in update format. I deliver news about my job (I think I have carpal tunnel syndrome), my band (we are bad), my friends (Jose thinks he has carpal tunnel). Kevin listens actively, sagely, and because he's the best, responds with an imitation of a donkey. It's like this: *Eeeeaaaaawwww.* I can't do it. It comes from the diaphragm. Deep inside.

Kevin's news is of the fast life. Sometimes I can get him to tell me about his job at the zoo, and this is what I like best. The invertebrate house is his beat, and when he is catching me up on Sylvester, the giant octopus, who plays with toys, who pulls toys to his giant rolling head for inspection, whose tank is surrounded by AstroTurf on which he can enjoy no traction and thus no escape—when Kevin is telling me this, I do not worry about his future, what he will smoke, what he will jump off. I relax among images of octopus feedings, a realized life, safety, my brother holding shrimp on a stick and not scaring me to death, really, to death.

I don't have sex in the back seat of anything. I'm twenty-four. Seasoned. Graceful. An owner, now, of folded road maps and hand soap. (The hand soap, technically, belongs to my roommate, but I do use it, because I am seasoned, graceful.) I used to dive headfirst into the waves from the rocks, but now I ease in slowly, but I could dive into the waves headfirst from the rocks again. I might do it tomorrow. I will work on my brakes, buy more cottage cheese, drop off the film, call the guy about the gas line, pick up the drywall, get that recipe for the goulash, and dive headfirst into the waves from the rocks.

BORN TO POP PILLS

Elissa Schappell

HERE IS WHAT I hate: pain. Here is what I love: extra-strength anything. Believe me, if it were socially acceptable, I'd name a baby Codeine.

It all started with baby aspirin—St. Joseph's. I was twelve. The sweet orange tang, the transformation on the tongue from pill to sand to a velvety pinkish stripe—I was hooked. It wasn't just the taste I craved, it was the imagined fortification those little peach-colored pills imparted. I was a ridiculously morbid child, acutely aware of my own mortality. On my tenth birthday I had locked myself in the bathroom and sobbed, refusing to come out. The pink cake, balloons, Barbies—it all seemed pointless. I would be two digits now, forever. I was no longer a child. I was dying.

By the time I was fourteen, I was sucking mentholated euca-lyptus cough drops and starting to smoke Salem Lights (I thought they kept me skinny), imagining that in some crazy way the cough drops were rebuilding my lungs. That's right, healing me. I was, by then, a fool for pharmaceuticals—anything that would make life sweeter, hazier, less scary, more exciting. In no time at all, I got into heavier stuff, sneaking around, copping extra-strength Tylenol and Vicks cough drops at Happy Harry's pharmacy.

The rest of my family had—still does have—a very Yankee approach to pain. Medication is strictly limited to uncoated aspirin, Pepto-Bismol, gin and bitter lemon, and a lot of fresh air. If your shrieks of pain are drowned out by the wind, they don't exist.

I, however, did not inherit the gene for stoicism. I've never been terribly brave. Even thinking about death as a melodramatic teen girl—Will I be able to see my friends, or will I be forced to sit in alphabetical order for eternity? What if there is no God!—put me over the edge. All the existential dread an adolescent lint trap of a brain can spin out got me chomping Flintstones chewables and taking tugs on the Robitussin.

My crush on pills turned into a full-blown love affair the year I turned fifteen and my father was diagnosed with lymphoma. A tumor as big as a cocktail onion nestled under his jawline. Almost overnight, I became even more obsessed with taking medicine. I needed it. I made myself chew adult aspirin, and as I gnashed my teeth, choking down the sour, chalky tablets, I felt impervious to harm. I envisioned surviving a crash landing in the desert and being the sole survivor able to ingest painkillers without water. I imagined building up a martyr's level of painkiller in my blood that would protect me from feeling anything.

Because my father was a Ph.D. chemist, I believed myself invested, by proxy, with some kind of unique knowledge of drugs. All those little experiments he'd brought home from the lab for me and my sister to play with—a stupendous concoction that made bright pink foam bubble out of a test tube, and two liquids that, when united, created a terrific bang—had made me a scientist. Forget that I couldn't do math. I was arrogant. I knew best.

"Suggested dosages" were for suckers. After all, pale flower that I was, I felt pain more intensely than others. So I took slightly more than was prescribed—always. I also had to figure, pill popper that I was, that there was a level of tolerance that had to be accounted for.

My father's doctors took a high-tech melon-baller to the lump and sent him home with bright orange silos full of pills—a low dose of chemotherapy. He didn't even have to take them for a month, that's how well they worked. It was astonishing; he never even looked sick. For one weekend he let the lawn go and he took a nap, something he never did. But not one dark hair fell from his head. He was cured, I believed, by both his Superman-like will to live and those pills.

My father was in remission when I went off to college. I felt weak and guilty as I popped my pills at keg parties or in the library stacks. In addition to my off-the-shelf pain relievers, I had phenobarbital for anxiety and panic attacks and Zantac for an ulcer brought on, no doubt, by my double major of English and Middle American partying.

I was a Girl Scout in pursuit of my pharmaceuticals badge. I was a walking medicine cabinet; I nearly rattled when I walked. I trusted pills. I could have kissed the chemist who created gel caps. Two blue-green gel caps—meditate on that. I mean, was there any image more soothing? Not for me.

I liked feeling as if I had my own little army of soldiers ready for deployment at the drop of a boyfriend, ready to storm the beaches of reality. I liked being able to delude myself that I could take care of myself, that I was really taking control of my life. I may have been heading for the express ramp, but I was in control.

Until the cancer came back, six years later, my father took aspirin for pain, plus a little Bengay for post-squash-game aches. The second time around, the cancer was an almond-size tumor in his lung. (Why is it that cancers always come in the shape of fruits and vegetables? Is it less frightening to hear you have a green-bean-size tumor vs. a tumor as big as a AA battery?)

After the surgery to remove half his lung, my father started on morphine; but for fear of getting addicted, he took only half his prescription. Also at this time, my father did break down and add a new drug to his wee host of pharmaceuticals—a seasickness pill for the scuba diving he took up after his lung surgery.

In his case, cancer was like a mangy dog you keep thinking you've left on the highway but keeps showing up at your back door. It took six years, but the cancer showed up again, filling my father's lungs, metastasizing to his spine.

It was only then, in considerable pain and under the doctor's orders, that my father began popping steroids and painkillers. As my father got sicker, I began to develop psychosomatic symptoms. His back and neck hurt; the length of my spine felt as if it was being forced through a meat grinder. He couldn't draw deep breaths, and his throat was sore; ditto for me. He had numbness in his extremities, and he had nausea; me too, me too.

I suppose I wanted to be close to him. At the slightest threat of pain—headache, stomachache, a swollen gland—I was certain I, too, was dying. After all, I was his daughter. I was sure I loved my father more than any other girl, and so how could I live without him? I took a pill.

I popped pills in defense, I popped pills in solidarity. It was a bonding thing, although I never confessed my ailments to my father. I liked to think that, sometimes, as I took a pill like Wellbutrin—a bit of smiling sky—perhaps my father and I were dosing at the same time. One part of me knew that I was going to lose him, but there was still a part of me that held out some hope of a miracle. I was desperate for even the most tenuous connection.

Returning home from the hospital after my father died, the first thing we did was go through the house with a giant green trash bag, rounding up all his pills, from morphine to Benadryl, and throwing them out. We blamed them, in some small part, for failing him, for failing us. I was punishing science, turning my back on pills. I didn't believe in them anymore.

It didn't last. The fallout from his death was overwhelming, and I found myself back on an antidepressant; but all my other drugs, all my little friends, I shunted to the back of the medicine closet. I wanted to feel pain. How much more could I possibly hurt? To not feel pain felt like a betrayal.

After a couple of years, I started to realize I didn't need to carry an arsenal of painkillers and mood modifiers. After all, the worst I could have imagined had happened, and it didn't kill me. I could, if I chose, handle anything. Pills didn't hold the same sway over me.

Not that I am reformed. I haven't kicked pills altogether, oh no. To this day I usually have on hand at least two types of tranquilizers—Ativan, a white tepee-shaped, slow-pitch anxiety reliever, and Xanax, a white, blue, and peach take-'em-down-at-the-knees pill for attacks of panic. I also occasionally carry Klonopin, a cheery safety-orange disk with a cutout "K"; it's highly addictive but good to have on hand, just in case.

When I travel, this is what I pack: green-and-white Sudafed Sinus, for any close encounters of the pollen and mold kind, and a muscle relaxant (the name long erased from the bottle, as a result of my talismanic rubbing), just in case I should find myself moved to engage in some kind of activity I usually eschew, like swing dancing, capricious movement of heavy furniture, or the occasional "Hey, I'm not that old" back walkover, usually performed after a couple of mai tais. I've got a few penicillins in there (yes, I realize you must take the entire prescription), because at times one sallies forth without shoes, or a scarf at the throat, tempting all sorts of mayhem. There's the two blue Zoviraxes, in case I should forget my parasol—my quaint protection from the rude sun—and begin to sense a slight tingling in my lips, the doomed harbinger of dastardly cold sores.

Also tucked into the first-aid kit is a tin of chalky tummy

drugs such as Titralac, Gaviscon, and their poor relation, Tums; two pretty pink Benadryl capsules, should I be beset by hives or insomnia; Atenolol, a performance-anxiety drug, because you never know when you will be called upon to do an impromptu recitation or have to commandeer a classroom of roaming creative writing students. Finally, and most banally, I have red-and-white Excedrin Migraine tablets for headaches and the strangely orangey brown Advil for everything else. Advils are the M&Ms of the pain pill world, slightly sweet and easy to swallow—you can take fistfuls of these.

While I am a lot slower now to pop just any pill or tuck into codeine syrup, in my heart I still believe in the power of the well-chosen pill. If that means I am just one step away from getting a Burroughs-Wellcome tattoo on my fanny, well, so be it. Though I don't take half of what I used to—and though I am still devoted to over-the-counter pain pills—I do like to have some big-time pharmaceuticals on hand, just in case. It's like having a hit man in the family. Those pills are like an old friend you know you can rely on, someone who has seen you at, and through, your very worst.

Recently I was spring-cleaning my bathroom closet and happened upon a bevy of Ziploc bags in a box at the rear of a shelf. As I went through the bags I found a sample of nearly every prescription I've ever had. Romantic that I am, I'd kept them the way you'd keep a corsage from a fancy dance, to remind you of a love affair, a tempestuous and dangerous flirtation, a bad mistake. I shook the jars and listened to their songs.

IDENTITY CRISIS

Theresa Pinto Sherer

MEMORY IS so indelibly bound up in words, the symbols that stand for the objects that make up remembrance. Twenty-five years ago, I spoke a different language in a different country and lived a different life. Yet I have no memory of it. I was just three, and by the time I was four, I had been adopted by an Italian-American family living in south Florida, I spoke flawless English, and I had neatly forgotten my past. I began rebuilding my identity from scratch.

Twenty-two years later, my mother revealed to me that just before I was adopted, I had been found on the streets, wandering alone with a note pinned to my shirt that read, "Kim, Won-Hee. August 20, 1972." It was handwritten, not in the letters of the English alphabet, but in the calligraphy of Korea, the country where I was born.

Upon hearing this news, the writer in me immediately snatched it up as something to develop and spread around like so much confessional compost. But the little girl in me was scared and a bit sad. Up until the age of three, I lived with someone—a guardian? a parent?—who cared for me. Then, for some reason, I was abandoned.

I could refashion the story to my liking, giving it elements of adventurousness and tragedy, claiming ownership of an exotic past that would never settle into a neat little pile of events and facts. But in reality, my past became an even bigger black box than it had been, for I had always been told that my parents were dead, and now that story was a symbol of mendacity.

One of my adoptive mother's habits is to spring news like this on me, but in a guileless manner, as if she assumed I already knew what she was about to tell me, her mind forgetting that she once colluded to keep certain things a secret. On this occasion, she responded with astonishment when I appeared shocked at her admission. Perhaps as a gesture of consolation, she proceeded to give me a box of official papers, aging documents with seals, stamps, and signatures on them. They are all I have to tie me to my Korean past.

All my life I have fought against what I perceive to be normal and conventional, because I have feared that if I did not struggle, my true self, which would undoubtedly be average and nothing special, would begin to show. I was afraid that I would be what novelist Frederick Exley was afraid of being, and what drove him to alcoholic insanity—a fan, someone to sit on the sidelines and cheer for those who take the center stage in life. After my mother told me about my inauspicious beginnings, I clung to the scant details and added them to my ever-changing identity; it was a way of knowing that I, too, had an extraordinary story to tell.

Then I learned, after some journalistic digging, that my situation was not peculiar for the time or place; most children who were orphaned in Korea were orphaned in much the same way I was, since it was essentially illegal to give away children who had existing relatives. The thousands of children who were eventually adopted usually had been left covertly on street corners and in alleyways.

Korean intercountry adoption by Americans and Europeans came into existence because of the Korean War, which also is nothing unusual. In numerous and obvious ways, war makes orphans of many. But Korean adoption was the second and largest wave of intercountry adoption since German and Greek children came after World War II. It was also the most noticeable wave (which I experienced through the racist taunting of my primary school years); the European kids, for apparent reasons, were less conspicuous.

It was almost fashionable to adopt Koreans after the war, much the way adopting young girls from China or children from Eastern Europe is in vogue today, and more than 100,000 kids— the majority of them female—are estimated to have made the trek from Korea to the United States or Europe since 1954.

If you visit one of the many websites devoted to tracking down and reuniting Korean families with the children they once gave up, you see the emotional damage laid bare. Women who do not remember the exact year they gave birth plead for help in locating their child, who may be twenty-six or twenty-seven and may or may not be living in the Netherlands. Young adults seek out details of their heritage in desperate hope of enlightening themselves about themselves.

Strangely, I have never felt the urge to find my own biological family. I admit that I am a little afraid of such a search, but mostly I am just apathetic. While growing up, I often mentally perceived myself as "white." What surprised me is that in this, I was not alone: a recent survey of Korean-Americans adopted between 1955 and 1986 shows that more than half saw themselves in the same skewed way, describing themselves as Caucasian. Many times I too forgot that my origins lay halfway around the world. But I am not ashamed of my heritage. Over time I have become very proud of my slanted eyes and flattened face, but these traits are not central to my existence or my common bond with society as a human.

When it was my turn to be given up, I was one of the "lucky ones." My note very specifically spelled out my name and my birth date; I spoke full and flawless Korean so that I could communicate my needs; I had been found not long after I was abandoned. My younger, adopted sister, who came into the family two years after me, was one of the unlucky ones. Her note was lost, and no one knows exactly how long she was left to survive on her own, but it was long enough to bow her legs and weaken her bones from malnutrition, to put disease into her gums, and to essentially break a young child's spirit.

The lone picture of me taken right before I left Korea for the first and last time, snapped outside of what I assume are the walls of the orphanage, shows me to be a petite girl with remnants of baby fat still clinging to my cheeks, ostensibly healthy and striking an almost military pose, arms stiffly at my sides. My hair has that slicked-down, Louise Brooks *Diary of a Lost Girl* look that is probably common to all such places, and my face has a shine to it. It's as if the photographer asked me to smile for my new parents, and maybe relayed to me that I was going away to America. But, sad and perplexed, I could only give him a mild look of defiant confusion. My picture, so different from my sister's, at least shows that I was not defeated; hers limns out a bleak existence, with her standing forlornly against a white wall. She just looks lost.

In 1976, I came to New York, literally with the clothes on my back and a single, official "travel certificate," which permitted me "to pass freely without let or hindrance . . . for the purpose of adoption." I was approximately three feet tall and weighed twenty-eight pounds, only three pounds more than my ten-month-old son weighs now. I am told that I adjusted very quickly, that Korean Social Services, the government agent responsible for my adoption, must have taken good care of me, though I arrived carrying scabies and with a bandage on my forehead. Two years later, almost to the day, my younger sister arrived, and I was there to greet her. I felt part of a family once again, and I strove to ensure that she would shortly feel the same.

What I ask now is, why at the age of three? If I had been left as a newborn, my Korean family would have been abandoning an infant, an almost blank slate, unable to express who she was at this nascent stage. And I can understand the circumstances that may lead a person to do that, such as the financial inability to feed and clothe and take care of a new baby.

But by leaving me at three, they were abandoning all I had become in those years; they were forsaking me as a young person, a girl named Won-Hee Kim. They were not saying, "We cannot take care of you," but, "We no longer want to take care of you." And I wonder what I was like, what it was about me that caused this action, since in our solipsistic society, I know in the end it must have been my fault. Like a child of divorce, I fear the blame rests on my shoulders, even if, rationally, I know it's likely they just wanted a better life for me, and saw America as a shining beacon.

On this side of the world, I had a ready-made family waiting: a twelve-year-old sister, two parents, two sets of grandparents, one aunt and her son. When you meet me, you meet all of them, embedded within my personality. Most noticeably, I talk with my hands and stuff food down people's throats. Yet I believe in the theory of evolution, having studied it for nearly seven years, so I know that the nuances of my personality were predisposed before I was walking and talking, before any environmental influences had time to take hold. But we all know that a person develops as a confluence of nature and nurture, so I wonder: What behaviors do I have that are a remnant of my first three years of life? What still connects me to that far and distant country?

One thing I know is that I don't have a solid foundation in

myself. I never quite know where I belong, and this I definitely attribute to my chaotic beginnings. Like many people, I have always felt isolated and apart, trying a bit too hard to find my rightful place in the group. But my new knowledge of my initial start in life has helped me to reconcile this aspect of myself, putting a cause before the effect, showing me that my rootlessness does not come out of nowhere.

I occasionally wonder why my mother adopted two Korean girls to begin with. When I ask her, she will respond, "Because I love children and would've adopted dozens more if I could have." Yet I look around and see her slightly improper infatuation with all things Asian and the picture on the wall of a birth daughter that she lost at the age of three. If I ask her about the Asian fetish, she swears up and down that she is not obsessing, but that she was one of us in a past life. She just knows it. By this I am to understand that she has an unspoken kinship with Asians, even though she won't eat bean curd or shrimp heads.

When we talk about the death of her second biological daughter, Diane, she claims the loss had nothing to do with our adoption and the coincidental age of three. She would have adopted anyway, she says, because she wanted a houseful of children and planned on sending for two boys after Diane was born—before she found out that Diane suffered from the rare genetic disorder that would kill her. Though I can't help wondering what subconscious motives lay about, when I see her loving and familiar face, the one that has been with me for twenty-five years, the one that has never abandoned me, I neatly forget all that.

Unquestionably, I am happy to be here, and I am happy to have become the person that I am. The recent turn of events, the attacks on the World Trade Center and the newfound insecurity that has befallen us as a nation, have only cemented my identity as an American and in an ironic emotional twist, left me more secure than ever as to who I am and where I belong. Since I am an Italian-American Korean from New York, I have an immigrant's appreciation of America, but also now an American's appreciation of America.

I have never doubted who my "real" mother is. (Ironically, four years after I came to America, my adoptive father left, so he is somewhat of a nonentity in my life.) But now I have a son of my own, and my mind more and more wanders over territory littered with terms that purvey a sense of a knowing past, like *family medical history* and *genealogical tree*. My curiosity about my roots has increased a thousandfold, so that I am compelled to seek out more knowledge of my other short past, but from a safe and objective distance. I am not yet to the point of looking for my birth parents, and I may never be.

I consider myself a survivor of all that has been heaped upon me through no volition of my own, no different from the rest of society, moving from one event to the next, whether good or bad. I mean, I don't carry around many emotional bruises from these humble beginnings. I adapt quickly. My sister slept with a bag of bread, among other things, for years, while my only visible scar, if it can even be attributed to the healing of a wound, was my use of a night light throughout my teenage years. Really just a carry-on, not true baggage.

But I still like to sleep with the lights on, perhaps to make sure that I won't be left alone in the dark once again.

A HERO'S RETREAT

Margaret Finnegan

THEY SAY that parenthood is about choosing your battles. So is childhood. The only difference is that parents can choose from a more extensive set of weapons than children. Parents have words. They have money. They have brute strength. They have power. Children are like occupied territories. Their claims to autonomy often exist at the whim of what can seem like imperial potentates who set their bedtimes, choose their clothes, control their whereabouts, and set their limits. And, like residents of occupied territories, children learn that the more oppressive the state, the more will and ingenuity it takes to find liberation. Even then, you sometimes need a miracle.

For my father, parenting wasn't about choosing battles. It was the battle. He was a soldier descended from a long line of soldiers and heroes. His ancestors fought in the Revolution. They fought in the Civil War. His father, a general, was the first American officer to arrive in Munich during the Allied invasion of Germany.

Like his three younger brothers, my father enlisted in the army; but he had the bad luck of serving during the late 1950s—peacetime. By the time I was born in 1965, he worked as an electrical engineer for Sylvania Electric. He made televisions. At least that's what I believed, and that's what I told the polite grown-ups who asked.

Funny industry, TV manufacturing. You have to jump through a lot of hoops to get ahead. We relocated all the time. By the age of seven I had lived in New York, North Dakota, Montana, Utah, and Montana again. The working conditions were outrageous. On the odd occasion my father needed a ride to work, the whole family would pile into Betsy, my mom's beloved red Volkswagen bug, and we'd cruise out of town, past the farms and ranches that skirted the city limits, past the nearby campsites. We'd drive until we reached an isolated stretch of highway surrounded by a flat expanse of long, wild grasses imprisoned behind an endless barbed-wire fence. At no place in particular my dad would say, "Stop here."

Mom would bring Betsy to a stop in the hard, dry dirt beside the road. My father would get out and wave, and we would wave back as the car swung a wide U-turn and headed home. I didn't know if my father walked from the road to a hidden, secret TV-making plant, or if a car with official, secret TV-making people would come by and take him there. All we ever saw was Dad standing by the edge of the road, waving.

Years later I learned that my father did not really make television sets. He worked for a defense contractor that made nuclear missiles. In particular, he worked on Minuteman missiles buried in deep underground silos scattered across the western half of the northern United States. In the paranoid frenzy of the cold war, my father's missiles were our nation's salvation.

And in my father's thinking, a doubled-over black leather belt was our family's salvation. Used repeatedly and forcefully on our bare, red bottoms as we lay on his lap or leaned against a piece of furniture, the belt was his main line of defense in the war against spoiled-rotten, back-talking, disrespectful, lying, ungrateful, careless, lazy-ass girls by the names of Laurie, Lynne, and Margaret.

In the litany of childhood sins, I would call the offenses of my sisters and me laughably innocent and small. I think the worst thing one of us did was change a D-plus into a B-plus on a report card. It didn't fool anybody. My father was like one of those police departments that haul in criminals for small crimes in the hopes of deterring big ones. He didn't let anything by him.

As a parent, I appreciate his intent. Who doesn't want to nip their children's antisocial tendencies in the bud? But what my father did was wrong, and not just because he hit us. He ignored the context of our actions. It didn't matter if I furiously threw a glass against the wall or if it slipped out of my hands and onto the floor while I was washing the dinner dishes. The sanction was the same.

What my father didn't realize is that a state controlled by fear and perceived injustice is destined to fall. My sisters and I tested the boundaries of authority in the subtle and not-so-subtle ways that marginalized people always do. As much as the sting of leather against flesh hurt, we never cried. Control over our tears was the one response to violence we could assert.

Beyond that, we approached our powerlessness in different ways. Laurie, the oldest, was boldest. As she stepped into adolescence, she began to rebel. My father called her a liar. Lynne took on the Neville Chamberlain role by always seeking appeasement. She's the only eleven-year-old I've ever known to voluntarily do the laundry and buff the linoleum—anything to keep the peace.

I hid. When I was very small, I hid under my blankets, convinced that what I could not see could not see me. I hid in the dog-food closet, under desks and beds, in the darkness of the basement. I learned to like the solitude, and sometimes I hid just for the peace and quiet of it. I also retreated into a world of imaginary friends and lands. I wrote plays and stories and pretended I was a rock star. I invented so many worlds safer than my own.

My sisters and I were, and are, very different. Because of the differences, and because powerless people fight in the only arenas they can, the three of us battled one another ferociously. We yelled. We pinched. We scratched. We hit. We kicked. I freely admit blame. As the baby of the family, I played the older girls off each other like nonaligned countries used to play off Communists and capitalists.

But when it came to my father, we adhered to a common spirit of resistance. We looked out for one another. We knew what information to hide and what information to share. The house-key incident comes to mind. When I was in third grade, Sylvania wanted to transfer my father to an army base in the San Francisco Bay Area. My California-born-and-bred mother couldn't wait. The base was mere minutes from her parents' home. No fan of big-city living, however, my father quit the defense racket and opened a laundromat in a small Montana town. My mother went to work at the new business, and my sisters and I became latchkey kids. We each received a shiny red key, but since my older sisters got home after I did, I became the key master.

Unfortunately, I kept losing my key. It fell out of my pocket. It fell out of my shoe. Mom put the key on a metal chain that I wore around my neck. I lost that too. Each time I lost the key, I got spanked. It wouldn't have been such a problem except that my dad, the now self-employed ruler of his domain, sometimes came home early to check up on us. I feared going home. I enrolled myself in catechism, even though my family never went to church. I hung out on the playground. I took new and longer scenic routes home.

But this is Montana we're talking about, and it could get really cold. Besides, an eight-year-old girl has got to pee sometime. So after a while I would head home. On good days my dad would be working. I'd sit on the back porch and wait for Laurie or Lynne. On bad days he'd be home. That's when the sisterhood kicked in. If I saw his car, I'd hide until my sisters returned from school and could slip me in the window or throw me a key. These weren't big heroic deeds, but they were risky, and they bespoke a valued, if often uneasy, loyalty.

The laundromat days were bad. First Dad traded Betsy for a gigantic blue van used to transport motel laundry. Then there was Laurie. Each year she sought more independence and became more rebellious. Too old to be spanked at fifteen, she found herself grounded for weeks, even seasons, at a time. She'd hide in her room and scowl, and then she'd sneak out and end up grounded longer. But the worst problem was my mom.

My mom was hip and wholesome, with a great, easy laugh. She dropped out of college to become a stewardess when being a stewardess was about as glamorous as being a movie star. She hobnobbed with airline executives and reporters. She met my dad at an embassy party in Washington—an embassy party! Yet she gave it all up to get married at the spinsterish age of twenty because she already thought herself over the hill.

She was a good mom. She made a cake or pie every Friday and a roast every Sunday. She encouraged us, laughed with us. She sang all the time. She made us believe in magic. In the days before salmonella-poisoning scares, she had us convinced that the stretchy bands that held together roasting chicken legs were good-luck charms. We fought over wearing them on our wrists.

But she was complicit in my father's war. She wanted to be Switzerland. She wanted to be neutral. But when you live on a battleground, you have to choose sides. Inaction implicitly rewards the powerful. I'll say this, she hid or ignored evidence of our misbehavior when she could. But not always. Sometimes, to assert her own authority, she ratted on us. She never stopped him from hitting us. I don't think she considered it a possibility. And it killed her, because she knew we deserved better. She deserved better.

So, at the sunny age of thirty-six, with three scared, bickering kids, a troubled marriage, and a job she never wanted or asked for in a town she hated eating at her soul, she started to drown.

She took the ubiquitous "nerve pills" that ladies in the '70s took. She drank a scotch on the rocks every night. And she still cried into the German sausage she stood frying for dinner.

I could put up with a lot of things. But I didn't even know how to begin putting up with that. When the Republic of Mom fell, the occupied territories surrendered. When he hit me, I cried.

Then the miracle happened. Mom chose to win. She won by doing what women in her situation often do. She ran. She went home for lunch one day, packed everything she could in the trunk of our unhip boat of a Buick, pulled us out of school, got on the interstate, and never looked back.

She drove to California and moved in with her begrudgingly supportive parents. She had no job, no friends, no prospects. She threw out the nerve pills and scotch. All she had was a trunk full of clothes, toys, silverware, and three members of the resistance who needed to be liberated. It was her moment of courage and her finest hour.

I'm a soldier's daughter, and I know this much is true. You don't have to be a warrior to be a hero. You don't even have to raise your fists. You just have to believe in something better. And you have to elude the enemy in the ways that you can.

WORLD WITHOUT END

FAITH IN THE BABY

Kristin Ohlson

I IMAGINE my son swaying at the counter, shifting from one foot to the other. He says "Huh?" when the cashier tells him how much the boom box costs with tax, and when she tells him again, he stares at her. Then he pulls a credit card from his wallet, rattles it on the counter, spins it between his thumb and forefinger, and puts it away again. He asks the cashier if this boom box is the most popular model. He asks her if she thinks he should use his credit card or his checkbook, and she frowns slightly, not just at the questions but at the timbre of his voice, which sounds as if it comes from some node of tissue not typically used for sound.

Maybe she figures it out. Maybe she realizes that this young man is special in a way not implied by the sign over the cash register proclaiming: "All our customers are special." Maybe she relaxes a bit; maybe she even enjoys suspending her routine to watch my son as he prints the store's name on the check in letters like sticks thrown on the sidewalk, as he pauses to ask her how to spell *forty*. Or not; she might exchange annoyed looks with the other not-as-special customers who are piling up behind him with their boxes of computer peripherals and televisions. She might even grin when one of them brays his impatience.

How much of this does my son notice on this day of firsts— his first time taking the five-mile bus ride to this store from his new apartment, his first time making such a large purchase on his own? I'm not there, but my guess is, not much. My guess is that he's thinking of the burly electronics inside the box, of the spot he's cleared for the boom box on his dresser between the Special Olympics medals and the bowling trophy. He's thinking of the well-ordered plentitude of his music; he's deciding which tape or CD he will play first, and he knows exactly where it rests, in which case, in which Plexiglas slot. He doesn't notice the stares and grumbles, and they won't change the way he makes his way through this checkout line the next time he visits this store. These are details nearly as arcane to him as the rules of punctuation or boccie ball.

This kind of oblivion has been both a curse and a blessing during his twenty-five years. On this day, it would be a blessing. Matthew leaves the store's mutterers behind. He grips his boom box under one arm, and he tromps to the bus stop as his other arm pistons into a January fog. After he finds his seat on the bus, after he settles his package on his knees, he raises his fists and shakes them around his face like maracas. This is how he expresses joy.

I WAS A little girl with apocalyptic visions. I was also very practical; every night, during my last moments of clarity before sleep, I worked out strategies to avert disaster. Worried that people were frittering away the world's supply of fresh water, I imagined household systems that caught lightly used water and piped it into gardens. Mindful of the burgeoning pile of human waste, I imagined adding a mystery ingredient to ordinary poop and turning it into something useful like bricks or asphalt. And then there was overpopulation: I imagined peeling away all the layers of humanity that made life harder or less pleasant. I made whole categories of human beings vanish: the bad people who were in prison, the crazy people who shouted from street corners, the retarded people who didn't really do any harm but weren't able to contribute much, either. Before I fell asleep, I always amended this last final solution: my older cousin Stephen could stay in my emptier, ideal world. He was retarded, but he was always very sweet to me.

My Matthew, my first child, was born nearly twenty years láter in a hulking old Cleveland hospital. The pregnancy was lovely until the final, ponderous weeks, and the delivery was unremarkable until Matt slid into the doctor's hands. Then, from way up at the head of the bed, I heard all the voices in the room assume a quiet, measured urgency, as if they were creating a blockade of words to keep something quick and terrible from being said. They didn't bring him to me, at first. Then someone came to tell me he had been born with the umbilical cord wrapped around his neck and that my amniotic fluid had been stained with his excrement. I'm sure I asked if he was all right, and I'm sure they told me something, but it wasn't until days later, after he spent his first days in an isolette and had been observed and tested, that they told me he was fine.

I don't know that I ever believed them. Although I never saw Matt lined up with all the other newborns in the hospital nursery, he seemed different from the other babies I knew. He was pale, his eyes were puffy and bruised looking, and his waking moments were filled with noise—not the howling his father and I had braced ourselves for, but chirps and grunts and twitters. He generated his own white noise. When I'd tell other people about this, they'd sometimes pat my arm indulgently and tell me each baby has its own enigmatic little personality. Give yourself time to get to know him, they said.

I tried to get to know him, but he seemed uninterested in either his father or me. When I'd pick him up, he'd startle, his arms jerking like small featherless wings, and he never seemed comforted by my touch. When I'd talk or sing to him, he often didn't even turn his head; if he did, he soon turned away without interest. Instead of looking at me, he'd stare at the lightbulb or the glare coming in a window or, as he asserted more control over his limbs, the restless movement of his own tiny fingers. We could get him to smile or laugh, but with great effort, usually after his father had thrown him in the air over and over again. It seemed to be the movement, not his parents' adoration, that pleased him.

It seemed that my fears about Matt would be confirmed if I spoke them out loud, so I didn't. Still, I felt like the unnamed differences that set him apart from all those other babies lurked around corners; I felt that if I left him unguarded, these differences would snatch him away for good. The playpen that well-meaning relatives gave us held unfolded laundry in the corner of the living room. Instead of using it, I would hold Matt often and carry on a hopeful monologue. I would set him down on the floor and crawl around him in circles, trying to make contact with his disinterested gaze. When Matt woke up at night crying, I would pick him up, but he'd cry even harder and push away. I'd put him back in the crib to comfort him, then sit on the floor weeping as he flailed himself back to sleep.

When he was eight months old, I took him to the pediatrician for a routine checkup. My mother-in-law from New York came too. We were in high spirits: we had big plans to go antiquing in Amish country after the doctor's appointment. But instead of the usual pleasant chitchat about appetite and bowel movements, the doctor studied Matt's face and called his name from different parts of the room. He snapped his fingers near Matt's ear, then watched him startle, look up, and turn away. He wiggled a toy over Matt's head and made a fake, falsetto laugh, then sighed as Matt frowned in the other direction. I was afraid that the doctor was searching for something I didn't really want him to find.

"He should be more interested in people," the doctor said, looking sad. "He should be looking around for Mama or laughing with me at the toy. Instead, he looks at the shiny handle on the cupboard."

My mother-in-law was able to ask all the important questions. I couldn't speak or even follow what she and the doctor were saying. I picked Matt up and rubbed my face against his hair, wishing he would nestle against me just this once.

We didn't go antiquing, of course. We went home and made phone calls to the neurologist the pediatrician had recommended. Then we made the harder calls, the ones to my parents in California and to our friends and to all the others who loved this baby and his parents from afar. My mother-in-law stayed for many days, and then my parents took a shift, and then my mother-in-law came back for a while longer. I stayed in bed with the curtains drawn as much as I could, thinking sometimes of the girl who had gone to sleep with Hitlerian schemes for a perfect world. By the time Matt was born, I didn't believe in God, luck, or fate. Still, I had some kind of certainty that those long-ago thoughts had ruined my baby boy.

MY MOTHER-IN-LAW tells me that I said something very wise during that first year. At some point in the ongoing conversation about syndromes and specialists and our wrenching shift in expectations, I lifted my head and looked at my son. I said, "We have to have faith in the baby."

I don't remember saying this, and I don't know that the next few years showed great faith. We worked with a neurologist, we found a wonderful pediatrician who specialized in children with problems, we went through a slew of speech therapists and music therapists and psychologists and the like. We took Matt to odd-ball practitioners, too—a hypnotherapist in Minneapolis, a listening therapist on Cleveland's East Side, a pediatrician on Cleveland's West Side who immersed a lock of Matt's hair in solution to look for chemical irregularities. Matt was tested and observed over and over; today's health-care system would never allow such vast duplication of effort.

In the end, there was no culprit to pursue—no smoking gun among his chromosomes, no malfunctioning organ, no negligence or error by the hospital during delivery. There was only a description. He was retarded—significantly so, in the early years—with what they called autistic-like behavior.

It seemed like a betrayal when we stopped looking for cures and began to accept our child as he was. Matt reached most of the developmental and social milestones, albeit later and with greater fanfare than most babies. He walked when he was one and a half. He said his first word after he turned two. At three, Matt succeeded in using his potty chair, with me, his father and my in-laws watching. We cheered so much that Matt's great-grandmother abandoned *Perry Mason* and came running; she thought we had won the lottery.

When Matt was about four, we were walking down the street,

and all of a sudden, he was not beside me. I turned around to see him saying something to an old man who was sitting on a blanket by the side of a building. "Friendly kid," the man said, waggling his fingers at me. "He came right over and started a conversation." This was a milestone as important as the others: without prompting, without anyone calling his name or waving a toy, Matt had approached another human being.

We had our second baby, Jamie Rose, when Matt was nearly three. That initial year was lovely but sad because it forced us to relive all we had missed with Matt. When Jamie grinned as I ran my finger over her lips that first week, when she began to watch intently as I walked from the sink to the table to the stove, when she cried as I left the room, I mourned again the gulf that had separated me from baby Matt.

When I took the two of them out, the comparison was even more painful. Jamie's lashes grew in long and black, her hair glowed in golden ringlets, her eyes shone an opal blue, and she soon learned to enjoy the attention of people in grocery stores. They'd let the ice cream melt in their carts as they cooed over her. The same people looked at her brother uneasily, not sure what to say to this child who flinched from their gaze and whirled in ceaseless activity at the end of my arm.

He grew, they grew, we all grew. Matt and Jamie were pals during their early years. She came along to all of Matt's therapeutic play groups and classes, tumbling in with the other "special" children as well as their siblings. In addition to these activities, I dragged the two of them through the full array of middle-class enrichment. I enrolled them in classes at the art museum, the natural history museum, and a dance studio; they took ice-skating lessons and joined Pee Wee soccer. I stayed through each of these activities, ready to herd Matt back into the group if he ran off, wincing every time one of the other children would stop to stare at him shaking his hands around his eyes. Still, I persevered: I had a foolish hope that one of these activities might tap a hidden source of brilliance in him, make neurons dance the way they had when Mozart first heard music or Einstein saw stars. People were fond of suggesting these duckling-into-swan analogies to me.

When he was seven years old, Matt was placed in a public school class for multihandicapped children, a cozy nest of eight such mysterious ducklings with a teacher and two aides. A bus pulled up in front of our house every morning, driven by a cheerful man who sang "Volare" along the route, and Matt rolled away from me without a backward glance. I visited his class often. The teacher was droll and matter-of-fact about her assortment of quirky characters; she was fond of dismissing their quirks as an overdose of their parent's tendencies. "Look at him," she'd say, as Matt raced from one activity to another. "He's just like his father!" Enough time had passed since the shock of Matt's diagnosis that I found this funny.

I met other parents who were also at this stop on the road from grief to acceptance—confronted by the things in our children that we couldn't understand or change, it helped to laugh. I remember going to a festival once with Vincent, a boy in Matt's class, and his mother, Carol. She and I walked together, the boys walked in front of us, and we could hear their animated nonconversation. Vincent was talking about baseball, Matt was talking about cartoon characters, and neither listened to the other. Carol said that she imagined that in some mirror-opposite universe, two boys were also leaving a festival with their mothers. "Those boys are saying, 'Mothers, might we stop for a snack?'" Carol pantomimed the boys' exaggerated courtesy. "And one mother answers by repeating the score of yesterday's game ten times, and the other answers with 'Go, go Gadget!'" It was an apt way of describing how estranged we sometimes felt from our children, how cosmically and comically mismatched.

Matt stayed in the multihandicapped class for three years. Toward the end of the third year, the psychologist we'd been taking him to ever since he was a toddler administered a routine IQ test. The next time we saw her, she rushed into her office with a bulging file of papers and a look of great excitement. "I have wonderful news," she announced. "Matt is not retarded!"

In a way, this was meaningless: Matt was the same person he had been the day before, but his unanticipated ability to match like objects in one part of the test had pushed him over the threshold to the bottom tier of normal. "That's great," I told her, but more to be polite than out of any real feeling. Even though there had been a time when I would have cherished this new, improved labeling, I knew by then that my son was a complicated being who defied categorization, that even though a new hole was being offered, he would still be the wrong shape for it. And I can't say that what followed was good for him, although it's still hard to tell. He was now ineligible for the multihandicapped class. The option suggested by our school system was to put him in a regular classroom in our neighborhood school with pull-out hours in the learning disabilities resource room. In other words, he was mainstreamed.

Mainstreaming isn't so bad if you're part of the mainstream. The next four years of public school were difficult, and I take little solace in the possibility that all those other kids got a lesson in compassion by being around Matt. It was a rude shock for him to be snatched from his multihandicapped haven, in which every little triumph was celebrated and every deviation calmly corrected. In contrast, his years in the academic mainstream were ones of nearly unremitting failure. Even though his IQ had climbed slightly higher, he still made odd noises and had a hard time staying in a chair, his reading was below grade level, and his math and penmanship were hopeless. He had two good teachers in the elementary school and one bad one, but none was equipped to do much for him. They didn't know anything about kids like him, and they hardly had enough time to devote to the rest of their students.

Most of Matt's elementary school classmates never quite figured out what to make of him, so they kept their distance. They knew he had some kind of disability, but it wasn't one they could easily understand—it wasn't like he was blind or lame or even severely retarded. He wasn't different enough to solicit their tenderness; he just made them nervous. Matt had a few friends who came over after school, but most of them were also marginalized, kids whose miserable family lives stunted their own ability to fit in. One of them could spend the weekend at our house without anyone in his family wondering where he was; to the outrage of all his relatives, he later turned in his father to the police for being a drug dealer. But even these guys, his fellow wretched, didn't want the stigma of being seen with him at school.

As time went on, Matt became less otherworldly but more aware of how different he was from the children in this world. He was the one who could never finish the test, the one who couldn't remember how to get from one part of the building to another, the one who completed the project last, no matter what his class was doing. I believe he was also the one child who didn't receive some kind of award or recognition at the school's graduation ceremony for fifth-graders; I noticed and hoped he didn't and fumed all the way through the ceremony.

He also had the most painful comparison right in his own home: his sister, whose abilities had outstripped his years before. When she grew old enough to get letter grades instead of S or U, he was dismayed by how easy it was for her to do well. One day he came home from school and looked through a pile of her papers on the dining-room table, each one perfect. "A's, all A's," he wailed, flinging her papers to the floor. "Why does she get all the sweet life?"

By the time he reached the middle school's learning disabilities program, I felt like I was sending him off every morning for a day in Beirut. It's not that the children were so much more vicious to him than they were to one another—or to my daughter, by the time she went there—but they had richer opportunities for torment, and Matt had fewer resources to fall back on. He had always been excitable, but now he had epic tantrums, both in the classroom and at home. All the therapists' advice didn't seem to help. Finally, Matt's father and I met with a psychiatrist to revisit the idea of medication—Matt had tried Ritalin before—and the psychiatrist talked to the three of us, then the two of us, then Matt alone. His recommendation was to get Matt out of that school. "He's depressed," the psychiatrist told us. "It's no wonder—his life is miserable."

We looked at other public school programs, then at private schools, but found no local options. Finally, we heard of a boarding school in upstate New York that sounded perfect except for the fact that it was a twelve-hour drive from home. Matt and his father and I visited for a day, and Matt decided he wanted to try it for a week. The house was peaceful when we returned home; we felt a little guilty for enjoying it so much. But when I went grocery shopping, it struck me how very different life would be with my son gone. I made a spectacle of myself, weeping in the aisle with the cans of anchovies, remembering how we couldn't leave an open tin in the refrigerator when he was little, or we'd find a trail of anchovy oil from the kitchen to the television. Life without him and his odd little ways seemed bleak.

His dad and I went to pick him up at the end of the week. We held each other's hands as he played basketball with a team, instead of just watching others play, and we saw people jump up and down when he almost made a point. We saw tables full of kids call his name in the cafeteria and ask him to sit with them. We saw him speak with confidence in a history class and even help another boy find the answer to the teacher's question in his book. Three girls trailed behind him as he showed us around campus, pretty girls who giggled and seemed to find him a fascinating stranger. He told us he wanted to stay at the school, and I cried when we left him there, not just because I would miss him but because we had finally found a place where he fit in. Matt spent the next four years at this school, finding blissful respite from the rigors of being different.

He was a much happier boy when we moved him back home at the age of eighteen. As a special-education student, he was eligible for four more years of public school education. We hoped things would be easier for him in the high school than in the middle school, and they were. The high school draws kids from all the city schools, plus it pools special-education students with other districts. There was a critical mass of kids like Matt at the high school. They weren't the mainstream, but they were a sizable and exuberant stream of their own.

Matt had four good years there, which is more than you can say for most people. He made lots of friends, had two girlfriends, and got work experience through the school's vocational department. He had three excellent teachers and did well in his classes. He was a minority in more than one way—our high school is about 70 percent African-American, and he is not—and he absorbed the school's mantra of racial harmony so well that he now buys just about anything marketers pitch to blacks. I'm sure he was the only twenty-two-year-old white guy to buy a copy of the movie *Waiting to Exhale* the day it was released, and this is just one of the things I love about him.

When he graduated, my entire family from California and his dad's entire family from New York came. At the ceremony, a school administrator warned the three thousand people in the audience against rowdy applause, but there were enough of the people who love Matt to do the wave and to make enough noise, and we did.

AFTER MATTHEW was diagnosed all those years ago, my aunt Helen sent me a letter right away. "When Stephen was born," she wrote, "he was our greatest sorrow. Now he's our greatest joy."

Lucky me, I have many joys. It would be hard to say which is the greatest, but I can say unequivocally that Matt is one of them—at least, most of the time. He has the kind of life that many of us wish for our children. He's in good health, eats a lot of vegetables, and changes his sheets once a week. He has an apartment, a compatible roommate, two sports channels, and season tickets to the Cleveland Indians. He has work that he enjoys, a job bagging groceries that showcases the almost courtly good manners he must have picked up from some of his well-bred boarding-school friends. "It's been a pleasure to help you today, ma'am," I hear him say to customers as I hunker near the forty-pound bags of dog food to watch him work. His customers like him: he receives an extraordinary amount of money in tips, something I've decided must be some kind of cosmic compensation for middle school. His bosses like him, too: he was named "Employee of the Month" once and then "Employee of the Year," for which he received a gas grill the size of a golf cart.

People point to Matt's successes and tell me they have something to do with my great mothering skills. I don't feel I can take that much credit for this complex young man; I can only marvel at the ways in which my "faith in the baby" utterance was prescient. The essence of Matt was there from the beginning, written into his genetic code and embellished by the unique events of his gestation. He has his father's concern for order and cleanliness as well as—surprise!—his ability to charm a room full of people. He has my lack of enthusiasm for talking on the phone, but also shares both grandmothers' and my feeling for words, especially big Latinate bombs. While his reading level is about that of the average American—good enough to read *USA Today*—his speech is loaded with words like *fastidious* and *apprehensive*.

Of all my father's eleven grandchildren, I think my son is the one who resembles him the most. Matt tells a joke just like my father does, he walks like my father, and even his few remaining noises remind me of my father. Matt often makes a low, nasal humming sound; people who don't know him hear it from another room and think a machine has gone bad. My father also hums a lot, a kind of mysterious drone while he's gardening or washing the dishes that my siblings and I think might be "Santa Lucia." When the two of them sing at family functions, the rest of us exchange glances.

At the very least, Matt has taught me as much as I taught him. I've always been shy, with hardly enough nerve to face the world with my own imperfections. It was harder still to face it alongside my son's more unorthodox flaws, which drew attention to the two of us even when he wasn't setting off fire alarms in airports (just once) or playing with five-year-old toys when he was fifteen (many times) or doing a little Rumpelstiltskin dance as he walked down the street (still does it once in a while). I'm used to faces whipping around for a second look, and there are many times I would shrink from rather than champion him. It was hard for me to be in public with my son. It is still hard at times, and that's a terrible thing for a mother to admit.

My daughter almost never has such qualms. Jamie was raised not only with her brother's differences but also with those of his peers and has always been comfortable with the range of alterations on "normal." One of Matt's friends is the king of trivia— ask him who sang "The Duke of Earl," who held the National League record for home runs in 1972, what the capital of

Mozambique is, anything, and he knows, but he can't button his shirt. Another can't add two and two but can drive a car. Jamie learned early on that abilities don't come in clumps, that just because someone can do one thing doesn't mean he can do another. She became sensitive to these hidden surprises and was unfazed by the scorn of people who weren't.

Early on, Matt's father and I decided that the world has two camps: those who sneer at our son's differences and those quirky souls who enjoy them. It's gratifying when we meet strangers in the latter camp. A few years ago, I took Matt to a ball game in which the Cleveland Indians clinched the championship for the American League Central Division. The Indians were playing the Baltimore Orioles, and Matt and I had great seats between home and first, just four rows from the field. The only drawback was that the row in front of us was filled with guys from Baltimore, who sat there watching glumly as the Indians hammered their team. I was afraid that Matt might piss one of these guys off. Matt is almost always on his feet. He loves to recite the provenance of each player—the various teams and positions he's played, the honors he's received over the course of his career. I often tell him to shut up and watch this game, the one we paid to see, but he's in thrall to the Game, all its players, all its moments.

At the Baltimore-Cleveland game, I was sure Matt was driving the guys in front of us crazy, especially the one guy he leaned over every time a batter took his stance. The guy would turn his

head toward us slightly, which is sometimes a polite indication—
like a skunk shaking its tail—that something bad is in the works.
I kept pulling Matt down; he kept standing up again. Finally,
after Matt spat out a long string of past engagements for Kevin
Bass—that he had started with Milwaukee in 1982, then moved
on to Houston, then to San Francisco, and then back to Houston
before he got traded to Baltimore—the guy turned all the way
around. He removed his cap and set it on the seat next to him,
and I got ready to block a punch. But the guy grinned. "You forgot New York," he told Matt. "Kevin had a stint in New York between San Fran and Houston." Matt's mouth dropped open as he
considered this, then he shook his fists around his eyes. I almost
did, too.

We still run into members of the other camp, and it's still as
painful as ever. Not long ago, Matt and I were at the airport waiting for a flight to California. The plane was delayed, so we decided to go back to one of the fast-food counters in the lobby and
get something to eat. It was crowded, and I figured it would take
us ten minutes to reach the counter, but was afraid Matt still
wouldn't have figured out what he wanted by the time the
woman asked for his order.

"Look at the menu," I instructed, pointing to the pictures of
sandwiches over the counter. "Figure out what you want now so
that you don't keep everyone waiting." He rocked on his heels
and hummed.

By the time the woman asked what he wanted, he was still

rocking. He looked at the breakfast side of the menu. He looked at the lunch/dinner side of the menu. I gritted my teeth and stepped away.

Then a man in the line started making long, operatic sighs. He looked at the people around him to find a kindred spirit in exasperation. He settled on me, not realizing that Matt and I were together. Matt was still trying to decide. The woman at the register was patient. The man made large gestures of annoyance—a hand thrown to his forehead, a slight kick at his briefcase. He looked at me again and groaned.

I realized I could just look away and pretend that this man wasn't making ugly faces at my son. I've done it in the past. Instead, I gave way to twenty-four years of anger at such boorishness. "Do you have a problem?" I asked him.

He pointed to my son. "You'd think after all this time in line, he'd know what the hell he wanted. What is he, a retard or something?"

"Yes," I said. "Do you have a problem with that?"

The man was only slightly abashed. "Are you his mother?"

I nodded.

"Then you should be helping him or something. He shouldn't do this. He shouldn't be able to just stand up there and . . ." He sputtered and stopped. The other people in the line regarded us carefully.

"He has as much right as anyone else to order lunch." It felt as if the whole airport was listening.

By that time, the woman behind the counter was handing

Matt's order to him. Her arm hung in the air as he looked back at me, his mouth a slightly whiskered circle of wonder.

The man's face deepened from capillary-streaked pink to purple. He shuddered inside his black suit. He fiddled with his watch. "I'm sorry," he finally said, looking back up.

"No, you're an asshole." I was calm as the words left my mouth, but as soon as they did, I started to cry. Matt was shocked. He almost walked away from the cashier without his change.

"What happened?" he asked several times as we walked toward our plane. He knew how unlikely it was for me to make a scene—he makes scenes, his father makes scenes, but his mother usually keeps quiet. He touched my shoulder a few times. He unwrapped his burger and offered me a bite. He put his arm around me. Then he forgot about the confusion twenty feet back. He hummed and began to walk a little faster, his thoughts already in California, his feet already touching down in a circle of people who love him.

ASPIRIN FOR A SEVERED HEAD

Suzanne Finnamore

I HAVE BEEN divorced two years this Thanksgiving. (The irony is not altogether lost on me. Bear with.)

I did not believe I would ever get over my divorce, which couldn't have been more painful, squalid, or banal. We had just had a baby—not to save the marriage, I might add, but for the usual joyous, traditional, and misguided reasons.

I did not know the marriage needed saving. This shows my general naïveté, something that divorce cures one of forever.

I became a single mother overnight, which is nothing like becoming famous overnight: I believe it is the emotional equivalent of having a stroke. While my estranged spouse recuperated at the requisite tropical island where frothy drinks are served with miniature parasols, I was left holding the diaper bag.

The timing could not have been worse, as I was left to raise our beautiful son at a time when eating or grooming seemed difficult and perhaps unnecessary. (Other activities, such as swan-diving off the roof, or driving my car into a cement piling, seemed easy and sensible.) I wanted to die. Unlike my spouse, I did not want Club Med. I wanted Club Dead. Life as I knew it was over, my bills were doubled, and my fear and loneliness and sense of complete failure rose like bone dust into the night air.

In a true universe, there would be a place where love and marriages go to die, rapture's own version of the elephant's grave-yard. They should not be allowed to dissipate on their own, to float away on some random moment, irrevocable as seed from a dandelion.

There ought to be a body you can bury.

At the grave site: Here Lies the Marriage of Mark and Suzanne, 9/21/96–11/22/00. One could visit the grave, say a few words. Maybe plant a flower, or defecate. It would be up to you. Instead, we are faced with a vague sense of loss and the feeling that a passage has been missed. There are so many marriage cere-monies; there ought to be one for divorce. Instead of rice, people could throw Xanax, Mercedes keys, and money for the mortgage.

DURING the first few weeks, my mother came to stay with me, positioned on the Pottery Barn Chair-and-a-Half, a kind of an-gelic sentinel in sweat clothes. She drank Diet Coke, and she lis-tened, telling me stories from her own divorce. These stories were not terribly encouraging, seeing as how my father remarried twice and dropped dead at forty-four. But although my mother wanted to part my husband's hair with an ax, she was happy; I noticed that. She had survived.

Of course, I did not die. Instead, I focused on my extraordi-nary son and drank midrange chardonnay every night. From the couch, which had become my battle station, I ordered a barrage of mail-order items. I felt like hammered shit every day.

I asked my mother, How long? Two years, she said. My brain did not accept this as viable information. Yes, my mother had been left at thirty-six with two kids, but that was in the '70s. I announced I could not last that long, that even next month was pushing it. She said, "Oh. Well. Everyone's different, honey."

I walked around my small town with a thought bubble over my head: Person Going through a Divorce. When I looked at other people, I automatically formed thought bubbles over their heads. Happy Couple with Stroller. Innocent Teenage Girl with Her Whole Life Ahead of Her. Content Grandmother and Grandfather Visiting Town Where Their Grandchildren Live with Intact Parents. Secure Housewife with Big Diamond. Undamaged Group of Young Men on Skateboards. Good Man with Baby in Baby Björn Who Loves His Wife. Dogs Who Never Have to Worry. Young Kids Kissing Publicly. Then every so often I'd see one like me, one of the shambling, sad women without makeup, looking older than she is: Divorced Woman Wondering How the Fuck This Happened.

I remember thinking, This just can't last. Sooner or later my life is going to have to come back from the cleaners. I waited. I was not patient, but I waited. If there'd been someone in a position of authority to upbraid for this, I would have. I would have upbraided most severely.

I asked my divorced friends, How long? Two years, they said.

No no no no no, I thought. This is the new millennium, after all, and I felt certain things could be moved along if only the right therapists or books or audiotapes or workshops or aromatherapy could be found. I was open to seminars, Deepak Chopra, Marianne Williamson, Persian Sufis, and Doctor Phil. I was as open as one can be without coming apart entirely. I was the village idiot of self-help.

I got all the books. *Spiritual Divorce, How to Rebuild When a Relationship Ends, Dumped, Crazy Time,* and even something called *The Good Divorce,* which at the time struck me as the Good Holocaust.

Luckily, I had a good therapist. One with the ability to dispense Xanax.

My therapist said, People tell you to get over it, but they don't tell you how. His insight that there is no magic bullet that will erase the pain and propel one into spanking-new shiny lives, free of lingering trauma, fear, and humiliation, was one I could certainly relate to. I felt relieved. I was not doing it wrong.

Time passed slowly, as when one is waiting for aspirin to work on one's severed head.

I got through the first Christmas (or "fucking holidays," as my mother referred to them at the time, incensed on my behalf that Christmas was coming and all I had gotten was abandoned). The first Valentine's Day. The first wedding anniversary. The first divorce anniversary. The pain slowly eased up; the psychic damage was beginning, if not to disappear, then to taper. I stopped wishing him dead, and started wishing him rich so he could send us more money. This did not happen.

And then, just as my mother said would happen, one day I walked down the street with my son and realized I felt happy. Out of the woods.

When people say it takes two years, believe them. Statistically speaking, this is the point in time when one has gotten through it. There is some truth to this—also some rather flamboyant falsehoods, especially when you have a child running around wearing his face and yours, entwined forever: You have done this, it cannot be undone. You will always have children together; they will almost certainly outlive the marriage in terms of years. It's beautiful and hard all at once. It's marriage and its Siamese twin, divorce. Divorce, which apparently has become the antidote to marriage, although the jury is decidedly out. In the end, it's just life.

Still, I easily relate to what Karen Karbo wrote in *Generation Ex*, "There is no statute of limitations on wanting to strangle your ex." I would add that no such statute exists on feelings of affection, anger, and even love. You learn that you can love someone and be divorced from them at the same time, in the same way that you loved them before you were married—except now you know they are capable of ripping your heart out. This changes things considerably. It gives you what time gives you: perspective.

After a couple of years, you can appreciate your ex for who he is and realize that he is separate and distinct from you. You can feel a certain amount of warmth for him, as you do your alma mater, or your car. You can love a car, but you do not attach yourself to the car. You do not buy little gifts for the car, thinking you can win the car over. You do not lose sleep over whether the car thinks you are attractive or if the car is thinking of you too, right now. You do not especially care whether someone else drives the car.

Kierkegaard muses in *Love and Marriage*, "We read in fairy tales about human beings whom mermaids and mermen enticed into their power by means of demonic music. In order to break the enchantment it was necessary in the fairy tale for the person who was under the spell to play the same piece of music backwards without making a single mistake. This is very profound, but very difficult to perform, and yet so it is: the errors one has taken into oneself one must eradicate in this way, and every time one makes a mistake one must begin all over."

Right.

Or, you can wait two years.

ISLE OF SKYE

Mary McCluskey

I REMEMBER the day before there was a mackerel sky over Edinburgh; later, scudding clouds and mists. But when we traveled to Skye, it was clear, cloudless, a canopy of blue.

You can reach the island by bridge from the Kyle of Lochalsh. Not for us. We take the ferry instead from Mallaig and stand on the guardrail looking at the glinting edge of the waves, the sunlight on water. And we arrive five minutes after the bus to the village has left.

In America, or England, the bus would wait for the ferry. But this is the Highlands, the Islands, and the bus left five minutes before. We have traveled the Road to the Isles. We are here. We have no need for buses. We drag the suitcase, and a wheel is wobbling. When your backpack drops off, you stop, frustrated.

"Mom! Mom!"

I turn. Your face is a warm pink and wears a cartoon scowl. It's my fault, of course, for not booking ahead, checking schedules. I have come back to myself here. I have come back to what I was before, to what I am at the very core. My rebel Scottish blood reasserts itself against order, sensibility, good planning.

"Only a few more minutes," I say. "There'll be a hotel, a pub." At least let there be a pub, I pray.

And there it is!

A coach house with an old pub sign, swinging in the breeze from the loch. I don't remember the name—King's something, perhaps. It is an old white building, overlooking an inlet. We can see gray water and hear the sound of it lapping on the mossy banks. The voices from the rooms have the lilting sound of the Highlands. And the room is light, comfortable, with a little bath.

"Yeah! All right!" you say. We are happy to have found so good a place.

It's late, we've missed dinner. In the bar they serve chicken in a basket or fish and chips. We order both. We'll share. A shandy for you, a glass of wine for me. You love the shandy, gulp it down, then look around for a waiter.

I smile. "Hey, this isn't Los Angeles," I say. "You have to get it yourself. It's a pub."

You go to the bar, counting money in your palm, anxious. An L.A. youth, just sixteen years old, waiting to be asked for ID. The bartenders serve you easily, of course, smiling at each other.

You come back toward me in the warm pub, holding the drinks high with a wide smile that says, "I am the man."

I remember we talked about plans for hikes, boat trips. We ate, we smiled. You had rhubarb pie, and the locals waited for your American response to something so tart. "It's good," you said. "It's cool." You grinned at me, not wincing once. I loved you so much.

Did you know that?

In that pub on the Isle of Skye the locals exchanged glances with me, nodding, "He's a good lad, a good wee laddie." They saw the pride on my face. "Yes, he is. Yes." They knew that I loved you.

Freeze that moment. Go back. Rewind to that point.

Go fast, past a midnight in May. A Los Angeles highway, a car veering out of control, a truck crossing three lines of traffic to hit one corner of a Mustang convertible with its top down. To slam into it, to shatter it, to extinguish one young life.

Yours.

Had I known that was your destiny, in that pub in Skye, I would have held you so fast. I would have asked them to help me, those kind people with their warm Highland voices. Help me hold this boy. Here. We'll live here. Live here forever. There are schools. And girls. You can go to university in Edinburgh. Or Inverness. It will be wonderful.

It will be life.

A WORLD OF HURT

Earl R. Mies

DURING the darkest hours, when my anger burned hottest, I learned to pray. Surprisingly, for someone who never regularly attended church, the prayers came easily. "Please, God, make her stop drinking. Please God, don't let her get into another car accident. Please keep her from harming our daughter, or anyone else. Please remove this anger and restore peace."

When I recited my newfound litany of prayers, I closed my eyes and imagined addressing a person stronger than me, someone able to endure endless days and nights of tension, mistrust, disappointment, and abuse. Someone possessing a magical arrangement of words or a secret phone number. Someone who knew a certain someone who could rescue a family that was drowning in a sea of alcohol.

Maybe these were the wrong prayers. Perhaps I should have asked, "Please God, save this precious soul so afflicted with the disease of alcohol, a disease now linked to other brain diseases such as Parkinson's. Show me a way to help her." But I was too filled with anger and disgust to think compassionately, to really believe that I was dealing with a disease instead of a poor life choice. And I was just beginning to learn how to pray.

God may have heard my prayers, but my requests appeared to be granted only on those occasions when my wife was arrested for a DUI and jailed overnight. Her confinement was my respite. I knew my seven-year-old daughter was safe at home with me. We could both sleep, and I could let my boiling anger simmer until the morning. Those few hours of peace were priceless.

Her drinking began about the time we stopped following whims and commenced being adults: the time our daughter was born. Life became serious—as it should when you are responsible for the future of a child. She entered a rigorous professional program. I earned a college degree and went right to work. I was exhilarated; she was stressed. I attended professional conferences and won some honors. She sat in friends' cars and started drinking. I never saw her alcoholism coming until it was too late.

At that time we resided in a small town with a skyline of grain silos, church steeples, and steep, grain-covered hills. Apple and plum trees shaded our yard. Train whistles and bird song punctuated the dry air. I could depend on pheasants calling in March, lilacs blooming in April, and the cleansing rains of October. Shouldn't that have been enough to sustain us?

But like so many American families, we had no relatives within five hundred miles and could rely only upon our marriage, our young daughter, and ourselves to survive whatever life threw our way. Our margin for error was slim. The three of us were adrift in a lifeboat bobbing on precarious waters. When we sprung a leak and the raft filled with alcohol, no one knew how to bail and find land.

Anger is exhausting. I was tired all the time. I dragged my feet on the short walk home from work to our sinking ship, never knowing which spouse would be waiting: the doting wife and mother, the serious college student, the reeling drunk, or (the worst scenario) a conglomerate of all three? I often paused at the edge of the driveway to contemplate our wood-frame house, sitting so serenely on a spacious one-third-acre lot. Outside were signs of normalcy: the tree swing I built for my daughter, the bed of lipstick-red tulips that signaled spring, and a south-facing garden plot where I once grew a gallon's worth of pinto beans.

As I looked at the house with its two glassed-in porches, I wondered, How could such a solid house hold so much instability? I waited for an answer that never came. Then I plunged forward into the chaos that my life had become.

Love led me to dysfunctional vigilance. At the onset of her newfound love of beer and wine, I believed I could control my wife's drinking and stay one step ahead of her. No matter what I tried, I was never prepared for her next move. I took control of the checkbook. She went to the bank and got more checks; soon the overdrafts came. She hid all the bills. I opened a postal box so bills and important correspondence would come directly to me. On my hands and knees, I sifted through the trash in search of grocery receipts, corks, and bottlecaps that would contradict her assurances about not drinking. Pleading and begging were also part of my arsenal. "Please seek treatment. You need help." "No," she said. "I don't have a drinking problem."

Dramatic contrition is a major part of an alcoholic's roller-coaster behavior and helps enable the enabler. After an overnight in the drunk tank, my wife would wander back home, ready to make amends. "Things will be different," she said, vowing never to buy a twelve-pack or a gallon jug again. "You'll see," she added tenderly, tying an apron on, holding my hand tight in hers and pulling me back toward her, to a place I never imagined existed.

For a few days, things would be better. Calmness would settle over the three of us. I would let up on my prayers, even though I knew the peace was temporary. In a few days an odor gave her away: not a beery scent, but earthy and decomposing, like death itself. Soon her clothes and hair looked oddly arranged, as if dropped from the sky with no thought to tidiness. Her gait was awkward; the timing was all wrong. She lurched and swayed heavily on her toes. Bald patches appeared, revealing the red gouges she had dug in her lovely black hair. Her speech became aggressive and confrontational.

"You will have to leave me! I will never leave you," she shouted gleefully, as if she had set an inescapable trap for me. After all, the one who leaves the marriage is usually seen as the culprit, the villain who couldn't "stick it out." In retrospect, however, I stayed far past the point of being useful, or safe.

I stayed, even once the violence began.

To be hit, hard, by a woman is the ultimate test of anger management. As a man, you are allowed to be punched, kicked, slapped, scratched, or made the bull's-eye of flying objects such as cast-iron skillets, lamps, and chairs. Movies and television shows often try for a cheap laugh with a diminutive woman clocking a guy in the jaw or in the groin. I'm not sure why, but audiences love this scene, yet the reverse—a man belting a woman in the face or kicking her below the belt—is never funny and never shown. A father, a husband, and a son cannot throw, under any circumstance, a retaliatory punch, even if the woman stands over you and dares you to strike back by calling you a coward and questioning your manhood. Theoretically, a woman is physically weaker, but in practice, a drunk, angry female has awesome strength.

Aside from my own decency, I was further guided in my restraint by the constant presence of my daughter, who took in our battles like a sponge. I reasoned that if I struck back at her mother, the trauma would be worse for my daughter than if I was hit. (Who knows if I was correct?) I learned to cover my face and stifle my anger. So I took one, and then another, for the family. And, at the time, I never told anyone.

I am not a saint. I wanted to hit back, and I wanted to hurt her. I wanted to throw her out the door, along with the hundreds of empty cans and bottles hidden away in the shed. I wanted her to perish alone in a one-car accident and be done for good with this slow death. But restraint was key. After all, I knew the deputies would almost always haul off the male in a domestic fight. Instead I left, said good-bye to the picturesque house, the south-facing garden, the tulips, the fruit trees, and the tree swing.

I left my daughter, too, believing that our separation would last only as long as it took me to find a good attorney. This was a mistake, I think, one of several that I made as panic seemed to overwhelm reason. I thought my wife would only harm me and her. And although she did not physically harm our child, I can only imagine the damage that must have been done in many other ways.

At the time I believed there was a home-court advantage, a safe harbor for a child asleep in her own bed, in her own room among her cats. I was camped out on the floor of my office, surprising the janitor at five in the morning when he came in to empty the wastebaskets. I now understand that a safe harbor, presided over by a sober person, can exist almost anywhere.

But I was hooked, too—on anger. It was my best friend during those terrifying months after leaving home. As I plunged into the divorce proceedings, I leaned on my rage to compile what I thought was convincing evidence for the court to grant me full custody of my (I stopped using the pronoun *our* after the first DUI) daughter. Rage fueled my life, it filled every cell of my being until it became an overdeveloped muscle that felt, well, intoxicating. And I never wavered, even when my wife paid a visit to my new apartment in the middle of the night, declaring she had pancreatic cancer and I should take her back. She was lying, of course, which made me even angrier.

Fear still accompanied me, the fallout of too many dizzying

punches that came out of nowhere. Soon after the late-night visit, I went to the county courthouse to request an order of protection to keep my unpredictable wife from tearing apart my new life. As I made the request at a clerk's window, a woman who worked in the office said, looking at my six-foot-one frame and, I suppose, my gender, "He needs an order of protection?"

This insensitive aside from a public official was devastating. I immediately phoned Alternatives to Violence, a local organization mainly concerned with abuse toward women. Much to the organization's credit, a woman rushed down to the courthouse and, after chewing out the county functionary, walked me through the hearing, where I received a piece of paper that, in theory, was supposed to keep me safe. In practice, the piece of paper was as valuable as a napkin, but still I felt as if I had finally won my first battle in a war that leaves no one standing.

Eventually, though, I hit an emotional wall and a moral dilemma. To be granted sole custody of a child in a state not known for progressiveness in these or any other social matters would involve further destroying my wife's reputation at a time when she was drying out for a month in a state hospital. Attorneys required more money, and I would need an even larger reserve of anger. I could muster neither. Nor could my young daughter, who only wanted stability and, of course, a sober mother. I settled for joint custody.

And then one day, maybe a year after the ink was dry on the dozens of divorce papers, I woke in the morning, and the anger was gone—just like that. There was no epiphany. I can't remember if the sun was shining or if rain was falling or if a rare spring blizzard had blown in from the mountains. I simply rose off my futon, made my usual cup of strong coffee with cream and sugar, and everything was different. "Time to feel good and have some fun again." By then I had added up the lawyer fees and counseling bills, and I knew that anger had saved me but also cost me dearly. No wonder I felt lighter.

My former wife finally stopped drinking, in part because some of her remaining friends held an intervention that led to her month-long residency in the hospital. By that time, she had lost everything. The abstinence held for a couple of good years that were vital to my daughter, but it wasn't long before there were more wrecked cars, half-truths, and angry friends. Instead of obsessing about those dramas, I concentrated on my daughter's mental health and on maintaining my own fragile emergence into light. Perhaps I should have been more sympathetic to my former wife's continuing messes (after all, she is my daughter's mother), but once that first punch was thrown my way, all vestiges of support and concern disappeared.

At times in the first few years of being single—times that I will never be proud of—the anger returned, like sparks flaring up following an old forest fire. Standing in line at the grocery store, I would see headlines about the latest Hollywood-Nashville-L.A.-NFL-NBA bad boy or girl just released from Betty Ford. "Clean and Sober and Back to Work!" "New Attitude, New Baby." "Grate-

ful for Second Chance!" "Loving Life Again!" There are no headlines for the rest of us, I would think, rage building. We sober
ones have to keep it together: keep the job, pay the bills, console
the children, clean up the messes, talk to the insurance man, deal
with repossession, foreclosure, humiliation. We have to be
grown-ups. Addicts can get high, and I hate them for it.

I would stomp around during these episodes, exploring self-
imposed misery until I got tired of it. But the passage of time
threw dirt on the smoldering ashes, and just as I forgot what I
had loved so much about this flawed woman, I eventually forgot
what it was that had kept me so angry for so long. Time had
worked its amnesiac balm on me, or perhaps God had finally answered my prayers.

A MOTHER WITHOUT A CHILD

Robin Wallace

THE SNEAKER salesman asks me about my exercise preferences—aerobics? running?—and I'm halfway through a detailed history of step classes and speed walking before I realize how ridiculous the regimen must sound considering the heft I'm carrying around. I want to explain that my excess flab is the product of recent childbirth, but stop myself midsentence.

I can't tell the sneaker salesman that I'm shaping up postpartum because, unlike most new mothers, I don't have a baby. One day after my son was due, his umbilical cord became entangled around his neck. He died, still snug in my womb, before he could be born.

It's just not a thing you toss into casual conversation. Yet this self-imposed, socially correct silence is painful to maintain. I attend showers and cocktail parties, where women I've never met are talking about their pregnancies and their kids. I don't want to impose the burden of my personal tragedy on strangers, but I also don't want to have to stand in these circles denying who I am.

I craved oranges and had burning pelvic pain, too. My epidural also didn't take on the first try. But of course the natural progression of such remarks—Congratulations! Did you have a boy or girl? What's his name? How old is he?—makes such contributions impossible. So I stay quiet. And with each incident of forced, unnatural muteness, of pretending I did not have a baby, I lose my son all over again.

You don't realize how many strangers you chatter with each day until you must guard each word to avoid mentioning the most significant event of your life. You do not appreciate how many acquaintances you can go a year or more without contacting until the specter of a chance encounter turns routine functions like grocery shopping or visiting the local pub into perilous exercises of anxiety and avoidance. You cannot know how important your physical appearance is to you until you cannot provide every person you meet with the excuse of pregnancy for your fat.

My husband refuses to be robbed of the heartbreaking pride he still takes in having sired a child. I watch him tell old friends and associates. I watch his face contort with the effort of reconciling stubborn traces of joy with the awkwardness and discomfort that comes from sharing this information. But my husband keeps himself in a pretty tight orbit of friends, family, and colleagues. If my world is to extend beyond the safe cocoon of people who know what happened—and for me, it must—I have to be prepared to suppress the most distinct part of who I am.

A full-term stillbirth is not the worst-case scenario in pregnancy; it is the unfathomable. You skip that chapter in the pregnancy book, not so much because the idea is too awful to consider but because it is too improbable, too horrible—you think—to actually happen. When it does happen, you learn that the unimaginable does indeed happen, that there is no reason to really believe that it can't or won't. The basic human inclination to hope for the best—in times of eager promise or fearful anxiousness—is not only exposed as a sham, it is also no longer available to you. You become proof of the foolishness and naïveté of such faith.

My son did not look dead. He was pink and round and perfectly formed and appeared only to be deep in a peaceful baby slumber. His eyes were closed, but there was an expression on his face, a thoughtful one, as if he had spent some time pondering his future, planning his entry into the world. The secret of who he would have been was permanently trapped inside him, but its presence was unmistakable. Personality, humor, intelligence, talent—potential my son would never have the chance to realize, potential from which the world would never benefit.

I see his face every minute of every day, and when I see it—when he was born, and now, in my memory—I think of what happened as some sort of payback, a restitution for past sins or transgressions. Yet I have no sense of any cosmic debt being paid, of karmic accounts being settled. Instead, my little baby hovers above me like an angel of foreboding, a warning to heed the message of his death. I cannot figure out what that message is, what lesson I was supposed to learn, and the fear that these lessons will keep coming until I decipher the meaning of my son's death is paralyzing.

I had been very proud, almost cocky, about the speed with

which I had conceived and the ease with which I carried this baby. For so many of my closest friends and relatives, procreation had become an exhausting medical process resulting from infertility and miscarriage. My pregnancy was romantic, natural. My son was going to squeeze into the world two months before my thirty-fourth birthday, six weeks before my first wedding anniversary. I had beat my biological clock and breezed through forty weeks of tests and examinations without a complication or concern.

Pregnancy, for me, was a process in which I cast off my old self, with its mundane inadequacies and failings, and regenerated a spectacular new me in its place, a me empowered with awesome, preternatural capabilities. By the end of my pregnancy, I could not remember or imagine the reliable efficiency and functionality of my prepregnancy body. I could not recall an intellect that could be engaged by any subject other than the baby I was carrying. I spent the last six weeks of my pregnancy in severe, immobilizing discomfort, but that only seemed to reinforce the importance and seriousness—the privilege—of the condition. I could not imagine a life that was not defined by this experience.

Instead I am distinguished by a grotesque mutation of the experience. What was to be my ultimate triumph is now my most abject failure. The onset of labor did not send me to the hospital; the eerie stillness of my child, the absence of his familiar squirms and kicks, did. A team of nurses and doctors frowned at the screen of a sonogram scanner with mounting dread and alarm, and some essence of myself, something innocent and optimistic, drained away. Whatever my pregnancy had been or meant, whatever memories or expectations it had brought into our lives, collapsed into a mangled pile of useless rubble in the few seconds it took for an obstetrical resident to look up from the sonogram screen and say, "I'm sorry. There doesn't seem to be a heartbeat."

Whether a woman believes motherhood to be her most significant experience, or mothering to be her most important role, she is redefined, her identity permanently altered, once she gives birth. I am stranded in a lonely purgatory between the worlds of motherhood and childlessness. I carried my baby inside me for nine months and pushed him into the world. I know the surge of all-consuming love and pride that rushes into every cell of a person's body the instant her child is placed in her arms. But I never fed my son or changed his diaper. I never heard him cry or saw him smile. I have not had to adjust to the stress and exhaustion of this awesome new responsibility.

Everyone I know is having babies, and I imagine I can hear the cliquish scorn of the other mothers I thought I'd be joining: "You're not really one of us. What ever made you think you could be?" I had been the dutiful and faithful pledge of this elite sorority, but ultimately I was only permitted to push my nose against the glass. I've had a child, but I don't have my child. I fit in nowhere.

Sometimes it does feel as if the pregnancy did not actually happen, as if the whole ordeal was simply a disturbing, vivid dream or the product of my own imagination. I could be the protagonist of a science fiction thriller, my identity stolen, the last year of my life erased by mysterious evil forces. I can remember nine months of pregnancy, but other than some medical bills and excess weight, there is no real evidence of it. Sometimes, for a second, I think I'm still pregnant and just haven't had my baby yet.

Sometimes, however, my whole body will just ache for my son, a ravenous craving. I find myself at these times taking huge, deep breaths, as if I could catch a whiff of his essence in the air. I know what my husband smells like. I know the comfort of being able to summon a memory or a place, or the spirit of someone, through the power of a familiar scent. I hold the blanket and knit cap my son was wrapped in at the hospital up to my face, and I inhale until my lungs are bursting; but these remnants of my baby are eerily odorless, not the faintest trace of olfactory evidence remains. Everything else in the world has a smell, or at least a scent that evokes presence, but my son did not leave one behind. I cannot even have that simple connection with him.

I sometimes see myself as a freak, the pathetic subject of a nature documentary, the slow, sad female of the species who, tricked by a cruel twist of biology into believing she has reproduced, spends her life roaming her habitat in search of her phantom offspring.

My son was born at one o'clock in the morning, an induced labor fast and painless under heavy dosages of epidural medication. My husband and I named him Luke Michael. We were able to hold him and kiss him and baptize him and keep him with us for hours after his birth.

They were agonizing hours, filled with fantasies that Luke's eyes would open, and punctuated by a horrible sound that I later realized was our wretched, unhinged wailing. But Luke was beautiful, and he was ours; there was still a joy in holding him, still a thrill in seeing him for the first time.

I spent the next days, even the next week, trying to celebrate Luke's birth while simultaneously mourning his death. I could not stop myself from brimming with the pride of a new mother. It was a part of me that could not be kept down. Hours after I held him in my arms for the first time, I showed off my son, taking extreme advantage of a hospital policy that allowed families unlimited access to their dead newborns. Luke was held by his grandparents and aunts, passed around my hospital room in a ritual that seemed perfectly sound to me at the time, but that probably permanently traumatized my ambushed relatives. They saw his long legs, his giant feet that had jabbed my ribs, his full head of red-brown hair (light like mine, not dark and thick like his father's).

My husband and I have photographs of ourselves holding Luke; we have his lanky footprints and a lock of his hair. I sent clothes to the funeral parlor—a diaper, an undershirt, and the special homecoming outfit I had chosen for him—to make sure he was dressed properly when he was buried. We honored him with a formal funeral, and laid him to rest in a small white casket covered in downy feathers like angel wings. I tried to be as much of a mother to my son as I had the chance to be.

But all we really have of Luke is this suffocating sadness. The hospital professionals—the counselors and nurses and clergy—tell us that we did know our baby, that we do have memories of him, but it's just not true. As time has passed, Luke has become more real to us, more of a presence in our lives, but what we have bonded with is the sadness, the emptiness that, like a growing child, keeps taking up more and more space in our lives. All we have to remember Luke is sadness, so we cling to it so as not to abandon our son.

We are not so selfish or self-absorbed not to know that our pain is barely a blip on the meter of world suffering and tragedy. But our small world revolves around our missing baby. Even as I struggle with the sadness that the loss of my son has unleashed in my life, I am comforted by the way my grief returns with faithful potency every time I fear I may be forgetting. It is the gaping hole in my life, where my baby and I were supposed to be together, that reminds me that I am still very much his mother. Whatever I fear now, it is not that my grief will never heal. My greatest fear is that it will.

J. B. Orenstein

A PIERCING shriek cut suddenly short, a car flipping sidelong against its natural direction. For an odd, hanging moment, nothing else happened. The sky overhead buzzed as a helicopter changed directions. On the ground, asphalt sparked in an infinity of rising dust and fallen glass crystals around a dusty brown car; a palette of reds splattered and dotted the windshield, and then began to drip.

The car tumbled to a halt in a precarious stance on the passenger side, all four tires airborne, after one-and-a-half turns on the highway. The truck had recoiled back into the mouth of the crossing. The next thirty seconds or so following the helicopter's departure were still. Police records indicate several calls registered to 911 nearly simultaneously.

That's how it ends, or that's how it begins.

The intersection, at Route 1 and Rippon Boulevard, was long familiar to 911 operators. Route 1, three lanes in each direction on a slight elevation, bends gently to the south and east. Rippon Boulevard enters blindly. Route 1 traffic is hidden by a twenty- or thirty-foot hill at the intersection, a mound of dirt and tall reedy grasses. A left turn is a grope until the middle of a lane in which cars stream by at fifty miles per hour. It's a setup. A meat grinder.

The nearest rescue squad, three blocks south, can get there in under a minute. The first vehicles arrived as the second round of calls lit up the 911 switchboard, and they knew, before they even got there, that it was going to be a bad one.

The paramedics were ready for anywhere up to four or five occupants. The statistics of vehicle occupancy dictated that chances were good there would be a single victim, the odds on two a lot lower but possible. Three or more would have been a rare stroke of bad luck. As they shot out of their truck and scrambled over to the driver's side of the smashed car, a single occupant—and a horrible surprise—awaited them. It was instantly apparent. The lady's huge belly was moving.

First-responder protocols include perhaps one paragraph on the pregnant trauma victim: (A) It is a rare situation, and (B) get her the hell to the hospital as fast as humanly possible. The woman's body would take a minimum of five to ten minutes to extricate from the wreckage. It was already so busted up they might only have attempted to find a pulse to confirm the fact of instant death, but with a living patient trapped inside their dead patient, they had to get her to the hospital no matter what.

A medic crawled in through the back seat to support the woman's head and stabilize her neck with a rigid-foam collar; a second medic broke through the windshield and produced a face mask and oxygen bag. Then, still at a crazy angle inside the vehicle, they attempted an awkward, ineffective CPR in earnest, one pushing in and falling back off her chest, the other blowing in oxygen from the bag and mask. The ambulance driver radioed for more help.

No one noticed that somewhere along the line the baby had stopped moving.

"Line one, Jul."

The call greeted me as I began my ER shift at 4 P.M. "They're working on what looks to be a near-term pregnant woman MVA out on Route 1. No vital signs, ground crew called for air backup. No ETA yet, they're still getting her out of the car."

Okay.

I turned around to look at the patient board, scan the nursing station. A reflexive move, a dodge. Okaaay. "No vitals because they haven't gotten to her yet, or no vitals?"

"No vitals." As in dead.

"All right." I paused again, because this raised a million questions. "I'll get NICU (the neonatal intensive care unit) down here. Do they know?"

"Not yet."

I hung up. Lynn, the charge nurse, hovered over me with her hands on her hips. "What's coming in?" She skipped a grimace and went for a poker face when she heard the details. "Coming by air?"

"Called for 'em. Still getting her out of the car. We've got some time."

The message from communications was clear: Mom was gone, but if everything broke right, there might be a chance to salvage the baby. Such rescues were rare, but not unheard of.

They'd have to be here in ten minutes max to give the baby a chance. Possibly the mother, too, if for some reason the prehospital info was wrong or overblown. So, in practical terms, the call meant we had to get the NICU, specialists in newborns and preemies, down to the ER in a hurry.

Activating a trauma team is as easy as pushing a button. The ER at Fairfax Hospital, in the suburbs of northern Virginia, is a Level 1 trauma center, a place where miracles can—and are expected to—take place. But the rescue about to unfold was going to push our limits.

Comm called again almost immediately with an update. "Air crew's there. ETA 15," she said and disconnected. We had fifteen minutes to get ready.

Kathy Kelly, the other ER doc who had been alerted to the coming trauma code, was on the phone when I found her. Her exasperated look, a too-calm "No, I need you now," signaled that the party on the other end wasn't cooperating. Her clipped tone, the *now* of her request, was the unique prerogative of the ER doc: when we call for help, we need help. Kathy set the receiver down and stared at it for a second before looking up at me. "That was OB. They'll try to make it."

"Try?"

"Do or do not," she said, in fair imitation of Yoda. "There is no try."

"So what's the scene here?" I asked.

In medical school, one of the fostering-nurturing things students are told ad nauseam is that there is no such thing as a stupid question. In the real world of medicine, 90 percent of questions are stupid, including the one I'd just asked. The "scene" was the New York subway, the F train at rush hour, and it was about to get substantially worse.

Lynn suddenly appeared from the mouth of the trauma room, dictating strategy and ready positions. With a double trauma on the way and every bed already occupied, her whip was already cracking. "Kathy, I'm moving the last two traumas out to the hall. Julian, the baby will go into Room 2 once he or she's out."

Because obstetric trauma occurs so rarely, neither obstetrics nor neonatology staff are used to the stop-drop-and-run drill that ER and trauma docs take for granted. A few obstetric and neonatal emergencies demand instantaneous care, but for the most part, their docs rarely need to go running to find them. When the neonatologist, Dr. Huntington, returned my page she, too, sounded busy, and her tone left me less than completely reassured that anyone would show up to help.

I had performed resuscitation on critically ill newborns and preemies during my pediatrics residency years before, but I had gotten a little rusty, and hoped the skills would come back to me. A lot of life hung on the results. I didn't need the NICU so much, but I prayed for them to arrive. I doubted any ER doc had ever done a crash cesarean section. A trauma surgeon, yes, probably, because trauma surgeons are accustomed to emergency surgery, but even then it might not be smooth.

An inescapable fact of medicine, unfailing as a law of nature, dictates that the more practiced a surgeon is at a procedure, the better the ultimate outcome. I had no idea at the time, really, how fast a crash C-section could be performed—two minutes? three?—but I knew that an obstetrics resident performed them far more often than a general surgeon.

Given the situation, doing it in two minutes was infinitely preferable to doing it in four minutes. And given, too, the grim fact that the mother, already dead in the field, had no realistic chance of resuscitation whatsoever, the only point of this whole exercise would be to immediately remove the baby in the remote-to-unlikely chance it had not already suffered irreversible brain damage.

All trauma patients, upon arrival in the ER, are given a name, Alpha through Zulu. All receive the surname Doe. The woman headed our way was Sierra Doe; her baby, if she made it, Tango Doe. Once the helicopter bearing Sierra Doe landed on the roof of the ER, it would take less than sixty seconds for the team to bring her down from the landing pad and into the trauma bay.

The only job I absolutely had to do was to check that we had a functioning warmer for the baby and a neonatal resuscitation kit ready. Residency training had ground into me that checking one's own resuscitation box is like packing your own parachute—only the life at stake was not mine, but a newborn baby's. I had five or six whole minutes to get ready. An eternity.

Matt Minoli, the senior trauma surgery resident, had already been in the ER all day. He had just left to tend to a crashing patient in the surgical ICU, leaving Prabhu, his junior resident, sewing up the head of the last trauma patient, who had arrived twenty or so minutes earlier.

Matt responded loudly to the page, "Fuckin' motherfucker. They're thinning the fucking herd out there today."

"OB's not here yet, and they sound busy," Lynn informed him on his return. "Ever done a stat section?" she asked.

"I've done C-sections once or twice," he said, folding his arms.

"Well, here's your chance to do another one," she said.

He rubbed his chin, eyes sliding to the trauma room, where his junior resident was still sewing the scalp laceration. He patted his pockets, found a surgical stapler. "Prabhu!" he called out. "Catch!" The silvery packet sailed across the ER. Prabhu's puzzled look turned to a nod of understanding. The head wound was closed in an instant.

The Comm nurse had an update from the flight crew. Sierra still had no pulse, even with CPR. There was a "downtime" of fifteen-plus minutes, which meant she'd been pulseless—dead— at least that long. There was a lot of blood.

The only one listening besides the secretary, several patients, and their families was Donna Rotondo, our social worker.

When a trauma patient arrives, one critical team member waits in the background, eyes and ears alert, arms folded, hands idle: the social worker. He or she watches from a corner, picking up bits and pieces of information, awaiting the family's arrival.

Social workers routinely embrace the family's misery and loss, standing by through the ordeal and interpreting the goings-on. Depending on the gravity of the situation, they offer condolences, tempered pessimism or reassurance, accompanied by advice on whom to call for emotional support.

"You knew this was coming in, didn't you?" the Comm nurse asked.

Donna shook her head no, her face registering alarm.

Donna's task was to find the husband and arrange for him to get over here if the 911 rescuers had not dispatched police to do that already. Maybe the woman's wallet would help someone from the ambulance crew find the guy. If not, Donna would make first contact. This delicate art requires her to prepare him for a brutal shock without telling him the worst of it. After all, none of us knew yet what was coming our way.

Donna is the person you want in the room at the moment your life is shattered. The daily, close contact with vulnerable and confused people facing their most primal fears is not for the faint of heart. The trauma code could last a matter of minutes at most. Intense, hairy as it might be, it would blow over quickly enough. Everything afterward, preparing the father to cope with the hours, days, months, years ahead, fell on her shoulders.

With Donna dispatched, the Comm nurse repeated her update. Sierra Doe had taken the full impact of the oncoming car. There was a subtext: In the science of crashes—and car wrecks are meticulously referred to as crashes, not accidents—somebody is always at fault. When a car runs a light, the driver of that car risks being crunched under the force of an accelerating vehicle, the caving door just inches away from his or her body. The innocent driver is at least a hood's length way from impact. By the harsh logic of vehicular crash statistics, our girl may have run the red.

We didn't want to believe it. Prehospital information is sometimes sketchy, inaccurate, or just plain wrong. (Subsequent accident-reconstruction investigators later did, in fact, find otherwise.) But the news distracted us.

That's when we heard it. The helicopter carrying Sierra Doe chopped into our thoughts, and at that moment, despite all the commotion, not one true specialist who could help her in a meaningful way was present.

The baby box was under the warmer, and everything seemed to be ready: tubes for the airway, IV catheters, prefilled medication syringes. My thoughts were racing so fast at that moment, I was only half-aware of what I was checking. I didn't want to miss the action in the next room. At first, I nervously registered a couple of syringes, a bunch of tubes. I forced a deep breath, then focused on each item one by one. Each medication syringe appeared to be properly labeled, none expired or outdated, all the correct tube sizes. Very few items are needed to rescue even the most gravely ill newborn.

Kathy, Matt, Prabhu, and select nurses began to rip open sterile packs containing turquoise blue surgical gowns, matching booties, masks, and caps. An obstetrics cart had been wheeled in, and Matt headed there first. He was soon joined by two women I did not recognize, both skinny and blond, neither one in trauma garb, who had followed us in without our being aware of their arrival.

The obstetrics team—finally.

Their belated arrival added to the crackling air of anticipation. Our patient was being unloaded from the helicopter, rolled into the elevator. In another moment, she would emerge into the corridor a few yards away. NICU was still AWOL.

Matt and the obstetrician reviewed their strategy. The trauma surgeons were to be at Sierra's head and chest as the OB team, at the belly, sliced and grabbed. "Who's going to take the baby?"

"Me."

The surgeons whirled around and seemed to see me for the first time.

Prabhu, lacing and unlacing his fingers, looked across an empty stretcher to Matt. "She won't make it," he said. "Right?"

"Bet she will," Matt said.

"A beer," the junior rejoined.

"You're on."

"Prabhu," Kathy said softly from immediately behind his shoulder, "don't bet on patients. Don't bet on death."

A few students and residents had been trying to squeeze into the room so as not to miss out on the rare experience. Lynn, assuming the role of recording nurse, shooed them out one by one, from a podium at the back of the room. Each time a swish of a body came through the door, all eyes turned in anticipation, fol-

lowed by grumbling at the inconsiderate idiots breaking their attention, stretching their nerves.

Lynn, getting exasperated, yelled out into the ER for someone
to keep everyone else out of the room and then pulled the door
closed. The trauma record, a massive, three-page document, un-
scrolled in front of her.

The door opened again, and Lynn countered with a lunge of
her own. "I told you to keep out!" she snapped.

A dark-blue-sleeved arm, bearing the insignia of the AirCare
rescue team, forced her arm backward. Sierra Doe, the guest of
honor, had arrived.

The fifteen or so sea-blue bodies packing the room—doctors,
nurses, techs—distinguishable only by their eyes, parted for the
stretcher and paramedics. As if choreographed, a gap opened
around the trauma bed, and the phalanx of dark blue rescuers
marched in with Sierra Doe.

My first glimpse was of a small mass—a swath of skin, a tan-
gle of hair, and a plastic tube. The head and face. Next came a
huge mass, a thunderhead—her gravid belly. Dried and not yet
dried blood covered her face, her hair, every inch of her flesh, the
middle part of the dark blue flight suits surrounding her. It per-
meated the fabric of her dress. The torso of one of the paramedics
rhythmically pumped up and down on her chest as the effort at
cardiopulmonary resuscitation continued.

Fifteen bodies closed in on Sierra Doe as swiftly as they had
parted. Exhale, inhale. A pair of heavy-duty scissors hacked

through the remains of her blue jeans up to her blood-soaked maternity top. The bloody rags were pulled aside.

Simultaneously, the chief flight paramedic stepped back and gave his report, his the only voice in the room for the moment. Standing just beyond the patient's head, he described the scene we all knew by heart: T-bone collision, high speed in an intersection. Driver-side car door into her side.

Matt and Prabhu were on opposite sides of her chest, talking in voices loud enough to be heard over the paramedic. Matt apparently didn't like what he saw and called, "Thoracotomy tray!" The paramedic performing CPR was waved off by Matt, who intended to slice open her chest and explore for heart wounds—the first swirl of chaos in the otherwise orderly proceedings.

The obstetrics surgeon had not said a word. Standing immediately in front of me, next to the enormous belly, she started her procedure. My eyes snapped from Sierra Doe's chest to her belly; the mental sequence of neonatal resuscitation stopped running abruptly. In another two minutes, maybe three, I would have the baby.

"Probably twenty-five minutes realistically," blared the voice of the flight medic over the din. Dead for twenty-five minutes. An eternity. What are we all doing here? In just that flick of an eye upward, I missed half of the cesarean.

Epidermis.

Dermis.

Subcutaneous fat.

Linea alba.

A scalpel raced through them, a single horizontal slice. A brown-black mass appeared through the incision; the obstetric resident's assistant's hands shoved back the ecchymotic flesh, further exposing the darkened uterus.

Lynn barked irritably from her podium: "Tell me what you're doing, people." A nurse holding a bag of blood spiked it with an infusion set, called out to the nurse closest to the body to open up. At the nod, she squeezed the bag with all her might, and a cord of red—transfusion no. 1—began snaking its way into Sierra Doe's broken body.

Fascia sheath.

Myometrium.

Amnion.

The OB resident deftly flicked the scalpel handle around in her hand and passed it off to her assistant. Then, equally swiftly, she produced a fine pair of scissors, poked the point of the blade through the uterine fundus, and guided the scissors down vertically from umbilicus to pubis. A slice first this way, then that. Thirty seconds, tops. She reached into the black waters and brought out a baby.

It's a girl.

No wail, no cry, just a purple slippery form.

"Time of delivery four-thirteen," she called loudly, and the room froze momentarily.

In a final display of dexterity, the OB resident's hands again appeared, this time at the improbable reed dangling beneath the baby. She clamped the umbilical cord once, moved up an inch, and flicked the second clamp down, closing it on the cord. She cut the cord a moment after the second clamp was on, and Tango Doe was free.

I had been standing just behind the OB doc, stepping in closer as the startlingly brief cesarean unfolded. As she wheeled around, holding aloft the newborn girl, I raised my arms to receive her. Before I could lay gloved hands on her, Dr. Huntington, the NICU herself, darted in, grabbed the baby, and fled.

A single, graceful arc traced her journey from mother's dark womb to isolette landing pad. I saw the baby's assessment had already started: a pair of the NICU doc's fingers fixed at the base of the umbilicus, feeling for a pulse.

The infant flopped down limply, and it was clear, without a nod or grunt from Huntington, there could be no pulse, no heart rate, no cry, no respiration. She was the same deeply saturated grape hue as mom. Lifeless, stillborn. Dr. Huntington had brought along just one nurse, and they began their work: an endotracheal tube down the throat to breathe, a long IV catheter placed through the umbilical cord. Reflexively, my fingers were on the baby's chest, performing rapid compressions.

The nurse applied monitor pads, connected IV fluids, accepted medications from me. The quiet of Trauma Bay 2, punctuated by brief, staccato comments and replies, was a stark contrast to the rising din in the next room. They must have found something.

Sierra Doe, epicenter of the frenzy, lay paralytically still. Her color was an ashy purple, ashy from the rivers of blood drained through her many injuries, purple because the little blood left in her body had been depleted of all its oxygen. Her short brunet hair was matted in blood. The thin rim of her dilated pupils was too small to register a color.

Her arms were extended at both sides, the better to receive blood and fluids, the better to expose her flanks for various and sundry crash surgical procedures. The rest of her features were vague and distorted by the circumstances of her death: her face swollen and cut up, her body similarly disfigured and opened in unnatural ways.

But she inched closer back to life each moment. Matt found several fractured ribs and a gaping chest wound, perhaps sheared by glass, perhaps from the door itself crunching under the impact. Like the OB doc a few moments ago, he made a hasty slashing incision to explore. If the worst of her injuries was only a lacerated heart muscle, he would know the moment he held it in his hands. Fixable. The brain and its starvation for oxygen—screw it. Never believe the worst until you see it for yourself.

With one hand inside her chest, Matt used the other to shove away the medic doing CPR. Sierra Doe's chest relaxed, allowing Matt's fingers to crawl deeper into her thorax. Maybe there was a chance for a good resuscitation after all.

The second unit of blood arrived, then almost as quickly began to leak through the sieve of her wounds. Prabhu spiked a needle into the right side of her chest and was greeted immediately by a rush of air and a stream of blood, and the right lung re-expanded. A step closer.

It was with the third unit of blood, the third of eight eventually muscled in, that the miracle occurred. Matt's fingers, caressing the woman's heart, failed to identify a tear, and for a moment his spirits fell. The woman would not be tricked from death by something as easy as a lacerated heart.

As his fingers withdrew, he perhaps tickled a fiber, a sensitive spot. Something. Kathy's eyes, still darting briskly, flicked up to the monitor above.

A beat. A pause. Another. Another.

"Is there a pulse with that?" Kathy asked, her voice rising through the din.

And there was. As the heart resumed its ceaseless motion—contract, relax, contract, relax—the pallor of Sierra's face transformed from purple to pink, from ghostly death to flickering life, from a gargoyle into a pretty, young mommy.

"God must not have wanted her," Lynn said, tears pouring forth from her eyes.

Everyone in the room froze as Richard, Sierra's husband, stepped in. The only movement was the flare of a white bedsheet as it was hastily thrown over Sierra Doe's gutted abdomen and thorax. The nurses, docs, and techs met his eyes with a blank stare. We had assembled for the sole purpose of giving this man a chance to be with his wife and baby, but no one seemed to know what to do with him once he got there.

Kathy sensed her cue and approached him, softly, telling him about the broken ribs, the internal bleeding. She pointed to chest tubes. He nodded, possibly understanding, possibly following what she was saying. The sheet covering his wife's belly was turning red as Kathy pointed to it; the surgeons needed to get her to the OR right away to explore for other injuries, like a lacerated liver or spleen. Again a nod. He looked around nervously. A rainbow of reds splashed seemingly everywhere, on towels thrown to the floor, smearing the sea-blue surgical gowns and hanging from the last two transfusion bags into the body of his wife. Too much blood. No baby.

We don't know yet if any head injuries have been sustained, Kathy continued. There's no obvious sign of head injury, and the tube coming from her mouth is for breathing. Once more, a nod.

Then she handed him off to me.

He engaged my eyes first. He was so young.

"Here. Come with me," I said, guiding him by his shoulders through the cubicle between the two trauma rooms.

The view in Trauma Bay 2 presented a far more antiseptic picture: here was a small baby, swaddled in blankets, in the arms of a nurse. We arrived just as Dr. Huntington and her nurse were preparing to take the baby to their unit. They didn't know the father had shown up.

I told him, "It's a girl," as the nurse handed her over, placed her in his arms. "Oh . . . a girl . . ." he cried. "A girl . . ."

He carried her stiffly, like any new father, afraid he might break her. It all looked so normal.

The long-dormant memory reawakened, the reflex of how to talk a new dad through a disastrous delivery that may—will—have lifelong consequences. I told him that his baby had revived as soon as we started to work on her, that her ultimate prognosis would be known better once some testing could be done in the NICU. *Prognosis* is a portentous, scary enough word, and I left it at that. He hadn't heard me, wasn't even listening.

"Her name is Elizabeth," he whispered, his eyes brimming. My eyes welled, too. "That's a beautiful name," I said. "She's a beautiful baby girl."

"Liebchen and I picked the name just a week ago."

Dr. Huntington explained that she was there to take the baby to the NICU in the mobile warmer just behind him. As he gave away his baby, he lapsed once again into a series of nods and "uh-huhs." The nurse placed Elizabeth in the isolette. I took the father by the shoulder and guided him back to his wife.

The collected surgeons, nurses, and techs were chafing to get to the OR, to get out of that room, finally. It seemed like an eternity since Sierra Doe had first rolled in, and the minute it took Richard to meet his daughter had been an excruciating pause. Matt and Prabhu were busting to get to the OR, a home turf of sorts, and be done with the ghastly nightmare. But they would be forced to endure it for another moment, as Richard took a step to his wife, and bent down to her ear.

"I've just been in to see our daughter," he said, choking on the word *daughter.* "Elizabeth. She's beautiful. Just like you."

Then he kissed her, lingering for a long moment, tears working their way down his face. "She loves her mommy. She told me to tell you."

And then it happened. Her eyelids twitched. Blinked. It was the last movement Liebchen ever made, and even now I think it was because she had heard him. In the darkening, closing paths and circuits of her brain, I am convinced she knew, just before she died, that she had given birth, was a mommy, and that her daughter was making her father so damn proud that she could finally let go.

No one else saw it besides Richard and me. I asked, and no one believes me. It hardly matters. She blinked. She acknowledged her husband's love and the birth of their daughter.

Richard stood up, ready to go, helpless and malleable once more. But halfway out of the room, he turned back to face us: a vast crowd, anonymous behind identical gowns, masks, and caps. He stopped and addressed the sea of eyes. "Thank you. All." He stuttered, trying to think of something else to add. "I mean, just thank you. All of you."

The door shut softly behind him. Sierra Doe's blink, her baby's flickering survival, the stunning synchronicity of these unexpected events for the benefit of a husband and father—it felt like perfection, like the apex of lifesaving, even with death, two deaths, around the corner. We had resuscitated battered humans before, but never with such graceful timing, never for such brief and rich reward.

As if a switch had been thrown, the team revived and broke into action, this time to disband. Someone kicked the brake from under the stretcher, releasing the wheels, and in another second the sea-blue and blood-spattered phalanx escorted Sierra Doe to the OR. A half-minute later, Dr. Huntington and her nurse rolled the isolette bearing Tango Doe silently away to the NICU. Both trauma rooms stood empty except for one or two housekeeping crew cleaning up.

Kathy and I exchanged glances, a few words, and we started to part company, too. The X-ray tech was hustling back toward us with a film's ugly truths and a confused, wondering look on her face. Everyone's gone, and she had something vital to share. "OR," I said.

"Look, though."

I held the black-gray film up to the light. "Yeah, okay." The head was attached only by skin and muscle, above a severed spine. Depending on where you stand, that's how it ends, or that's how it begins all over again.

Liebchen, once known as Sierra Doe, died at 9:46 P.M. She was taken to the operating room from the trauma bay, where a quick exploration of her abdomen turned up surprisingly little damage. The X-ray tech jogged in with the film revealing the fatal separation between head and neck. Matt studied it as he worked his fingers on her intestine. He sighed, shrugged, and instructed Prabhu and another junior resident to begin closing.

"See that?" he said. "Atlanto-occipital distraction."

The existing records fail to document how many times Richard held Elizabeth in his arms before she died the day after the accident. They are maddeningly dry with regard to her final moments: "The infant was removed from the ventilator, and within six minutes there was no heart rate. The infant made no respiratory efforts off the ventilator. Thus the heart stopped."

But I know what goes on.

The nurse takes the baby's isolette to a quiet room, picks a fresh blanket from the warmer, and sits the father in a comfortable rocker. She disconnects the monitors first—the alarms going off would be a cruel distraction—and then she caps off whatever IVs are running. This makes it a simpler matter to wrap the baby to make her look pretty and normal, and only then does she hand the baby over to the dad.

In a minute the nurse stops the ventilator. She breaks the connection between breathing tube and machine, and the baby's color fades, pink to ashy to deeply cyanotic, and the mingled sounds of crying and grief might fill the room. And then sometime later they will fade, too.

Almost to the day, four years later, Richard remarried. And almost to the day, two years after that, he held a baby girl in his arms once again, healthy, pink, kicking and crying. Which was the greatest act of faith? Getting married again? Crying for joy upon learning his wife was pregnant? Or something as subtle as watching her drive off to work one more time?

If asked, I'll tell you the most beautiful thing I can think of is this: At night, Richard puts his baby, Serena, to bed in the crib Liebchen's father made for another baby in another house in another life. Richard sings his daughter to sleep, and sometime later on he'll check on her once more.

PAPA DON'T PREACH

Benjamin Cheever

GEORGE W. BUSH said he'd kept his bust for drunken driving a secret because he didn't want his twin daughters to know. When the question arose if it wasn't better to tell children the truth, Dubya didn't answer. It pains me to say good things about George W. Bush, but I don't think I would have answered either. Not if the children were listening. Nor would I write this, if I thought they read Salon.

I used to be a full-disclosure father. I delighted my tiny sons with stories about shooting friends with BB rifles. I trotted out my nastiest and most obscene jokes. We laughed and laughed.

Then I heard that one of the boys had been repeating the jokes at school. He might easily have been suspended. "What if they don't find the BB gun stories amusing either?" I thought. "What if they find them instructive instead?"

Since then I've inhabited that anxious purgatory of half-truths and omissions where most of today's responsible parents with "youthful indiscretions" seem to dwell. Information is released in my house on a need-to-know basis. I don't want my boys to drink. If they do drink, I don't want them to be alone with their remorse.

When my fourteen-year-old drank scotch at a sleepover, he told me about it. So maybe this method is working. Besides, it's only fair that I should know when my children are drinking. I certainly knew when my parents were drinking. Does "always" ring any bells?

What strikes me most forcefully about the Dubya bombshell is that it is a bombshell at all. It's extraordinary how far we've come, or gone, depending upon your point of view. And how quickly we've forgotten.

"Here is the last of that generation of chain smokers who woke the world in the morning with their coughing," my father wrote in the introduction to *The Stories of John Cheever*, "who used to get stoned at cocktail parties and perform obsolete dance steps like the 'Cleveland Chicken.' " And boy, did they get stoned.

Nothing secret about it either. I was very little when I was taught how to lay my fingers along the side of a crystal glass so that if my father needed four fingers of Bellows Club bourbon, I knew how to get it. Flattered to be asked, thank you. Nobody had thought up the word *enabler* yet.

I remember one festive evening when a close family friend—a full partner at Morgan Stanley, if memory serves—fell down the stairs to the dining room. It wasn't the fall that made the evening remarkable, but rather the fact that the banker's highly polished shoes left scuff marks above the handrail. Scuff marks, which could be seen and admired the following morning.

My parents lived in a house with a drive that was lined with stone. My mother still lives there, although on more temperate terms. I remember standing out in the drive in the evening and watching as the dinner guests backed up until they hit the stone wall, crushed the lenses of their brake lights, and then drove off, the tinkle of broken glass playing against the roar of exhaust.

Home from boarding school, I went barhopping one night, and woke up at 5 A.M. with a splitting headache and the vivid recollection of having been in an accident. I was terrified. I knew boys who had been threatened with Culver Military Academy for less. Finally, I got out of bed. I went down to the drive and examined the car. Then I breathed a great sigh of relief. The family Studebaker was so badly scraped up, you couldn't tell which was my accident, or even if I'd had an accident at all.

I remember sitting in the boot of my father's red Karmann Ghia when he was driving my girlfriend back to her parents' house. The car jumped off the road and went right over one of the wooded islands sometimes left where several roads come together. Large rocks rushed by, branches swept over the hood. We bumped back onto the road and went on as if nothing had happened. Nobody said anything either. What was there to say?

Yes, I'm perfectly aware of the dangers of alcohol. My own beloved father had a terrible fight with the hooch, a fight he very nearly lost. "Allied to my melancholy is my struggle with Demon rum," he wrote in a letter to his friend, the novelist Josie Herbst. "There is a terrible sameness to the euphoria of alcohol and the euphoria of metaphor—the sense that the imagination is boundless—and I sometimes substitute or extend one with the other. My performance is sometimes comical. I leave my typewriter at a quarter after ten and wander downstairs to the pantry where the bottles are. I do not touch the bottles. I do not even look at the bottles and I congratulate myself fatuously on my willpower."

Drinking seems to me a little like driving a motorcycle, or jumping out of airplanes. Maybe you'll get tagged. Maybe you won't.

Please don't conclude, from all this, that I was primarily a victim of my father's illness. I was, of course, a victim of my love for him. But then so was he a victim of his love for me. I was a fat, arrogant, lonely little boy. During dinner, I'd get my feelings hurt and go upstairs and hide under the bed. My poor father would climb the stairs after me, lie down on the floor, and talk at me through the dust bunnies.

I'd violate parental edicts, go to a neighbor's house and see Wolfman movies, which left me horrified. I'd wake up at night screaming. I'd go into my parents' room, crawl in between them, fall asleep, and wet the bed.

We did the best we could.

It's great that people don't drink or smoke the way they used to. The gains in health and sanity should be substantial. I'm afraid sometimes, that we've lost something also. We're all so scared now. More scared than I was of the Wolfman. We're frightened of cancer, and of BB guns. We seem also to be afraid of the truth.

Which may be why we so rarely get it.

CURSE OF THE HIPPIE PARENTS

Sarah Beach

ONE SUMMER when I was ten or eleven, a boy I'll call Jackson befriended my brother and came over to our house frequently to play in our pond. After a few hours of splashing around, naked as usual, we went up to the house to dry off and have something to eat. Jackson plopped down on my mom's platform rocker, grabbed his penis, and started to masturbate.

"Hey!" I yelled, and threw a pillow at him. "Don't do that right in front of everybody!"

"My mom says, 'If it feels good, do it,'" he said, whacking away.

If it feels good, do it: a rallying cry of the '60s and the root of a lot of really awful parenting. Jackson may have been admirably comfortable with his body, but like many children of hippie parents, he was in the dark about some very basic social rules, such as the one that says "Don't jack off in public."

Growing up with no boundaries will do that to you. In their effort to raise children without inhibitions, my parents and their peers eschewed the teachings of Benjamin Spock and went for a more anarchic, Fellini-esque parenting approach. Sometimes this meant noodle dancing to Ravi Shankar into the wee hours of a school night, or spending whole days swimming naked and gorging on blackberries. But there was a dark side to this intoxicating rejection of rules and boundaries. With everyone embracing spontaneity and the mandates of the id, there was no one left to assume the adult role. People like my parents may have had the best of intentions, but in a wide-eyed quest for social change, they became children. And their actual children suffered as a result.

Sure, the benign neglect of hippie parenting had some side benefits. If you wanted to stay home from school, you could—as long as you had a really good excuse, such as, "I just can't get behind school today, Mom." Hippie kids also got to run around in the woods a lot, without being overly burdened by Establishment concepts like sunscreen or mosquito repellent. My mom took me on long walks, taught me to find wild huckleberries and to weave baskets out of sticks. She woke us up at midnight for impromptu waffle feasts. If we found something cool, like a dead dragonfly or a weird mushroom, she would be just as curious and amazed as we were. She was convinced magic existed, and since she was our mom, we absolutely believed it. That was wonderful.

However, the hippie creed of "no rules, no limits," combined with a horror of hypocrisy, sent groovy parents skidding down a dangerously slippery child-rearing slope. If you smoke pot, what are you going to do when your kids ask to try it? It would be hypocritical not to let them. And if pot's okay, why not mushrooms or acid? If you tell your kids sexual expression is great, and you yourself frequently "ball" (to use the mot juste) with abandon, how do you explain to your daughter that it's not okay for some crusty old guy at a Grateful Dead show to feel her up in the child-care tepee? The old standby "It's wrong because I said so" was out, because they'd taught us from birth that such a statement is fascistic. So, to avoid the hypocrisy of potentially arbitrary limits, hippie parents placed few or none.

And kids need limits. Someone in the family unit has to take the adult role, preferably the adults themselves. On the commune, I actually begged my mom for rules. "Let's have a rule where kids have to go to bed at a certain time every night!" I said. Or, "Let's have a rule that says children should be seen and not heard!" I think I'd read that in Dickens. It sounded like a great idea to me, not because I had some freakish desire to be silent, but because I knew I could never live up to it, and then perhaps I'd be punished. I longed for discipline, for someone to tell me, "That's quite enough of that, young lady!"

But in the hippie days, discipline was out, and wild Dionysian revelry was in. I can't remember the first time I smoked pot, though I do remember getting a joint for my seventh birthday, all wrapped up in a pink ribbon. And the love was certainly what they called "free." My mom tells me it was considered impolite not to sleep with someone when they asked politely. People would pair up, naturally, but relationships were strained by the constant lure of extracurricular screwing. The repression and conservatism of the fifties were rejected with a vengeance, and people coupled and separated and regrouped like pornographic square dancers.

This was presented to the children as the natural order of things, but we knew there was something wrong. For one thing, a dizzying number of people were always coming and going. Sometimes they'd say good-bye to the kids who had grown attached to them, sometimes not. We were terribly hurt when people we loved just up and left, and we were embarrassed by all the unfettered humping. Adults seemed so ridiculous with their balling and their toking and their weird wiggly dancing to the Grateful Dead. One evening at the commune, the grown-ups took Quaaludes or mescaline or something, and they all ended up in a big horny, writhing, drugged-out mass on the living room floor. At some point, my mom says, they heard an angry little throat-clearing sound. They looked up, and I was standing in the doorway, fists on my hips, glaring at them. "What exactly do you think you are all DOING?" I yelled.

Things weren't much better when my brother and I visited our father in San Francisco. Despite fairly clear evidence of some early heterosexuality, Dad had always had homosexual leanings. Just as the hippies violently rejected social norms at least partly in response to straitlaced convention, my father exploded out of the closet like a rocket fueled by repressed yearning. With the gay sexual revolution in San Francisco, he was finally free to express that side of himself openly. This was a wonderful thing, but the effects of it were confusing and bizarre for my brother and me.

With him, the Love That Dare Not Speak Its Name became the Love That Would Not Shut Up.

My father marched, he swung, he went to bars, he talked incessantly about his sexual experiences, and he left copies of *Torso* and *Honcho* strewn liberally about his Victorian house in the Haight. At first, my brother and I thought they were just some kind of new mainstream magazine. Certainly, they weren't any more male-centric than *Time* or *Life*. Thus misled, we spent many a frustrating hour trying to figure out what was so funny about Tom of Finland cartoons.

Confusingly enough, Dad also had some straight porn as well. I can kind of track his acceptance of his gayness over time by the dwindling ratio of *Penthouses* to *Honchos*. By the time I was nine or ten, he was full-strength, concentrated, half-a-cup-does-the-whole-load gay, and living with a really nice guy named—I'm not making this up—Randy.

On arriving at his house for a visit, after months of cultural deprivation up in the boonies, my brother and I would drop our duffel bags at the door and head for the television like patients in an obsessive/compulsive ward. We had lots of cultural-reference catching-up to do, and devoured the subtleties of *The Brady Bunch* and *Speed Racer.*

The trouble really started when Dad got a VCR. He quickly amassed a large collection of movies, most of them pirated and hand-labeled, and he didn't bother to segregate the porn. Some, like *The Young and the Hung,* were easy to avoid. Others were more worrying. My brother and I would consult each other over ambiguous titles like *Twelve Angry Men*. We finally got up the courage to watch that one, but no way were we going near *The 400 Blows*. We loved *Arsenic and Old Lace*, but it was kept right next to *Run, Little Sailor Boy, Run*. Once we put in the wrong tape, and were treated to the sight of a guy being fellated in an alley. "I don't think that's Alec Guinness," said my brother.

The open sexuality and lack of boundaries of the hippie era, which many parents thought would encourage their children to be happy little free spirits, often had diametrically opposite results. At age eight, I had a big crush on a commune guy I'll call Bill. That crush included sexual fantasies. I had just learned about rape, by overhearing someone tell a joke about it. They made it sound like a fun game, and I decided I wanted to try it with Bill. I went and found him, and told him I wanted to rape him. "Okay," he said.

I took him into the kids' building. He took off all his clothes and lay down. He had an erection. I took mine off too and lay down on top of him. He kissed and fondled me. After a while, he got up, kissed me on the top of the head, and thanked me. I felt confused and embarrassed.

Over the years, I had many inappropriate sexual experiences, with different partners and levels of interest on my part. The confusion and embarrassment were a constant. Even in less ambiguous situations in which I was exploited by predatory adults, I blamed myself for what happened. I had been raised to think that saying no was uncool, and that my body was up for grabs.

The worst part was that even when I was really uncomfortable with a sexual situation, I would sometimes respond sexually. This sent me into an abyss of self-loathing before I grew up and learned that children naturally have sexual feelings, and that they can arise even when the child is scared and unwilling.

My parents wanted to raise a happy, sexually liberated free spirit. I took the "free" part to heart, anyway. By the time I hit puberty I was already sexually jaded. I can't remember not knowing what went where, complete with variations and subroutines. From age eleven until I whipped up a new batch of self-esteem in my late twenties, I slept with so many people that I lost count at around 150. To this day, I can be standing at the sink washing a dish, woolgathering, and something will trigger a memory of a long-forgotten sexual encounter: the guy I slept with in the bathroom of a Greyhound bus, or the taxi driver I screwed for the sole reason that he had a cute Irish accent and I had no money for a tip.

I slept with my friends' boyfriends, or their fathers, just because they asked. I alienated a lot of people, mostly women. I was lucky to dodge the scarier of the venereal diseases, but I got a lot of urinary tract infections and had a few unplanned pregnancies. Hey, man—love the one you're with. Right. I'm pretty sure that an overfamiliarity with Bactrim and cannulae is not the beautiful expression of sexuality the hippies had in mind when they rejected traditional parenting.

But all this has a happy ending. Paradoxically, the dangerous freedom I was raised with was the thing that allowed me to rebuild my self-esteem and set boundaries for myself. I had been told for so long I could be anything I wanted to be that I finally figured out I could, by that same token, get over the anger I had for my parents. They had no child-raising instruction manual, and they lived through one of the most turbulent, strange times in our country's history.

In the course of working on this, I finally found ways to shock my mother. At one point I decided to become a lawyer, and when I told mom, she looked stricken. "Oh, no! Anything but that!" she said. "Honey, be a painter or a poet or something else instead!" I felt like a tax-payin', job-havin' James Dean. All I have to do to freak out my mom is work too hard, or mention my 401K.

Now I'm thirty-five and happily engaged to a wonderful man I've been with for five years. Life is good. I impose boundaries on myself and try to stick to them despite an innate rambunctiousness that won't quite go away. I love my mom, who lives close by, and I live right next door to my "other mom," a woman we met on the commune, who helped raise my brother and me and is now my best friend.

People who were raised by hippies are writing books now, and I'm finding out how common my experiences were. Chelsea Cain's excellent collection of essays, *Wild Child: Girlhoods in the Counterculture,* is full of stories similar to my own. I've interviewed a lot of ACHs (adult children of hippies), and we all pretty much agree: Loved the God's eyes and the baby goats; hated the lack of Lucky Charms, boundaries, and discipline. We have nice traits in common, like adaptability, resourcefulness, and a tendency to be more open-minded than not. But we are all a little bit control-freakish, and we have no patience for people who romanticize the hippie era uncritically. An accidental Wavy Gravy sighting can send us into a frothing rage.

Which brings me to why I'm writing this. In the past few years, hippie culture has had something of a revival. Hippie music, hippie clothes, hippie politics, even hippie hairdos, are big. More and more, I see VW buses with cedar peaked-roof add-ons, lumbering up Highway 1 on their way to Reggae on the River, the happy scruffy singing hippies inside dandling little newborns in tie-dyed Garanimals.

It isn't surprising that in an era tinged with the paranoid ul-traconservatism of the fifties, people seem to want back some of the sixties freedom and revolutionary feeling. The George W. Bush presidency is almost enough to make me sell everything and buy one of those buses myself. Almost.

Growing out of the anger I felt has allowed me to admit that I also long for some of the feeling of that age, but I don't want nouvelle-hippie parents to make the same mistakes with their kids that the first hippies did. Once you have kids, finding your-self should never trump the goal of giving your kids a safe, thoughtfully limited environment.

So this is a cautionary tale. Go ahead, eat carob. Weave your own dashiki. Get off the grid. Open your mind to new experiences. But when your microbus pulls into the festival lot, don't drop acid and ditch your daughter at the child-care tepee. Sometimes your mind can be so open, your brain falls out.

SUPPLICANT

Kathryn Harrison

MOTHER, I still dream of you, and how beautiful you look. Thick dark hair that catches the sunlight, cheeks as pale and smooth as a funerary angel's, eyes that smolder with misery, lips painted with promises. Cosmetics can't achieve the kind of glamour you command. It's you in your twenty-fifth year, seen through my starstruck seven-year-old eyes, and even in sleep, I'm paralyzed by desire. How can I hold you? How can I keep you? I awake exhausted from the excitement of your presence.

Long ago, love made me a beggar, grateful for a glimpse, a touch, the hem of your dress brushing past. Because I've missed you all my life, your death feels, perhaps, less awful than another mother's might to another daughter. I tell myself it does. After all, I'm used to my longing.

When he was small, our son—your grandson—used to confuse the word *love* with the word *miss*. At bedtime, he would take my face in his hands. "I miss you!" he'd say, his voice ragged with passion.

"But I'm right here," I'd answer. "I'm right here with you." I couldn't correct him. Hadn't he, after all, gotten it right?

When you died, this is what I said to myself: It's over. At twenty-four, I was young enough to imagine that death would mark the end of our relationship. I'd looked forward to your dying; it seemed the one thing that might release us both—you from cancer, me from a vigil that began with my birth.

"Hostage," you called me. The word you wanted was *surrogate*, but you were in a hurry. We were driving through Coldwater Canyon, about to arrive at the end of the conversation. I was twelve, and you were trying once again to explain how things were the way they were. What had happened was this: You'd given me to your mother; I was the price of your freedom. But at eighteen you didn't know what a baby was worth, didn't know that you'd just rearranged the terms of your own captivity.

Hostage. I said the word silently to myself until the syllables collapsed into nonsense.

After your death, when I didn't know what a mother was worth, I determined that you would remain the only one to have brought me to my knees, to have made me beg. Not in front of you, never in front of you—I had my pride—but you knew that every star wished on, every prayer whispered, every candle lighted, was yours. A ransom's worth.

After your death, I tried to imagine what the circumstances might be that could tempt me back into a posture of supplication. As it has turned out, I bow my head eagerly. Each night, by my son's bed, knees mortified by Legos, elbows planted among stuffed animals, I'm being rehabilitated. Your grandson no longer mistakes *miss* for *love*. And as for your daughter, she is making progress.

MY FOUR FAVORITE PHOTOS OF MY MOTHER

Amy Bloom

PHOTO AT age six: My mother is in a dark wool coat, with fuzzy, ivory collar and cuffs and a matching tam. She wears baggy ivory woolen stockings and black leather lace-ups. She's leaning, fondly, on a huge, curvy white wicker baby carriage, which I believe contained my cousin Abby, who grew up to be the bejeweled, buxom, much-married, and eternally glamorous Elizabeth Taylor of the Bloom family (and of the Blume family—my uncle changed it out of some misguided sense of upward mobility).

My mother's misgiving is revealed in her dubious glance, which is not uncharacteristic, even now. She has the same wide face and dark brows for the next seventy-four years of photographs, and if you get tired of looking at her, you have only to look at photos of me and my daughters. We have the more assimilated noses, my girls have the more goyish eyebrows, and only my youngest daughter has my mother's astonishing skin, magnolia-blossom skin, which was smooth until she was in her mid-sixties.

PHOTO AT age twenty: My mother is sleeping on her bunk at Brookwood Camp. She is ridiculously lovely, like an exquisite infant, and I want to stop the world right here. Why should she have to have and lose children, suffer disappointment, arthritis, mortality? Her dark curls tumble about the pillow, and a loose grosgrain ribbon lies among them. She sleeps as I sleep, head at the edge of the pillow, left arm flung protectively over right shoulder.

On the little wooden table beside her is a coil of worn clothing—my mother's bra and T-shirt—and the casualness of the rumpled clothing is erotic, moving, and reassuring. We are a long line of untidy women, and it has always been a comfort to know that the thought of checking my furniture for dust and my pantry for order would no more occur to my mother than would hang gliding or making a pie from scratch.

PHOTO AT AGE TWENTY-FOUR: This is the killer. My mother the movie star. Makes Betty Grable look sick. Makes Ava Gardner look to her heels. Sleek, glossy dark waves. Slightly slanted hazel eyes (my sister and I make do with tinted lenses), long black lashes. Peach skin over high cheekbones, and that wide jaw. Outrageous, bodice-ripper lips painted dark red. Snug black blouse over discreet but unmistakably great breasts. Resistance heroine, Madame President, White House correspondent—all the lives I would have liked for her to have are almost possible in this picture.

PHOTO AT AGE FORTY: My mother's hair is shorter, worn in a 1960s updo and more auburn than it's been (but darker than it will be when she makes the leap to the middle-aged russet and ash blond that seems to appeal to dark-haired women when they begin to gray). She looks like a very successful queen of some Russian-French feminist empire—kind to her subjects, cruel to her enemies, and confident in her consorts.

She chose the fabric for that gown, as she did for all those ball gowns, and Mrs. Whosie, the seamstress in Great Neck, sewed a column of dark blue and gold cut-velvet flowers on a sheer dull gold net—and around her wide, white shoulders, over the still-beautiful breasts, a stole of dark-blue satin.

THESE seem to me to be my mother's true selves, utterly separate from her life as mother, almost invisible to her children, as real as uncut gems.

BEING FROSTY JR.

David Vernon

CHRISTMAS EVE, Hollywood, 1969: My mom, my younger sister, Tracey, and I sit in front of our brand-new ten-inch Zenith television. I'm seven years old, and Tracey is five. Our TV trays are still littered with the remnants of sloppy joes and Tater Tots. At eight o'clock a large voice, like the voice of God, booms out of the TV: "Our regularly scheduled program will not be shown tonight so that we may present the premiere of a new holiday classic, *Frosty the Snowman*." Tracey and I twist in our beanbags, preparing ourselves for what will follow.

I'm sure that children across the country were watching the same program that night, but this Christmas special meant something deeper to our family, because our father was the voice of Frosty.

Months before the special aired, I vaguely remember my father landing the gig that would change—or at least add an interesting footnote—to his career. He was an unusual choice for a holiday special. Jackie Vernon was a stand-up comic who had found success in nightclubs across America doing routines about how he used to be a dull guy, delivered in a slow monotone. His other famous routine was a nonexistent slide show that detailed his many disastrous vacations. Since Christmas and New Year's were my father's busiest months, I never associated him with Christmas trees or Christmas cheer. He typically spent the holidays by himself in New York or Las Vegas while we celebrated at home in Los Angeles.

Even my father seemed to be mystified by the fact that he was chosen to be Frosty. When asked, his standard and quite honest answer was, "Guess all the other fat guys were out of town that week."

My father was working a club date in Chicago the night Frosty debuted. He hadn't said a word about it, so as we watched the opening credits, we had no idea what to expect.

The show began with Jimmy Durante singing the "Frosty the Snowman" song. My sister and I, who had inherited our mother's cynicism, started criticizing the show right away.

"It's not much of a song, as far as holiday songs go," I said.

"It's a baby song," my sister Tracey announced.

"Lots of people recorded it, but I don't think anyone made it into a big hit," my mother told us, lighting her first postdinner Virginia Slim. " 'Hark! The Herald Angels Sing,' now that's a standard."

Finally a magician's hat flew onto a snowman's head, transforming the rounded lumps of sculpted ice into Frosty, a living, breathing entity. Delighted to be alive, Frosty opens his tiny, animated mouth and says, "Happy Birthday"—in my father's voice.

At first it was hard to hear my father's voice coming out of a crudely drawn walking, talking snowman. But soon I started to see that my father and Frosty shared certain physical characteristics. Frosty had a sly smile, the same expression that my father had when, for example, he was supposed to be on a diet and we'd catch him at 2 A.M. in his bathroom making spaghetti and clams in a portable coffeemaker. After a few minutes the only thing that didn't seem familiar was the kind, delicate way that Frosty spoke. Then I pictured Frosty in his jockey shorts calling from his upstairs bedroom, "Cripes, how many times do I have to ask, will someone bring me a can of Tab?" I was home free from there.

The show was upbeat enough. But then the plot turned, and something unpleasant happened. An evil magician had trapped Frosty in a hothouse. He began to melt. At first there were just tiny beads of sweat, but they quickly turned into a downpour. By the time Santa broke into the hothouse, all that was left of Frosty was a thick puddle and his tiny man-made facial features.

I stared at the screen in disbelief. The show wasn't supposed to turn out this way. My father was not supposed to die. Pandemonium broke out in our rumpus room. The cartoon girl on the TV started crying, Tracey started crying, then I burst into tears. My mother had a train wreck on her hands.

"Frosty's gone!" the girl on the TV bawled.

"What happened to Daddy?" I yelled.

"Daddy!" my sister wailed.

With the dexterity of a linebacker, my mother turned off the television, scooped Tracey up into her arms, grabbed me by the hand, and brought us upstairs to our bedroom.

No matter what our mother said, my sister and I were absolutely convinced that we'd just witnessed our father's demise on national television. "He's not dead," she said. "He's in Chicago, working the Playboy Club." My mother called my father in Chicago, but he wasn't in his hotel room, which only confirmed our worst suspicions.

We didn't hear from my father until the next afternoon. My mother made us both get on the phone extensions while my father explained that at the end of the show Frosty comes back to life.

"How does he come back to life?" Tracey asked.

My father admitted that he didn't remember. "It's the hat or some magic wind or Santa. Jeez, I did the show so long ago, I don't remember."

Our mother wisely decided to take us out on the night *Frosty the Snowman* played the following December, so it wasn't until two years later that my sister and I saw the scene where Frosty, aided by Santa and the magic hat, returns to life. But still the image of my father as a puddle of water haunted me for years.

Maybe in other parts of the country there are places where having your father be the star of a treasured Christmas special would make you the envy of the schoolyard. But not in Los Angeles. In our school, everyone's mother or father was some type of celebrity, and there were hierarchies of fame. You don't know the depths of humiliation until Helen Reddy's daughter laughs in your face and calls you "Frosty Jr." I'd get more general reactions along the lines of, "I wanted to watch *The Brady Bunch* Friday night but my mom made me watch that Frosty the Freakman instead. Frosty's a wimp! I hate that show! You suck!"

There was one area, though, in which my sister and I could claim a semblance of pride. Year after year, Frosty kicked snowman ass in the ratings. While other holiday specials fell into oblivion (*The Year Without a Santa Claus,* anyone?), *Frosty the Snowman* had undeniable staying power. Tracey and I kept track of the ratings. We made charts and discussed any upward or downward trends.

"We're down five points this year!" I'd exclaim.

"But all the specials are down. Rudolph's down twelve! It's still acceptable."

Tracey and I were having these conversations before we'd even reached puberty. There were a lot of other children of TV actors at our school. We figured that even if our father couldn't beat up their fathers, at least he could kill them in the Nielsen ratings.

My father also participated in a sequel to *Frosty the Snowman* called *Frosty's Winter Wonderland.* In it, Frosty falls in love with a snowwoman and gets married. Frosty's wife was voiced by Shelley Winters. After a promising first-year rating, the sequel eventually fell by the wayside without diminishing the appeal of the original.

Eventually I lost track of the Frosty specials. I never watched them and rarely told anyone about my father's role in them. Once, while at college in New York, I met a guy at a Christmas party who was flying high on something. We were playing that old "my family is weirder than yours" college game. But when I told him that my father was Frosty the Snowman, his mood shifted to one of nearly religious reverence.

"My brothers and I, we got it all figured out," he told me. "See, Frosty is Christ. The song says, 'Frosty the Snowman was a fairy tale they say.' Just like Jesus. Nobody thinks he's for real either. Frosty marches with his group of disciples, and teaches them how to love and stuff. My brother and I wind and rewind that tape. We've got it all down!"

I wanted to tell him that I was pretty sure that Jesus was not who the writers were thinking of when they created Frosty. Jesus at least had something to teach and some kind of message to impart. Frosty's most complex message was "Happy Birthday," a mantra he repeated whenever his magic hat was put back on his head.

"But the best part of it," the guy continued, "is the redemption. Jesus dies and is reborn. Frosty dies and is reborn. Jesus is going to come back. And Frosty's coming back. The last words of the TV special? 'I'll be back on Christmas Day!' Which is what?" The guy looked at me, annoyed that I needed to be prompted. "Jesus' birthday."

"I thought some scientists got together and decided that Jesus' birthday was in July or something," I said, excusing myself.

"What do scientists know?" he asked in disbelief. As if the world of science was much less conversant with absolute truth than the world of Hollywood Christmas specials.

Later, one thing from that conversation stayed in my mind—the concept of redemption. From my very first viewing of the special, I had missed Frosty's resurrection. And in the years that followed I had always found there to be something lacking in my Christmas holiday—a sense of completion, of redemption, perhaps.

The next year I was in Los Angeles over the holidays and decided to talk to Tracey about this matter. Tracey had gone in a completely different direction than I had in terms of celebrating the holidays. Her apartment was filled with Christmas cheer. She always bought the largest tree she could find and decorated it with antique ornaments. Her living room housed a miniature collectible Christmas village, filled with endless replicas of shoppes and cottages. Her windows were frosted with bottled snow that had been manufactured by Monsanto, and continuous Christmas music filled the apartment.

I went to visit her the day after Christmas and was surprised to see her Christmas tree outside the apartment near the trash. I went inside and found that every frosted window, every clipping of plastic mistletoe, every component of her Christmas village, any evidence of Christmas, had been cleaned up and boxed. When I arrived, she was furiously trying to yank strands of silver tinsel out of her vacuum cleaner. It was at that point that I realized my sister had probably missed out on the whole Christmas-as-redemption thing as well. Luckily my ailment was just a general ennui, while it seemed like Tracey was suffering from Christmas anorexia.

As my father got older, I was surprised to find out how proud he was about being the voice of Frosty. He would do his Frosty voice for children, sometimes without a request. Several times I was with him when strangers asked him where they knew him from. He'd always tell them about Frosty. I found this odd coming from a man who had worked with Judy Garland and Barbra Streisand, who was a sensation on *The Ed Sullivan Show* and had been a constant guest on *The Tonight Show* and *Merv*.

He returned one last time to do another Frosty special, a feature film called *Frosty and Rudolph, Christmas in July*. It paired up the two most famous Christmas characters, but to little avail. Like a movie matching up two aging idols who used to command their own films, this animated special carried about it a whiff of desperation and futility. It never made it to the theaters.

My father died in 1987. All of the obituaries remembered him as the voice of Frosty. I doubt that this was what my father was aiming for when he first ventured into show business, but I knew from talking to him that he was proud of the association.

A year later, I was surfing channels on TV, and landed directly onto the animated image of a puddle of water alongside a top hat. My first inclination was to change the channel; his death was too new for me to want to watch this. But I kept watching. Like the children watching it everywhere, I felt despair over Frosty's death. But then, even though I knew what was coming, I found myself surprised when Frosty magically returned to life. If my life were a Christmas special, this would be the part where my heart grows two sizes, or where, after seeing those three hoary ghosts, I'd march down the snowy streets, barking "Merry Christmas" at all my enemies. In short: I got it. Frosty was alive, so a part of my father was alive.

There is a new Frosty special, called *Frosty Returns*, voiced by John Goodman. I didn't watch it because I didn't want anything to challenge my memory of my father as Frosty. I was not alone. As petty as it sounds, Tracey and I were delighted to note that *Frosty Returns* was killed in the ratings.

Recently I watched the original with my five-year-old nephew, Gage. Frosty comes on the TV screen, and I tell Gage that Frosty is his grandfather. Gage gives me an incredulous look. "Huh? My grandfather's a snowman?" Gage laughs, and I laugh. I let it go for now. But I know in the coming years it will mean something to him. The voice of the grandfather he never met will march on throughout all the Christmases of his future.

MY FATHER'S LEGACY

George Packer

THE SUMMER before he killed himself, my father assigned me a reading list that was fairly daunting for a twelve-year-old. *Catcher in the Rye* was on it, and some Frost poems, and a short history of the Civil War, and Kenneth Clark's *Civilization*, which I still haven't finished. *Julius Caesar* was the highlight. The list was my initiation into the high-ceilinged sanctum of my parents' study, the grown-up world of books and ideas. Then it became my father's legacy. In despair over his paralysis from a stroke, he left the house one Monday in December and never came back.

In the months after his suicide I became obsessed by the idea that I now had to read every book in the world, because my father was no longer there to assign me some and not others. This prospect sent my head spinning. Sometimes, lying on my bed, I would become aware of my thoughts as if I were reading them in a book and then imagine (I was taking a typing class at school) my fingers hitting the keys that spelled out my ideas as I thought them.

I needed order, and it came from an unexpected place—the list of titles on the back of the Cliffs Notes guide to *Julius Caesar*, which I'd bought for advice in staging a backyard theatrical. This black-and-yellow friend of delinquent college students became my highest authority on great literature, and the number of books that had to be read suddenly dwindled to about two hundred: *Ivanhoe,* for example, and *Black Like Me* (but not *Remembrance of Things Past*). I sat down and assigned myself four listed titles a month, calculating that by the age of eighteen I would have read everything worth reading.

Almost immediately I fell behind (*The Aeneid* was heavy going), but the list itself wasn't discredited by this failure—only I was. My father's death had warped my relation to books—a love affair ever since *Where the Wild Things Are,* when I walked around the house for days believing I was Max—into something systematic and compulsory. I anesthetized the part of myself that was alive to literature's capacity for shock, delight, terror. The simple telling of a story no longer held any value; now I had to master each book, which meant wrestling its theme down to a single sentence. This sentence was often buried somewhere in the text, and I would spend tormented hours digging it up—unless it was available on the Modern Library jacket, which, for example, told me that the theme of *Crime and Punishment* is that crime is its own punishment. Once I had the theme under control, I would underline the title on the Cliffs Notes list and move on.

It was as if, by plowing through the world's great literature, I could keep the world itself at bay and stop the spinning in my head.

Ideally, reading means getting lost. The process of surrendering and then recovering the self might be the essence of growing up—being exposed to an alien world and, instead of being broken down and destroyed, absorbing it, making it your own. But that year, the thought of losing myself was quite real and frightening. I might plunge into the depths of a book and never come back up. "If phantasies become over-luxuriant and over-powerful," Freud wrote, "the conditions are laid for an onset of neurosis or psychosis." He added, ominously, "Here a broad by-path branches off into pathology."

So I read and read, checking off titles and hoarding themes, without letting a germ enter my bloodstream.

At the same time, I was discovering an entirely different sort of literary pleasure. It had nothing to do with the rational education I was receiving at home and school, and it gave me the crucial intimation that ideas might be no match for the power of feeling. In the year of my father's death I also came up with my own secret reading list. It included *Story of O, Lady Chatterley's Lover,* and *Fanny Hill.* It involved researching key passages in *Fear of Flying* and *The Godfather.* The books originated, like all literature, in the study, but they ended up in the bathroom, where questions of theme never came up.

There was nothing abstract about this reading. Instead of demanding impossible feats of self-discipline, it permitted brief escape from the confines of my other, classics-mongering self. Its satisfactions were easily available and quite concrete. It presented the same, limited, and always successful reading project every time. On the cover of *Story of O,* a critic called the book "a total literary experience." I snickered at this piece of adult hypocrisy; my experience was something else.

In a coming-of-age letter he typed out for me the summer of the reading list, my father had suggested that if I found myself doing this "once a day, or even more," I should talk about it with him or my mother. The suggestion seemed far-fetched, and the quota low. I carried out this secret reading like a criminal, pinning *Story of O* under my shirt as I made the dangerous journey from the bathroom down the hall back to the study, where I hastily returned Pauline Reage into the gap on the shelf and made sure her white spine was flush with those of her more respectable neighbors, to keep her (whoever she was) from betraying me.

In the summer of 1974, my mother took my sister and me to London. London meant ground zero of great books—half of the Cliffs Notes list came from London. But the literary experience I still remember from that summer involved neither Shakespeare nor Dickens.

My mother had a collection of contemporary short fiction called *The Naked I*, in which there was a story by Robert Coover called "The Babysitter," with a good deal of metafictional fantasizing about a teenage girl. The language performed its usual magic—too well, for one afternoon while my mother and sister were off doing something cultural, I accidentally stained the relevant pages of *The Naked I* beyond repair. The power of words to make us forget ourselves! In an instant the baby-sitter in the bathtub vanished, and the book became printed text on a page, which I had just defiled.

Panicking, I smuggled the evidence out of the apartment in a brown paper bag and went hunting for a garbage can. Block after block, there was no garbage can. My package felt as if it was about to blow up or start wailing like an alarm. At last I spotted a Dumpster—but it stood on the other side of a high chain-link fence. I looked up and down the street, then flung the brown-bagged book and watched with amazement and relief as it sailed over the fence and landed inside. I turned to run.

"What did you just chuck in that rubbish bin?"

A few feet away, two enormous bobbies under blue helmets were staring me down.

"What did you just chuck in that rubbish bin?"

"A book," I murmured.

"What book?" The bobbies looked tense and angry. As in a nightmare, their arrival made complete sense.

"A book of short stories."

"Why'd you want to get rid of it?"

"I was finished reading it."

I could see that they didn't believe a word. One of them narrowed his eyes. "How do we know it wasn't a bomb?"

This was the summer of the Cyprus crisis. The rubbish bin stood near the National Bank of Greece, which the police suspected me of trying to blow up. I swore it wasn't true, while the burning in my cheeks betrayed my real crime. Silently I resolved to spend the rest of the summer pursuing themes from the Cliffs Notes list. The bobbies had provided a perfect lesson in the danger of over-luxuriant fantasy. Mercifully, they didn't order me after the evidence, but instead let me go with a warning about not chucking things into rubbish bins and running away. I slunk back to the apartment and waited for my mother to come through the door looking for her short-story collection. But she never asked about it.

Like all splits, mine—between words and feelings, themes and stories, reading and living—was bound for a reckoning. It came ten years later, on the west coast of Africa, where I'd gone with the Peace Corps to teach English to village kids. From the first days, my head started spinning, just as it had after my father's death. Under the African sun, or in my room at the edge of the village, everything I once valued sounded as hollow as the hot hours in the middle of the day, when a crowing cock broke the silence like an insane herald of nothingness. As the rational world disintegrated, I turned for help to the only familiar things at hand—my books.

I had packed them with the malaria pills and snakebite kit, and they were lined up on the cement floor under a shuttered window that looked out on a papaya tree. In the early afternoons, while the village dozed in the peaceful sleep of the ontologically whole, I searched Kierkegaard's *Sickness Unto Death* for the causes of my despair. "When the enchantment of illusion is broken, when existence begins to totter, then too does despair manifest itself as that which was at the bottom." According to Kierkegaard, I wasn't even a self—which was why I was in despair. He explained my situation with dialectical beauty, and it made no difference.

I picked up Jung and found the archetype of the shadow, the antagonistic counter-self. "If we are able to see our own shadow and can bear knowing about it, then a small part of the problem has already been solved." I began to think that my problem lay in the period of my father's suicide—in all that had been repressed through things like reading lists. I went back ten years and tried to retrieve everything. But even as Jung explained the shadow, I noticed that it still rose with me every dawn, stood beside me before a classroom of African children, sat with me at night as I tuned the radio to the BBC.

I went looking for my frightened self in fiction. In Conrad I read: "How can you imagine what particular region of the first ages a man's untrammeled feet may take him into by the way of solitude—utter solitude without a policeman—by the way of silence— utter silence, where no warning voice of a kind neighbor can be heard whispering of public opinion? These little things make all the great difference. When they are gone you must fall back upon your own innate strength, upon your own capacity for faithfulness." And elsewhere in Conrad (Conrad knew everything about me): "The truth was that he died from solitude, the enemy known but to few on this earth, and whom only the simplest of us are fit to withstand. The brilliant Costaguanero of the boulevards had died from solitude and want of faith in himself and others."

I read late into the night, and while the wick of my kerosene lamp burned down, I entered the world of the imagination so deeply that for the first time since childhood I lost my way.

Everywhere words led, down through the *Inferno,* into *Heart of Darkness,* at *A Bend in the River,* they mastered me with their suggestive power. The themes had escaped my brain and slipped into my bloodstream. Those nights in Africa with a kerosene lamp finally acquainted me with the total literary experience, and it freed me to tell the tale.

SENTIMENTAL HOGWASH

Douglas Cruickshank

MOTHER'S DAY is sentimental hogwash. My mother taught me that. Those were the exact words she used. They were also the words she wrote in the notes she sent with me to grammar school every year in early May, starting when I was in Mrs. Eagerblade's fourth-grade class. (Yes, Eagerblade was her real name. And it had a sobering effect on bad boys with intense powers of visualization.)

Anyway, my mother, who was born in the same year—1914—that President Woodrow Wilson declared Mother's Day a national holiday, would send notes to school so that I could be excused from participating in classroom Mother's Day projects—card making, picture drawing, poem writing, and the like. She found Mother's Day maudlin, sappy, dull, and dimwitted, she told me, and she didn't want me observing it.

Needless to say, our family didn't go out for a special brunch on the second Sunday in May, nor did we bake a cake. "If nothin' says lovin' like somethin' from the oven," my mother once remarked, "I wouldn't have all these kids."

She was a typical mother, as far as I knew. Sometimes she'd take my siblings and me on picnics—to the local cemetery, where we'd eat salami sandwiches, then while away the summer afternoons searching for the tombstones with oval photos of dead people on them; the water-damaged ones were best. Other times, she'd pack up my pet tortoise in a shoe box and hike the three miles to my school so that my favorite reptile could join me during the lunch hour. "He's a quiet pet, isn't he?" she said once, looking at the soup-bowl-size creature, "but very good company."

We didn't take vacations, so when tortoises and tombstones were no longer enough, she'd commit herself (or be committed) to the local franchise of the state mental hospital for a month or three or five. It wasn't exactly a spa—the place favored electroshock treatment over exercycles—but it did afford a long-term, low-priced break from the rigors of life, and all the Thorazine you could eat. On weekends we'd visit her there.

This sounds drearier in retrospect than it seemed at the time. A child's reference points—to the degree they exist at all—are different from an adult's. You're eight, you're nine—what's normal? Who knows? Once the grown-ups calmed down (and her sedation kicked in), the weekend outings to the mental hospital, where there were many strangely attired, slow-moving adults behaving oddly and wearing Mona Lisa smiles, were not boring but novel, and therefore good. On visiting days, my mother's spirits were high, sometimes very high, other times very, very high. And the place had big lawns, big trees, and plenty of vending machines.

The electrical charges and chemical relief, however, did little to mellow my mother's contempt for Mother's Day. One spring Sunday when we were visiting, she asked a passing psychiatrist she knew for a pen and a sheet off his prescription pad so she could write what would be the first of many annual hogwash missives to my teacher. But she decided to interrogate the good doctor first.

"Mother's Day is sentimental hogwash, don't you agree?"

"Oh, I do," the shrink answered. "I really do." He was a good soul, and savvy.

"I'm glad to hear you say that," she said while she quickly scribbled the note. "I think we're the only two sane ones in here." The doctor chortled.

"Though I'm not so sure about you," she yelled after him as he walked off.

That got a big laugh all around. Even at nine years old, I knew that saying a head doctor might be out of his head was hilarious. It was a laugh a minute at the nut hut—much more fun than Mrs. Eagerblade's class.

The next day I walked into fourth grade and handed over the note. The teacher rolled her eyes. When I explained the situation to several classmates, they all said that my mom must be crazy, except for my friend Geoff, who was Goth a quarter century before Goth was cool.

The cumulative effect of those notes over my entire grammar school career was not only to relieve me of complicity in the great annual groundswell of sentimental hogwash that my mother found too saccharine to condone, but to illuminate the utility of a good bullshit detector, a bad attitude, and a degree of guerrilla jocularity when confronted with institutionalized nonsense.

As for my mother, her life continued for decades longer. She would go for years without a stay in the loony bin. There'd be long stretches of good times, travel, church activities, voracious reading. Then, as she once described it to me, the snake would begin eating at her heart (a paraphrased line, I believe, from her favorite author, Thomas Wolfe).

The last time I visited her on a psychiatric ward was in the early 1980s, a couple of years before she died. When I arrived, she was sitting in a hospital room, looking out the window toward the eastern hills of the San Francisco Bay Area, the hills where she lived.

"Oh, here's my brother," she said to a nurse who was just leaving.

"No," I said, "I'm your son."

"That's right," she said.

"Is this a Christ healing place?" she asked.

"It's a hospital," I answered.

"Really? It doesn't seem like one. There's all this funny equipment and the people and all. First I was down there, but then they moved me, and now I'm not sure where we are."

"This is Eden Hospital," I said. "You can almost see your house from here." I pointed toward the hills.

"Eden . . . ," she repeated.

A short time later a male attendant walked in, pushing a

wheelchair. "Hi," he said to her. "It's time to go downstairs for your spinal tap."

"That sounds fun," she said.

I walked beside her as she was wheeled down the hall to the elevator. "So where do you come from?" the attendant asked her.

"I come from Alabamy with a banjo on my knee," she replied.

I was returning home to Los Angeles that afternoon and wouldn't see her again for a long time. As we waited for the elevator, she reached over to me. "You know," she whispered, holding my hand, "they say I'm losing my mind, but I don't miss it."

AUTHOR BIOGRAPHIES

SARAH BEACH

Sarah Beach is a writer living in Berkeley, California.

AMY BLOOM

Amy Bloom is the author of *A Blind Man Can See How Much I Love You, Come to Me,* and a novel, *Love Invents Us.* Her work has appeared in *The New Yorker, The Atlantic Monthly,* and *Harper's Bazaar,* among other publications, and in many anthologies, including *The Best American Short Stories; Prize Stories: The O. Henry Awards;* and *The Scribner Anthology of Contemporary Short Fiction.* A practicing psychotherapist, she lives in Connecticut and teaches at Yale University.

GAYLE BRANDEIS

Gayle Brandeis is the author of *Fruitflesh: Seeds of Inspiration for Women Who Write* (HarperSanFrancisco) and *The Book of Dead Birds: A Novel* (HarperCollins), which won the Bellwether Prize for Fiction in Support of a Literature of Social Responsibility established by Barbara Kingsolver. She lives in Riverside, California, with her husband and their two children.

BENJAMIN CHEEVER

Selling Ben Cheever was published by Bloomsbury USA in the fall of 2001. A novel, *The Good Nanny,* will be brought out by the same house next year.

CHRIS COLIN

Chris Colin, a former Salon.com editor, is writing a book about his former high school classmates. Broadway Books will publish it in May 2004.

TIM CORNWELL

Tim Cornwell is the deputy foreign editor for the *Scotsman* in Edinburgh.

DOUGLAS CRUICKSHANK

Douglas Cruickshank is a former Salon.com editor. He lives near San Francisco.

MATTHEW DEBORD

Matthew DeBord is the author of *New York Wine.* A former editor at *Wine Spectator,* he has written for numerous magazines, newspapers, and websites. He lives in Brooklyn with his wife and daughter.

LAURIE ESSIG

Laurie Essig is a writer who has contributed to Salon.com, NPR's "All Things Considered," and *Legal Affairs*. She also teaches sociology at UVM and is currently working on a book on Coney Island, U.S.A.

SUZANNE FINNAMORE

Suzanne Finnamore is a native of North Carolina. She is the author of *The Zygote Chronicles* and *Otherwise Engaged,* both novels.

MARGARET FINNEGAN

Margaret Finnegan received a P.h.D. in history from UCLA. She has taught at various universities, and lives and writes in Los Angeles. She is the author of *Selling Suffrage: Consumer Culture and Votes for Women.*

LIZA WEIMAN HANKS

Liza Weiman Hanks is a writer and estate planner in California who is now the mother of two children.

KATHRYN HARRISON

Kathryn Harrison's novels include *Thicker than Water, Exposure, Poison, The Binding Chair,* and *The Seal Wife.* She is the author of two memoirs, *The Kiss* and *Seeking Rapture,* and of the Penguin Lives biography, *Saint Thérèse of Lisieux,* as well as a meditation on travel, *The Road to Santiago,* which is forthcoming this fall. She lives in New York with her husband, novelist Colin Harrison, and their three children.

HEATHER HAVRILESKY

Heather Havrilesky is Salon's TV and entertainment correspondent. Before joining Salon, she was senior editor of Suck.com, where she created the cartoon "Filler" with illustrator Terry Colon. Her writing has appeared in *Spin, The Washington Post,* and on NPR's "All Things Considered," and her Website, rabbitblog.com, is widely embraced by a select few.

JENNIFER BINGHAM HULL

Jennifer Bingham Hull is a Miami writer who reports on women's issues and international affairs.

ERIN AUBRY KAPLAN

Erin J. Aubry is a staff writer at the *L.A. Weekly* and a contributor to *Mothers Who Think: Tales of Real-Life Parenthood,* edited by Camille Peri and Kate Moses (Villard).

JILL KETTERER

Jillian Ketterer writes poetry and nonfiction. Currently, she lives in Pittsburgh and works as a psychology lab manager, but she hopes to relocate to Chicago in a few years to teach high school

English. Her interests include reading, studying human sexuality, and eating mushrooms.

CARA KLIEGER

Cara Klieger is a writer and attorney who has lived in Micronesia, Ottawa, and Liverpool, and has taught writing in both Memphis and New York City. Also a former talent manager, she has never abandoned her first love—pop music—and continues to pore over the charts from her uneasy chair on the East Coast, U.S.A.

JONATHAN KRONSTADT

Jonathan Kronstadt is a writer and stay-at-home father of two living in Silver Spring, Maryland. His essays have appeared in *Parenting, FamilyFun, The Washington Post,* Salon.com, and more. He has no cats, no dogs, no hobbies, just kids. It's enough already.

KIM LANE

Kim Lane is a writer in Austin, Texas. She is the creator and editor of the award-winning site, www.AustinMama.com, and an occasional commentator for National Public Radio.

STEPHEN J. LYONS

Stephen J. Lyons has been a regular contributor to Salon's Mothers Who Think/Life site since 1999. He is the author of *Landscape of the Heart,* and the forthcoming *A View West of the Divide: Everyday Life in America* (2004, Globe Pequot Press).

MARY MCCLUSKEY

Mary McCluskey is a British journalist, usually based in Los Angeles, presently researching in Shropshire, UK. Her short fiction has appeared in *The London Magazine, S Magazine (Sunday Express,* UK) *Atlantic Unbound, NightTrain, Gingko Tree Review,* as well as many other web and print publications, and she is contributing editor to *Literary Potpourri.* She has completed one novel and is working on another.

EARL R. MIES

Earl R. Mies is a pseudonym for a writer living in North America.

CALLIE MILTON

Callie Milton is a pseudonym for the writer of this story, who lives in Florida.

CAROL MITHERS

Carol Mithers is a Los Angeles-based freelance writer and author of *Therapy Gone Mad* (Addison-Wesley). Her recent work has appeared in *L.A. Weekly, Los Angeles Times Magazine, Ladies' Home Journal,* and *Parenting.*

SUSAN MUSGRAVE

Susan Musgrave's most recent novel is *Cargo of Orchids,* published by Knopf. She lives on Vancouver Island, in Canada.

DIANA O'HEHIR

Diana O'Hehir is the author of six books of poems and two novels; she has received several awards including a Guggenheim and an NEA and has taught English and Creative Writing at Mills College for many years. She lives in San Francisco with her husband, the writer Mel Fiske.

KRISTIN OHLSON

Kristin Ohlson is a California-born, Cleveland-based freelance writer with articles published in *The New York Times,* Salon.com, *Ms., O, the Oprah Magazine, Discover, New Scientist, Tin House, Food & Wine, Poets & Writers, Sojourners,* many regional publications, and fiction published in university presses. Her memoir, *Stalking the Divine,* will be released by Hyperion this August. She is also the recipient of the Ohio Arts Council's major fellowship for fiction for 2003–2004.

J. B. ORENSTEIN

J. B. Orenstein practices emergency medicine in Maryland and writes for the *Washington Post, McSweeney's,* and other fine publications.

GEORGE PACKER

George Packer is the author of two books of nonfiction—*The Village of Waiting* and *Blood of the Liberals,* which won the 2001 Robert F. Kennedy Book Award—and two novels, *The Half Man* and *Central Square*. A recipient of a Guggenheim fellowship, he has written frequently for *The New York Times Magazine, Mother Jones, Dissent,* and other publications. He is a staff writer at *The New Yorker.*

SRIDHAR PAPPU

Sridhar Pappu writes the "Off the Record" media column for *The New York Observer.* Previously he was a reporter for *Money* and a staff writer for the *Chicago Reader.* He lives in Brooklyn, New York.

HANK PELLISSIER

Hank Pellissier is the "Urban Animal" columnist for SfGate.com, his poetry is included in *The Outlaw Bible of American Poetry,* he is the founder/director of the Hyena Comedy Institute (www.hyenacomedy.org) and he's the founder/codirector of a preschoool called the Children's Lab in Bernal Heights, San Francisco.

ELISSA SCHAPPELL

Elissa Schappell is the author of *Use Me,* a *New York Times* Notable Book, a *Los Angeles Times* Best Book of the Year, a Borders Discover New Writers selection, and a runner up for the PEN/Hemingway award. She is the Hot Type book columnist for *Vanity Fair,* and cofounder of *Tin House* magazine where she is presently editor-at-large. Her work has appeared in *SPIN, The*

Paris Review, Nerve, GQ, SPY, Vogue, and many other publications. She teaches in the low-residency MFA program at Queens in North Carolina, and lives in Brooklyn, New York.

THERESA PINTO SCHERER

Theresa Pinto Sherer is a freelance writer who was born in Korea, and grew up in South Florida. She dropped her Ph.D. program to become a full-time mother and part-time essayist. She now is writing her first novel *(Woman Descends the Stairs)* and working as a federal agriculture officer.

JANE SMILEY

Jane Smiley is the author of many novels, including *A Thousand Acres, Horse Heaven,* and most recently *Good Faith.* Her hobbies are horses, horseracing, cooking, and writing irate letters about the Bush administration.

LORI STEELE

Lori Steele is a writer in northern Michigan. Her articles have appeared in a number of publications, notably the *Detroit Free Press,* to which she has been a contributor since 1997.

SUSAN STRAIGHT

Susan Straight has published five novels, the latest is *Highwire Moon* (Anchor Books). She has written essays for Salon.com, *The*

New York Times Magazine, Harpers', and others. She lives in Riverside, California.

DAVID VERNON

David Vernon is a writer of fiction and screenplays. He's currently finishing his first novel, a fictionalized version of his experiences growing up as the son of a comedian.

ROBIN WALLACE

Robin Wallace is a reporter and editor at FoxNews.com.

LISA ZEIDNER

Lisa Zeidner is the author of four novels, most recently *Layover,* and two books of poems, one of which, *Pocket Sundial,* won the Brittingham Prize in Poetry. Her essays, fiction and reviews have appeared in *Tin House, Boulevard, The New York Times, GQ,* and elsewhere. She is a professor of English at Rutgers University in Camden, New Jersey.

ACKNOWLEDGMENTS

THIS BOOK OWES its existence to a great horde of people—writers, editors, friends, relations—whose ideas, honesty and gall vibrate in its pages.

The unwavering faith of Salon founding editor David Talbot continues to make it possible for Life to flaunt the laws of "lifestyle" journalism, a tradition of rebellion established by the first "Mothers Who Think," Camille Peri and Kate Moses, in 1995. Other guardian editors, ready with faith and wisdom, are Scott Rosenberg, Gary Kamiya, and Joan Walsh.

Amy Benfer, my former co-conspirator in Life, a woman more gracious and kind with writers than I could ever hope to be, cast her editorial glow on most of these essays. Ruth Henrich, another brilliant editor, manages, with surprising good humor, to keep me sane. All other Salonistas—past and present—provide the inspiration and hilarity that make this the best job in journalism.

Many thanks also must go to Adrienne Crew, Suzanne O'Neill at Simon and Schuster, and Max Garrone, for conceiving of the book and getting it to print.

I am deeply grateful to the book's contributors—writers fearless, generous, and bright—for their patience and trust. In my years as editor of Life, I was honored, and amazed, to receive the best work of countless writers—from veteran authors to first-time essayists. To chose a handful of pieces for this book was torture.

To Lynda Barry, soulful artist of love, I say: "Without you baby, what good am I?"

Finally, I want to thank my family for all sorts of things. They are everywhere in my work; they make me happy and they make me think. Hannah and Jules and Kevin, I love you so much.